Babyproofing Your Marriage

How to Laugh More,

Argue Less, and

Communicate Better

as Your Family Grows

Babyproofing Your Marriage

STACIE COCKRELL,
CATHY O'NEILL,
AND JULIA STONE

ILLUSTRATED BY LARRY MARTIN

 Collins

An Imprint of HarperCollinsPublishers

BABYPROOFING YOUR MARRIAGE. Copyright © 2007 Stacie Cockrell, Cathy O'Neill, and Julia Stone. All rights reserved. Printed in the United States of America. No part of this book may be used or reproduced in any manner whatsoever without written permission except in the case of brief quotations embodied in critical articles and reviews. For information, address Harper-Collins Publishers, 10 East 53rd Street, New York, NY 10022.

HarperCollins books may be purchased for educational, business, or sales promotional use. For information, please write: Special Markets Department, HarperCollins Publishers, 10 East 53rd Street, New York, NY 10022.

FIRST EDITION

Designed by Elliott Beard

Illustrated by Larry Martin

Library of Congress Cataloging-in-Publication Data is available upon request.

ISBN: 978-0-06-117354-7

06 07 08 09 10 ID/RRD 10 9 8 7 6 5 4 3 2 1

For our husbands: Ross, Mike, and Gordon

CONTENTS

Babyproofing Your Marriage

ONE

How Did We Get *Here?*

Parenthood Changes Everything

"I expected to add diaper, pacifier, formula to my new
motherhood vocabulary—I didn't think f*!k and s#*t would
feature so prominently!"
—*Lisa, married 5 years, 1 kid*

"What I get from other women is what I need, and that is
help. I don't even have to ask other women for help, they just
volunteer. What do I get from my husband? I get a sink full
of dirty plates, a pile of dirty clothes on the stairs, and a child
dressed for church in a football jersey."
—*Katherine, married 8 years, 2 kids*

"My wife doesn't understand how important sex is to me.
Everywhere I go, sex is screaming at me. There are hot women
in advertisements on billboards, and before I know it I find
myself imagining Gina down in Accounts Payable wearing a
nurse's outfit."
—*Thomas, married 11 years, 1 kid*

We are three women who love our children. We love our husbands, and
they love us. Why on earth did we find ourselves so often at odds after
the babies came home? Our pre-baby marriages were really good, maybe
even great. So why weren't we talking the way we used to? Why were we
bickering? Why were we so infuriated at our husbands' inability to find
the sippy cups? Why were our husbands distraught that our enthusiasm
for sex had dwindled to "folding the laundry" levels? Were we normal?
Or was something seriously wrong?

Turns out we were totally, utterly (even slightly boringly) normal.

We figured this out because we started talking; first to each other, then to a handful of friends, and then, well, things got out of hand and we started writing a book about it. At that point, no one was safe. We accosted total strangers in checkout lines and captive fellow passengers on airplanes. We talked to legions of women who, just like us, dreaded their husbands' *Ten O'Clock Shoulder Tap*.* They wondered what had happened to *That Whole 50:50 Thing* and why the lion's share of the domestic crap was falling on their plates. We talked to countless men and learned that, like our husbands, they despaired that their wives had pulled a *Bait and Switch* in the bedroom. They complained that no matter what they did to help with the kids, the house, and the bank balance, *It Was Never Enough*.†

Through all the talking, it became clear that most couples, no matter how happy and secure their marriage may be, find the early parenting years a challenge (on a good day) or even seriously relationship-threatening (on a bad day).

In fact, if you read the latest studies, you'd think we have a national epidemic of miserable parents on our hands. A well-publicized 1994 Penn State study said that, "two-thirds of married couples report a decline in their marital relationship upon the birth of their children."[1] Ten years later, things hadn't improved at all. An August 2005 report from the University of Washington found the same thing.[2] Most recently, a December 2005 study of 13,000 people published in the *Journal of Health and Social Behavior* said parents reported being more miserable ("sad, distracted or depressed") than non-parents.[3]

How did so many of us wind up *here*? And, more importantly, can we do anything to avoid spending the next fifty years of our lives *here*? Parenthood changes us, and our lives, so profoundly. It changes how we view ourselves and each other; what we need from and are able to put into our marriages. This book is about understanding these changes and how we react to them. At its heart, it's about keeping marriages on an even keel

---

*Throughout the book, we use terms such as this one to capture a particular experience, sentiment, or frustration. Check out the Glossary for a complete list.
†We've changed the names of all the people who shared their stories with us (for obvious reasons) but not what they said.

after the baby bomb arrives. It's about the simple things we can do to stay connected as a couple after we have kids.

So, What *Is* Going On?

During our intrepid journey of marital discovery we learned—much to our relief—that many of the bumps couples might encounter along the way just can't be helped. The emotional, psychological, and lifestyle upheavals that accompany parenthood are unavoidable. *They're nobody's fault.* We're not necessarily doing anything wrong.

Topping the list of things we just can't help is our DNA, or as we three aspiring evolutionary biologists like to call it, *Hardwiring.* It took having kids for us to realize that men and women are completely different animals and, as a result, we respond to parenthood in drastically different ways. Our genetically-programmed instincts are at the root of many of our modern-day frustrations. They affect our post-baby sex lives, how we parent, and our relationships with our families, often in ways we're not conscious of. Secondly, there's the inconvenient matter of planetary rotation. Our sixteen waking hours are not enough to do everything we *have* to do, much less anything we *want* to do. And finally, it doesn't help that most of us are *Deer in the Headlights.* We're basically clueless about how parenthood will make us feel. An iron curtain of secrecy hides the reality. No one, not even our own parents, will tell it like it is. (Remember those cryptic comments you heard before you had kids: "Don't have a baby until you're ready to give up your life"? To which you responded, "Huh?") This *Global Conspiracy of Silence* means that most of us are ill-equipped to deal with the sea of change that a baby brings. No one prepares us for the *Parenthood Ass-Kicking Party.*

To some extent, we new parents are at the mercy of millions of years of evolutionary biology, the twenty-four-hour day and pure ignorance. These three factors set the stage for the various post-baby disconnects we'll describe in this book. Add in the facts that (a) we aren't very nice when we're tired and (b) we think we can get our lives back to the way they were before kids, and we can find ourselves facing some serious marital struggles. No matter how good our intentions are, most of us encounter some, if not all, of the following issues:

Deer in the Headlights

1. **How We Behave as Parents**. Those hardwired instincts we just mentioned, the ones we never knew we had, kick in when a baby arrives.
   A woman's *Mommy Chip* is activated and she gets compulsive. "Is this
   sunscreen strong enough? Do we have enough bananas in the house?"
   Meanwhile, a man's first instinct upon gazing into the crib is *Provider Panic*: "Gee, I better go make more money." She thinks he just
   doesn't "get it." He wonders why she's turned into a control-freak,
   bottle-wielding shrew.

2. **The Post-Baby Sexual Disconnect**. His sex drive doesn't change. She
   wants to shut down the factory while caring for the most recent offspring. To be honest, the three of us breathed a sigh of relief when we
   learned that ours were not the only marriages with some supply and
   demand issues. It was comforting to learn that like us, most women's
   libidos had also gone MIA after the kids arrived. Men, however, told
   us they still wanted sex just as much as they always had, baby or no
   baby. We were amazed at the level of anguish men felt when they
   were rejected repeatedly by their wives. When we heard guys like

Thomas say, "It's humiliating and painful when you are rejected at your most vulnerable, when you're naked. And when that happens three times in a row, it's soul-destroying," we rushed back to our own husbands to ask them if that assessment was accurate. Their response: "AbsoF'nlutely."

3. **The Division of Labor**. It's hard work, and there's a mountain of it. Dishes, laundry, feeding, changing, picking up toys, and keeping a job—every day is Groundhog Day. Not surprisingly, couples end up fighting about who does what, or rather who's *not* doing what. We keep score. No matter how spectacular the *Scorekeeping*, however (and the three of us have been fairly spectacular), no one wins.

> "Am I supposed to gush over what a fine job he did emptying the dishwasher? What does he want, a gold star?"
> —*Leslie, married 8 years, 3 kids*

> "What's the score? Ha. The score is always *zero* when I walk in the door at the end of the day."
> —*Nick, married 7 years, 2 kids*

4. **Family (aka: The In-Laws and Outlaws) Pressures**. Before we have kids, our extended families, for the most part, stay on the sidelines of our marriages. Have a baby and it all changes. Our parents and in-laws all jockey for a piece of the kid action. Their desire to be involved is another evolutionary imperative; each set of grandparents wants to leave the biggest mark on the child for all posterity. And plenty of us cheer them on. We want to make sure that our families have as great, if not a greater, influence than our spouse's.

No matter how wonderful and helpful they are (and for the record, all of ours are fabulous . . .) balancing the time spent with, and the respective influence of, our extended families is a challenge for most couples. Meddlesome in-laws can provoke an "If I have to spend one more weekend with them, I'm seriously going to hurt somebody" response from even the most tolerant of spouses. And some of us in-furiate our other halves with our exceedingly poor job of *Cutting the Cord* ("When Danny's mother is here, he turns into a complete lazy ass." "Why does my wife want to move back near her family all of a sudden?") as we don the new and unfamiliar mantle of grown-up-with-kids-of-our-own.

5. **Who Gets to Sleep In or Go for a Jog on Saturday Morning?** Naturally, "me time" takes a big hit after we have kids. We quite rightly give our children the time and attention they deserve, but doing so means the days are full and our tanks are empty. We often end up fighting over the precious scraps of free time that remain.

> "I really resent that he wants to take off for five hours to play golf on a Saturday, then he expects me to be oh-so-grateful because he watches the kids while I go to yoga for an hour. Big friggin' deal."
> —*Jane, married 9 years, 2 kids*

When we don't find the time for the activities that recharge us, we get testy, and our spouse's habits—once "cute and quirky"—become infuriating. A little bit of self-neglect can actually spell trouble for our marriages.

6. **What Happened to Us?** After kids, because we're so busy, it's easy to neglect our relationship. There are no more "deep and meaningfuls." Instead, it's "time to make the donuts" . . . every single day. When we don't spend time together, our marriage can slip into *Autopilot*. Destination: "Who are you and what are you doing in my bed?"

> "The people I know whose marriages are breaking up now have ignored their relationship like a houseplant that never gets any water."
> —*Mark, married 11 years, 2 kids*

Ultimately, we all want what's best for our kids. We'll do pretty much whatever it takes to make them happy. Many of us, however, overlook the fact that *a husband and wife's relationship is the linchpin of the family. When it falters, a child's world is unhinged.* We know that can seem counterintuitive when we're heading out for a date with one toddler clamped to our leg and another pleading for a bedtime story. But nurturing our marital relationship is central to our children's sense of security and happiness. Being a good spouse and a good parent are not mutually exclusive.

What Can We Do About It?

The dark, looming abyss that seems to separate us after we have kids is an impediment, but it is not insurmountable. We've learned that *there are many things you can do to improve your relationship, and quite frankly, most of those things aren't really all that hard.* This book will give you hundreds of suggestions, but we'll keep coming back to two essential points:

A Little Action Goes a Long Way

This is good news, because "a little" is usually all we have the time and energy for. Small, but strategic gestures (think of them as baby steps . . .) can transform a marriage, even one that is caught in a *Vicious Cycle* of low-burn resentment.

> "Basically, my first marriage failed because my first wife made it pretty clear that the kids were my replacement. She said that the kids needed her love more than I needed her."
> —*John, remarried 20 years, 3 kids, 4 grandkids*

Some actions we suggest in this book you will have heard before (have a regular date night, get away together), but we're here to inspire you to actually *do them* this time around because they can make a big difference. Others are new, exciting, and even controversial: like the *Five Minute Fix* or the *Training Weekend.* Your first reaction to some of them might be a raised eyebrow, or even a "no way in hell am I doing that!" Just keep in mind that we don't recommend anything that we haven't tried ourselves and seen yield major benefits to our marriages. Think of us as your crash test dummies.

A Football Metaphor for Men (and Southern Women?)

Understanding that men and women don't always speak the same language, we're going to make this key point again in a language we know guys *do* speak: the language of football. Well, it's kind of like football ...

In an ideal marriage, you'd meet each other's needs halfway, on the 50-yard line, all the time. After kids, though, that is somewhat unrealistic because they require so much time and attention. But if you make the effort to get as close to the 50 as possible, to say, the 35, the marriage improves dramatically. Warning: If you don't put any effort into meeting your spouse's needs and dig in your heels at the 20, it's a slippery slope back to the end zone. You can easily find yourself out of the marriage game entirely and sitting in the cheap seats.

The Marriage Bowl

The Right Attitude Is Essential

The three of us have to admit that, in some respects, a good response to our "what happened to our marriage after we had kids?" questions would have been a fairly swift kick in the ass. We were, *at times*, guilty of feeling oh-so-sorry for ourselves; or pining for the good old days; or reacting to our husbands' requests for whatever with a "well, what have *you* done for *me* lately?" It wasn't pretty and we're not proud of it.

We realized in the course of writing this book that our happiness with our married-with-kids life depends, to a large extent, on our attitude toward it, and we've adopted a few key mantras as a result:

- **Our children are the making of us**. Compromise and selflessness don't come easy to those of us who've been raised in a me-first, I-can-have-it-all American culture. When we have kids, we find reserves of patience, love, humility, and (ideally) humor that we never knew we had. They make us better people. Our children are and will be, quite literally, the making of us and our marriages.

- **The Getting versus Giving Equation**. It's the actions we take for each other that add up to a happier marriage. To paraphrase that great American orator (if not that great family man) John F. Kennedy: *Ask not what your spouse can do for you; ask what you can do for your spouse.* Easier said than done, we realize, if you're packing a couple of years of resentment under your belts.

- **Quit trying to get your old life back**. It's over. Kill the ghost of your past self. Surrender to the chaos and wonder of parenthood and embrace it wholeheartedly.

- **This is just a stage**. No matter how tough things are right now, no matter how little sleep (or sex) we're getting, it will pass. Plenty of parenting veterans told us that making the transition to parenthood is one of the toughest—if not *the* toughest—times we'll experience in our marriages.

- **Good enough is good enough**. Trying to have the perfect kitchen, bedroom, yard, wardrobe, etc. is just not possible after we have kids (if ever). Pursuing perfection can propel us into a cycle of "it's never enough," which just eats away at our happiness. There was a time when a husband dressing a child in pajama bottoms for school would have driven us into an apoplectic fit. Life is so much easier now that we've lightened up and lowered our standards a little.

- **Our happiness hinges on each other's**. It may seem obvious, but sometimes we don't act that way. We are our spouse's best shot at happiness. Whether or not your spouse is happy with his or her life depends, to a large extent, on you. Instead of competing against each other to have it all, we should try to help each other have it all.

What This Book Isn't: Legal Disclaimer Section

1. *We Love Babies!* Parenthood is a privilege that none of us take lightly. Raising children is hard work, but let us be perfectly clear: children are never the problem. The problem is how we grown-ups respond to the challenge of parenting. While none of the three of us grew up in fractured families, plenty of people we know did. We are mindful, at all times, that kids are highly sensitive to being at fault if their parents have troubled relations. That should never be inferred in anything we say.

2. *Work. Stay Home. Do Whatever Floats Your Boat.* This book is not about women's choices to work or stay home with their kids. We're not going there. We're afraid we'll get hurt. There *are* some differences, we've found, in the marriages of at-work and at-home moms, and we'll tell you what we learned, but we are in the reporting business, not the judgment business. After we became mothers, two of us stayed at home, and one of us worked, so we hope we've presented both perspectives fairly.

3. *We Are Not the Maytag Women.* This book is not intended to take the place of professional help if you need it for yourself or your marriage. Our only degrees in this subject are from the school of hard knocks. We are married to fundamentally decent, emotionally sound people and assume you are, too. None of us were contemplating divorce or even counseling when we started this book. We were just less than thrilled with how our post-baby marriages were shaping up and wanted to improve them. This book is designed to help couples talk about these

issues, and think about things they can do to improve their marriages. If your relationship is truly on the rocks—go see a professional.

OK, If You Aren't the Maytag Women, Who Are You?

We are three wives, mothers, and good friends, all muddling through the early parenting years together, who couldn't find the humorous, down-to-earth book we needed to help us make sense of what was happening to our marriages. We couldn't find it, so we wrote the book we wanted to read.

Honestly, the *last* thing any of us expected to do was write a self-help book. When we started this project we had no collective wisdom. All we had were questions and a willingness to listen. We've spent the better part of the last couple of years asking people how parenthood has impacted their marriages and adding their stories and insights to our own. Oh yeah, and we each had a second (or third) baby in the process. We have seven kids among us, the oldest of whom just started kindergarten. Needless to say, we lived this book as we wrote it.

A Balanced Perspective

An "It Takes Two to Tango" philosophy is central to this undertaking. We are all part of the problem and part of the solution. So we present both sides of the story. Men and women view things so differently. He thinks to himself, "Hey, look at me—I'm doing a great job, taking care of the baby on a Sunday morning and letting my wife sleep in!" She thinks to herself, "God, he does such a half-ass job! He's sitting there reading the paper while our son is sitting in a water-balloon diaper with Baby Einstein on repeat play!" It really helps when we know where the other side is coming from.

Although this book is written by women, men get a fair shake and a loud shout. This is not a girl's bitch session, though we don't pull any punches. We've done our best to get the guys' side of the story straight, too. We didn't always like what they had to say, but we can pretty much guarantee that, whether you are a man or a woman, something in here is going to tick you off. Fair enough. Just try to keep an open mind. We found that even the most inflammatory comments helped us learn something.

We're All in This Together

If you've ever asked yourself, "Are we the only ones not having any sex?" "Are we the only ones scrapping over dishes and errands and who gets to go for a jog on Saturday?" or "Are we the only ones who can't seem to do it all?" this book will give you the answer (which, by the way, is no).

We've talked to hundreds of people from different parts of the country in different stages of life and marriage. Everyone is going, or has gone, through variations of the same thing. You are not alone.

For the three of us, this realization changed our marriage dynamic for the better. It took the all-too-personal sting out of our arguments. Our husbands saw that we were not, in fact, crazy, and that our compulsive mommy behavior was normal. We, in turn, saw that our husbands' requests for sex were not ridiculously frequent. Realizing that we are all in the same boat reduced the "why are you doing this to me?" arguments and paved the way for "what are we going to do about this?" discussions.

We hope these stories will have the same effect on you. You might even find yourself saying, "Whew, we aren't as bad off as those people." Don't worry, the smugness won't last. You'll turn the page, read another quote, and say, "Ouch, that sounds familiar."

We hope this book will make you laugh. We hope it will make you think. We hope it will provide a framework for conversation (or more likely, ongoing negotiation) between you and the love of your life. Most of all, we hope—like us—you'll find some answers.

TWO

Baby ... Boom!

Welcome to the Foxhole

Kablooey

It's been said that having a baby is like throwing a hand grenade into a marriage. A hand grenade? Why the violent metaphor for such a precious, peaceful little thing? They're so beautiful. How could anyone defame such a cutie? But it's true. Those little babies just explode right into our hearts and lives.

Boom.

Do you have a new baby? Congratulations! Do you have one or more small people running amuck in your home? How wonderful. Does that home now more closely resemble a bomb crater than it does a dwelling place fit for human beings? Are you picking your way through the debris—the rubble of strollers, bottles, dirty clothes, and talking plastic gizmos—that now litters your domestic landscape?

Welcome to the foxhole, friend. Here's a helmet.

We know the feeling. The three (make that six) of us have endured seven major diaper-bomb assaults in the last five years and lived to tell the tale. Parenthood changed us, and our relationships, in the most unexpected ways. This is what they meant with the whole *for better or for worse* business at our weddings. Parenthood fills us with awe and humility and gratitude. It is also a soggy, uncomfortable, life-altering trial by fire. Babies are the great levelers. Like a drill sergeant who tears down his weak new recruits so he can rebuild them into soldiers, babies break us down and rebuild us into parents. They flatten everything in sight, and then make us better, stronger, and hopefully, wiser than we were before.

The Paradoxical Passage to Parenthood

It's the ultimate paradox, having a baby. It is at once the happiest, most breathtaking moment of our lives and the biggest mess we have ever gotten ourselves into (and been responsible for cleaning up).

The Best of Times

Once that baby is placed in our arms, we pass over to the other side. Becoming a parent is, without parallel, the single most beautiful moment in life (even if we are too busy throwing up, cursing, fainting, or just enjoying the drugs to notice at the time). We know that our lives will be richer because of this little person. We can feel it in an instant. And we can never go back.

"It's amazing how quickly the life before your baby fades. I think it took about two weeks. Then I couldn't imagine life without her."

—*Amy, married 3 years, 1 kid*

The Worst of Times

It's so wonderful, but at the same time, new parents can feel afraid, confused, and sometimes, downright miserable. How is it possible to stand there at the side of the crib, silently watching the rise and fall of your baby's breathing, and feel such extreme, and diametrically opposed, emotions—pure joy and sheer terror—rise within you? How is it possible to share moments like these with your spouse and think, "Look at this miracle we have created together!" and "You're nice and all, but you're driving me *crazy*," within the same synaptic flash?

We feel dazed, confused, and even demented. We are shell-shocked. We are wholly unprepared and painfully ill-equipped. It doesn't matter how many classes we attend. It doesn't matter how many books we read (in fact, in hindsight, most of them are a colossal waste of time and money). We are not ready. We never will be. Nothing prepares us for the baby torpedo.

Stage One: The Twilight Zone

This period is short, but it can be savage.

The Fear

We're amazed when they actually let us leave the hospital with little more than a shiny new car seat to show our readiness for parenthood. No certificate. No license. No nothing. *Can't they see we don't know what we're doing?* Somehow, we manage to get home with no major casualties, but the minute we leave the hospital and its fleet of medical staff, *The Fear* sets in. We look with horror at each other and whisper, "I don't think we're going to be able to do this."

We start our long vigil of "just checking to make sure the baby is breathing." Our fears range from the rational to the irrational. Stacie, worried that her cats would suffocate the baby, strung elaborate mosquito nets over the crib (nets that Cathy bought for her ... the fear is contagious). Julia cataloged every input and output; such was her angst that her baby was not eating enough. For a while, she was even afraid to leave the house. When kindly neighbors asked her husband, Gordon, how she was doing, "Hard to say ..." was his reply. Men are just as scared as women, though. Cathy's husband, Mike, admitted he harbored dark fears about baby snatchers.

The Parade

Many people get a soft landing into parenthood, as friends and grandparents line up to get a piece of the action. Hungry? Here comes a parade of people with hot meals. Tired? Just give little Sweetpea to Grandma and take a nap. Clueless? There's someone within shouting distance who can cast some knowledge on the matter at hand. How about a golf round for the proud new Dad? Here's Grandpa with his set of clubs. It's no big deal because, hey, Grandma is there to pick up the slack.

Unfortunately, the parade doesn't last long. Most of us are struck with abject terror when the grandparents and other supporting players leave. We are petrified at the thought of taking care of a newborn without backup.

> "My mother-in-law was with us for a couple of weeks and, yes, I was relieved to see the back of her. But when I actually saw the taillights of her car, I thought, 'Shit, no one in this house has raised a kid before.'"
> —*Gabriel, married 5 years, 2 kids*

You Will Never Sleep Again

We hear rumors before the baby arrives about the impact of sleep deprivation, *but no one can prepare us for this kind of pain and suffering.* As Gordon put it, "In many countries, sleep deprivation is used as a form of torture." Continuous sleep deprivation can make the most sane, level-headed people irritable, irrational, or just plain crazy. We all turn into zombies. It is a cruel irony that we are expected to deal with one of the most difficult challenges of our lives on a wing and a prayer and a thirty-minute nap. Couldn't Mother Nature have arranged things a little bit better?

> "I was so tired I actually tried to breastfeed Bob's arm one
>   night."
>   —*Louise, married 4 years, 1 kid (FYI: Bob is her husband,*
>   *not her baby.)*

The Cluelessness

Our general cluelessness compounds the fear. We really and truly don't know what we're doing. How could we?

- "I thought it would be easier to take care of a baby than a new puppy. I figured, hey, at least you can put a diaper on a baby."—*Margaret, married 5 years, 1 kid*
- "I thought the baby would be born with teeth. How else was it supposed to eat?"—*Alex, married 3 years, 2 kids*
- "I asked the nurse at the hospital, 'How will I know when the baby is hungry?' "—*Steve, married 8 years, 3 kids*
- "I said to my husband, 'Gosh, since Nina and Brian had little Natalie, they seem to be bickering all the time, even in front of us. I'm glad that won't happen to you and me, Honey, because we communicate so well. . . .'" —*Bethany, married 6 years, 2 kids*

First Runner-Up in the Cluelessness Category: Gordon, who, during a three-month hiatus between jobs, suggested that he and Julia spend that time taking a backpacking trip through Asia with their fourteen-month-old in tow. "We're really lame if we don't take advantage of this time off. Why can't we be more adventurous?"

And the Booby Prize goes to: Cathy and Mike, who actually forgot, *temporarily*, that they had a baby:

> "One Friday night, a couple of hours after I'd put our two-month-old, Kate, to bed, Mike asked me if I wanted to go get a video. 'Great idea,' I said. We both got in the car and drove the less than five minutes to the video store. As I got out, I suddenly remembered that (a) we had a baby and (b) we had left that baby at home. I was in a blind panic and close to tears. *How* could I have forgotten about Kate? Mike, however, thought that we should still get a video. 'It's not like she can get out of the crib and we're already right here …' I just left him there and high-tailed it back to the house. Of course she was still asleep and oblivious to our supreme negligence."

The New Job

Meet the new boss—a tyrannical (albeit cute) despot whose demands are incessant and often indecipherable. Whatever freedom we once enjoyed is gone. If we try to make ourselves a sandwich or, God forbid, sleep, that all-seeing, all-knowing tiny autocrat will yell his or her head off. And quite possibly take ours with it.

And how about that new job description—twenty-four-hour personal servant? We all know, or quickly learn, that the work required to keep our ten-pounder alive is astounding. They are truly phenomenal crying, eating, inputting, and outputting machines. All we can do is pitch diapers back and forth, go wash another bottle, and try not to lose our place on the assembly line. Just the thought of it makes us want to sit down and have a gin and tonic.

The New and Different Ways We Communicate

The Big Leagues (Cover Baby's Ears)

At times, we feel like we are under siege, and the pressure can take its toll. Remember when it was just the two of you and your biggest arguments revolved around whose turn it was to pick the restaurant, or who left their underwear on the bathroom floor? Friends, that was just battling it out in the sandbox. Caring for a newborn puts you right up there in the big leagues. It's a whole new ball game. At best there are testy exchanges: "What do you mean you didn't buy more diapers yesterday?" But often things get downright nasty. Doors are slammed and sofas are slept on.

Our friend Steve recalls feeling overwhelmed by the baby's cries and yelling at his wife to "Get the f*#king diaper!" He later asked her when she thought her mom-instincts would kick in, to which she quickly replied, "How the f*#k should I know?" They are among the many new parents who simply cannot avoid expletives in these crazy early days.

> "My husband had the unfortunate experience of telling me I should nap when the baby naps. I told him, 'F*#k you. You're at work. You take a nap.'"
> —Helen, married 11 years, 3 kids

This period of extreme parenting can cause severe *Scorekeeping*. "You're too tired to watch her for a couple of hours? Too bad. I haven't showered for three days. Just suck it up!" We'll talk in detail about Scorekeeping in the next chapter, and how it can set the stage for ongoing marital conflict.

Fascinating Conversation
Even if we aren't fighting, our conversation just isn't what it used to be. The day-to-day care of a newborn ushers in new and fascinating repartee. Now *all* we talk about is . . . *the baby and how to care for the baby—when to feed the baby, how much to feed the baby, whose turn it is to feed the baby, who's going to wash the bottles, when to change the baby, who's going to change the baby, when should the baby take a nap, when should the baby wake up, what should the baby wear, it's too cold, no, it's too hot, he needs a blanket, no, he doesn't, he threw up a few minutes ago, his poop was a weird color, he didn't poop today, we need to track his poops, why has he been crying for 3 hours.* It's endless.

Fun and Games

New parents resort to all manner of fun and games to keep themselves amused during this difficult time. Here are some of our personal favorites:

Midnight Chicken

Also known as Who Will Blink First? It goes something like this: It's 3:00 A.M. The baby is awake (again) and crying (again). You are both awake. You both hear her. But nobody moves. Women are tacitly calling in their chit (*Surely he knows it's his turn this time?*), but men, the masters of this game, simply play dead (maybe they throw in a little snoring). They can't hear the crying because they are *sound asleep*. Who will cave in and get up first? Needless to say, it's usually Mom.

Our friend Charlotte, however, plays a mean game of *Advanced Midnight Chicken*: "I used to nudge my husband when the baby would cry and say, 'Hey, you're up. I got her last time.' But there really was no last time." She'd been asleep all along, but he didn't know it. So don't get too comfortable there in the bed, Daddy-O.

Midnight Chicken

Tricks to Dodge the Poop

Then there are the guys who cringe at the thought of changing a poopy diaper and will say or do anything to avoid it. We know we women have a heightened sense of smell, but come on—that toxic-waste diaper passes your Smell Test? And how about Kyle, who has never changed one because, he claims, "It would make me throw up." How clever.

The Affair

John actually slips away from work an hour early just so that he can surreptitiously have a quick drink with his best friend before he heads home:

> "I feel like I'm having an affair with my best friend. I try to see him once a week before catching my usual train for the evening. Don't tell my wife. If she finds out, she'll insist I come home an hour earlier and I'll never see Pete again. It's just nuts."

The Fake Business Trip

Things can get so bad that some fathers resort to elaborate gamesmanship to survive, or more accurately, to get away from the baby-induced mania. The clear champion of this game is a new father, whom we'll call Ron, who got a little desperate:

> "When our first daughter was born I was so exhausted I couldn't keep it together at work. I thought my boss was going to come in and find me passed out on the keyboard. Things got so bad that I told my wife I had to go on a business trip to Chicago. There was no business in Chicago. But I took a day off work, flew to Chicago, checked into a hotel, and got a full night's sleep. It was heaven. I'm not really proud of lying to my wife, but it was a question of survival. I just couldn't take it anymore."

By the way, we absolutely and emphatically do not endorse this "solution," although we know husbands everywhere (our own included) are secretly in awe of Ron's ingenuity.

Sex

Huh? No one is having sex during this period (and if you are, it's nothing short of weird). Women have to heal, no one has any energy, and if there is any extra time, you are sleeping. Next.

Stage Two: The Dust Settles ...

The good news is that we all, with a little grace and a little luck, survive the state of emergency, shake off our zombie trances, and start digging ourselves out of the rubble. Things do start to smooth out. We start to see ourselves as a family. We get the hang of the parenting thing. The baby is absolutely adorable. We can scarcely remember what life was like without it. New Dads, especially, start to really enjoy a baby who recognizes them and can interact more. It's not quite throwing a football, but hey, it's a start.

... Or Does It? The Great Divide

The bad news is that even as we are in the process of getting our collective groove back on, it slowly dawns on us that things have changed, sometimes drastically, in our own hearts and minds, and in our relationships with our spouses. For some, the transition to parenthood is simply a short-term series of minor tremors in the earth. For others, it is a seismic shift, a great rumbling as tectonic plates rub against each other and produce some serious eruptions. We escape from the war zone, only to find ourselves inhabiting a new landscape that is still shifting, and largely unrecognizable. We are strangers in a strange land.

The New Landscape

"After I had Jack, I felt like a different person. I think and act differently because of the new responsibilities I have. It's like I have to reconfigure the whole picture of myself. And it definitely changed what I want from Matthew. Before the baby, I was unfazed by his long hours. Suddenly, I want him home

now. And it bothers me that he doesn't seem as interested in
Jack as I am.
    —*Erica, married 4 years, 1 kid*

"The baby's great and all, but when are things going to get back
to normal around here? When will my wife stop the control-
freak stuff? When will she be nicer to me and remember I exist?
And tell me this: will I ever again have a Saturday morning to
myself without being made to feel guilty?"
    —*Spencer, married 6 years, 2 kids*

Both men and women struggle to adapt to this new chapter in our
marriages. As we said, these changes are profound and they can take
some getting used to. In the process of changing, we often wind up taking out our fears, disappointments, and frustrations on each other.

Parenthood expands our lives, but it also shrinks our lifestyles. Lots
of us married later and lived ten or twenty adult years before we had kids.
We got pretty used to doing whatever we wanted. But when the margarita
and the sippy cup collide, we have to make a choice. We choose the sippy
cup, but, at times, we can't help but fantasize about collapsing on a lawn
chair with that margarita in hand.

What's more, after living much of our pre-parenthood lives as relative equals, it comes as a surprise when, post-baby, men and women start
to assume different and not always complementary roles. Hardwired instincts nudge women into the role of *nurturers* and men into the role of
providers. Given that we stepped out of the caves about 8,000 years ago,
just a nanosecond in terms of evolutionary psychology, it shouldn't be
surprising that when we become parents our most basic instincts rise to
the surface. But it is surprising. We find ourselves back in the prehistoric
suburbs, where women wonder if baby might be allergic to mammoth
and if there are enough wild berries in his diet, and where men stalk buf-
falo and question whether their hunting abilities will be good enough to
get the family through the winter.

HOW WOMEN FEEL

"It is the most important role of my life. If my kids don't turn
out well, nothing else matters. It really doesn't matter what I
achieve in my career or how much money I make."
    —*Danielle, married 6 years, 2 kids*

We are thrilled and terrified by our sweet babies. We wonder if we'll be
up to the task of motherhood. We wonder if we'll be able to maintain our
sense of self when it seems that motherhood will swallow us whole. We
see ourselves and our husbands in a whole new way.

The Mommy Chip

Whether we like it or not (and believe us, often we do not like it), when
we have a baby, a nurturing, domestic gene is activated. It's as if a *Mommy
Chip* is implanted in our brains. And we can't turn the damn thing off.
That microchip gives us supersonic hearing (Was that the baby?), x-ray
vision (Those pants are *not* clean.), lightning reflexes, and a relentless
internal dialogue (Do we need more formula? When's the next doctor's
appointment? Have I registered with enough preschools?). It also comes
with a *Worst-Case-Scenario Program* that plays into our newly-minted-
Mommy fears. And, if that's not enough, the chip is plugged into a *Guilt*

The Mommy Chip

Circuit that compels us to think we are never, ever doing all we could for our children, our husbands, and ourselves.

Once we become mothers, whether we stay at home, or work full-time, or anything in between, that chip is *always* humming.

Mommy Shock

Most women we spoke with said that the transition to motherhood was mind-blowing and life-altering. We feel shocked by the awesome responsibility of motherhood. We are shaken to our very core.

Instincts Take Over

Women are often overwhelmed by our visceral reaction to motherhood. We experience overpowering love and abject fear. It is hormonal. It is biological. It is rarely what we expect.

Julia put it this way: "I'd always prided myself on being a rational and in-control kind of woman, but after I had a baby, my instincts took over. I never expected myself to be super-maternal. I was amazed to find that that was how I behaved. I felt at the mercy of my emotions. I was definitely not in control anymore."

> "I just loved the way Alex smelled. I would carry one of his
> blankets to work with me and just smell it throughout the day."
> —Meredith, married 5 years, 1 kid

One of our children's pediatricians said new mothers "fall in love" with their babies. "The emotions a woman feels are as powerful, if not more powerful, than the ones she has when she falls in love. The child consumes her and occupies every waking thought, just the way her husband did, once upon a long time ago!" The besotted phase doesn't last forever, but the obsession can linger for a lifetime.

The fear is absolute. Women are deeply afraid that something terrible will happen to the baby. Often, the fear leads to overprotectiveness. The three of us refer to this behavior as *The Lioness Effect*, and again, Julia felt this instinct with great force:

"I felt like an animal—like a ferocious mother lion. I would
protect the baby's well-being if it killed me. I would have ripped
anyone to shreds, positively delimbed them, if they so much
as sneezed in the baby's presence. I said to myself, 'Nothing is
going to happen to this baby on *my* watch!'"

This common, though almost always groundless, fear that someone else
might hurt the baby compels many new Moms to do everything themselves—no matter how exhausted they may be.

Expectation vs. Reality

We go into motherhood with a set of expectations that rarely align with
reality.

We Don't Look Like the Women in the Mommy Magazines

During the nine months of pregnancy, if not our entire adult lives, we
are fed soft-focus images of motherhood. There are no dirty diapers at a
baby shower. When the baby does arrive, we are surprised by the noisy,
sleepless, messy reality. A real-life cover model would be a woman with
matted hair, stooped shoulders, a spit-up-stained bathrobe, and a look of
exhaustion on her face. She'd be lucky to have a coffee mug in her hand
because, hey, that means she had time to make coffee.

Pin-Up Mom v. Real Mom

"I thought I'd be fabulously stylish and a quintessential Earth
Mama at the same time. That was before I realized I'd only be
showering every second or third day."
—*Kristin, married 6 years, 1 kid*

It's Harder Than We Imagined

We are not complainers by nature. We're pretty tough, actually. But new
motherhood is relentless. The nonstop feeding and the no-sleeping gig
wears you down, no matter how robust a woman you are. Furthermore,
mothering doesn't necessarily come naturally, which frustrates us. For
example, we are all told that "breast is best," but who was forewarned
that it will hurt? Few of us can imagine what it feels like to become a
milk machine. It is, in fact, so difficult, that there is an entire profession
to feel you up and teach you about latch-on, the "football," and other
innovative holds. The paraphernalia that accompanies breastfeeding is
astounding: creams, nipple shields, pumps, pillows, and, let's not forget,
the whole "peek-a-boo" line of clothing. (There are pluses, though. Aside
from the many medical benefits and the incredible bonding experience,
breastfeeding will empty a room of visiting relatives faster than you can
say, "I'm going to nurse.")

The Questions

As we emerge from the foglike existence of the first three months, we
feel another sort of *Mommy Shock*. We constantly ask ourselves the big
questions: Who am I now? What should I do? Should I go back to work?
Should I stay home? What makes sense for me? What makes sense for my
family? How do the pieces of the puzzle fit back together?

Those of us who return to work, like Cathy did, and leave our
growing-cuter-by-the-day baby behind, at times, face conflicting feelings
of guilt (Should I leave her?), and relief (Thank God I am back with the
grown-ups), and more guilt (Should I be feeling so relieved that I get to go
to work?). Those of us like Stacie and Julia, who put our careers on indef-
inite hold while we care for our kids, sometimes experience withdrawal
symptoms as we go cold turkey from our formerly suit-wearing (or at

least non-sweatpant wearing), intellectually rigorous lives and board the time capsule that hurtles us right back to the 1950s.

"Things" Just Aren't What They Used to Be

Millions of women everywhere ask themselves the same question: will my body ever be the same again? It's like getting used to a new roommate that you don't really like very much, and you have to make your peace with her. Yes, the birth is miraculous. Yes, it's amazing what the female body can do. Blah, blah, blah. (Note to Mother Nature: What would really be amazing is if motherhood made your breasts perkier and your hips slimmer.)

How We Feel About Our Husbands (Oh Yeah, Them)

"It's impossible to put your husband first. Babies need you 24/7."
—*Kimberly, married 12 years, 2 kids*

The Warm and Fuzzies

"I finally knew what commitment was. I realized that no one would ever love this child as much as my husband would. No one else in the world could share that with me, ever."
— *Jody, married 4 years, 2 kids*

"Rick turned out to be a great father. I was kind of worried, because he's the kind of person who can't sit still for even five minutes. But he'll hold Sophie for an hour, just singing and talking to her. I definitely married the right man."
—*Robin, married 3 years, 1 kid*

As we cross over the threshold of new parenthood together, we feel a tremendous bond with our husbands. We revel in sharing this miraculous experience with them. When we asked women to recall the early baby days and how it changed their marriages, lots of them got misty-eyed. They talked of swooning on the spot as their husbands held their tiny babies in their big, manly hands. Allison said, "Getting married was one thing. Having a baby together is the real deal."

The Not-So-Warm-and-Fuzzies

"My husband was as useless as a tit on a boarhog."
*Liz, married 9 years, 2 kids. (Authors' note: Liz is from
Texas, which we hope explains this one ...)*

Those "wow, look what we did" moments sustain us. But the collective female consensus, and it was a resounding consensus, is that men *just don't get it.* While most husbands are thrilled about fatherhood, they seem to be one step removed from the work and not nearly as baby-crazy as we would like.

One of our mothers has said, "No matter how much a woman loves her husband, no matter how fantastic she thinks he is, when they have a child, he will disappoint her."

Ouch.

At first glance we thought that this was a terribly bleak and unfair assessment, but many women told us they *were* deeply disappointed with their husbands after they had a baby. Some reports state that as many as 70 percent of new mothers say they are less happy in their marriages in the first year of their babies' lives.[1] We think this disappointment is rooted in women's expectations that their husbands will share many of the same feelings and concerns about the baby. We also expect them to share equally in the work of parenting. Most guys don't do either of those things. And we are none too happy about it.

"He Just Doesn't Get It!"

Women want so much for their husbands to *understand* the radical change we have undergone. Our lives are upended by motherhood. We do a total 180. Our lives, our jobs, our bodies will never be the same again. By contrast, as Denise said, "I feel like my husband just took a couple of days off of work and then things pretty much got back to normal, or at least he wanted them to get back to normal." Yes, men are profoundly changed by fatherhood, and we'll talk more about that in a minute, but, relatively speaking, women feel their husbands' lives only shift about 90 degrees.

Do You Not See All the Work?

Guys, we know you can't share the experience of motherhood, but we often feel you don't recognize, unless we point it out, that the volume of work has gone up exponentially. Ideally, of course, we'd like you to help. When you don't see something that needs doing, or you wait to be asked (or told) to do it, it really burns us up. When that happens, we start keeping score: "I got up with the baby three times last night and you haven't done it for at least two weeks."

Babies . . . Wear . . . Diapers . . .

Most women are surprised at how little men understand about what it takes to keep a baby fed, clean, and happy. This lack of usefulness is, in fact, disappointing to most of us.

Case in point: Stacie remembers the time when her husband, Ross, packed the diaper bag for a three-hour plane ride. "During the flight, I took our baby to the back of the plane to change the Mother of all Diapers. But there was a small problem. He'd forgotten to pack the *diapers* in the *diaper bag* (Get it? *Diaper* bag?). That was a hell of a flight."

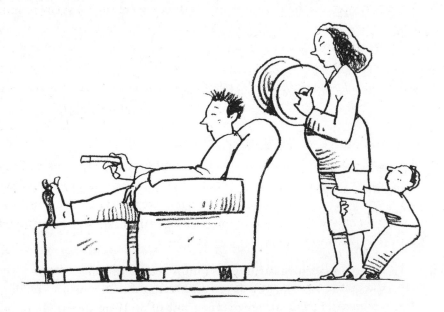

Clang, Clang, CLANG . . .

The Safety/Overprotectiveness Debate

Women's instinctive Lioness fears can produce a particular form of the "he just doesn't get it" sentiment. Guys don't necessarily feel the same degree of overprotectiveness. Women have been known to become apoplectic because they think their husbands are too lax in the general health and safety categories of child minding. Certainly, the "the baby needs a sweater, no, he doesn't" back-and-forth has raged in all of our homes. For Stacie and Ross, it's about checking (and rechecking and rechecking) the padlocks on the pool gates. For Julia and Gordon, it's about hosing down the boys with bug spray before they play in the Lyme-disease-carrying, deer-tick-infested woods behind their house. For Cathy and Mike, it's about the adequate application of sunscreen.

Why Do You *Say* Those Things?

Our husbands are all terrific, but all three of them, in the early days of this parenting thing, returned home from the land of work, grown-ups, and tall lattes with helpful comments like, "Why don't you just nap when the baby naps?" or (even better) "My mom had kids. Your mom had kids. Why is this so much harder for you?" Best-case scenario, these comments reduce a bathrobe-clad, unshowered new mother to tears. Worst-case scenario, they will be cited in divorce proceedings in the not so distant future. Until you have lived it, you can't understand it. And until you understand it, you'd do well to keep it to yourself, mister. We have big plans for you later in this chapter, so just sit tight and zip it.

Why Don't You Get Ga-Ga, Too?

Men don't have the Mommy Chip. They are not wired like we are. They don't care if the baby is getting a tooth. But it bothers us so much when they don't match us "coo for coo." A therapist we interviewed pointed out that a new mother can perceive any lack of enthusiasm by her husband for the baby as a lack of enthusiasm for *her*:

> "It works something like this—If I think you are rejecting the baby in any way, I think you are rejecting me. Or more accurately, I think you are rejecting both of us. There are few things more terrifying to a new mother than the fear that she will be left alone to raise a baby."

We think this is why we drive our husbands nuts pointing out the tiniest little baby details. Deep down, women have an underlying fear that their husbands might not be fully invested in this nest and will just fly off and make another nest with another bird. Some of us worry that they are not spending enough time with the children, that they are not bonding. We want him to be as ga-ga as we are. By the second child, we realize that our husbands aren't going to bolt, so we don't get ourselves into a state when he doesn't notice that the baby has a new hat. First-timers, though, can drive themselves and their partners crazy.

The Pressure to be Supermom
We put pressure on ourselves and try to live up to societal expectations about what a mother is supposed to do and be. The pressure so many women feel to reach superhero mommy status is one that we will revisit many times in this book. Societal expectations of Dads are still relatively low. As our friend Sean said, "I'd hate to be a woman, because you guys have to do so much. I wash a fork and people say, 'good job!'" Consequently, it's easy for men to dismiss our fears that we are just not going to be able to do it all, or do it all well. They tell us we are overreacting. Admittedly, we *can* get carried away. But a little more help and a little less advice would be better.

When we feel like our husbands don't get any of these things, we feel pretty justified in our complaining. We can start to sound like one of our kids' yammering toys pulling its own string—talk, talk, talk. Guys, we're simply looking for some empathy and assistance. But those aren't always easy to come by from you. It's hard to be a milk machine. It's hard to imagine how we'll go back to work when we can barely think straight. It's hard to imagine having sex again when we are larger, yet withered, shriveled versions of our former selves. We wonder, *how* can you not understand this—at least intellectually?

HOW MEN FEEL

"One smile erases the strain of a whole week."
    —*Dan, married 9 years, 2 kids*

"Marriage was a breeze—having children was by far the biggest
challenge I've ever experienced."
    —*Tobias, married 5 years, 2 kids*

"I was running on fumes when the baby was little. I remember
almost breaking down when friends came over with breakfast
one morning and asked how I was doing, because I felt like I
was barely keeping it together."
    —*Dean, married 8 years, 3 kids*

In many respects, upon becoming fathers, men don't feel all that different from women. They, too, feel great love and terrible fear. They, too,
are overwhelmed and exhausted. But they react in a different way. And
furthermore, they wonder, at times, if their lives, and their wives, will
ever get back to normal.

Provider Panic

"I would stand over the crib and the first thought that would
come into my head was: I better go make more money."
    —*Jack, married 7 years, 1 kid*

Although men don't get obsessed about their babies, they do have their
own internal hardwiring to contend with. Even if they are one half of
a dual-income household, most believe that providing for the financial
well-being and stability of the family is their responsibility. Now, before
anyone gets their feminist knickers in a twist, let's take a closer look at
that statement. Cathy, who has always worked, had a visceral reaction
to the idea that providing for their family was Mike's exclusive responsibility. As happened so many times in the course of writing this book,
she went to him and asked, "Is this how you really feel?" Mike told her
that even though she is willing and able to provide for the family, "the
buck stops" with him. "If we don't have enough money saved for the
kids' college, that will be my failing. I will take that personally." Mike's

sentiments resonated with many of our male friends. They described fatherhood triggering a sort of *Provider Panic*. This phenomenon often sparks a laserlike focus on work. Career and financial success become more important than ever. In those early months, women worry that the baby is not eating enough or not eating the right foods; men worry that they will not be able to put food on the table. (In many instances that is not a rational fear, but neither is ours that the crib mobile will fall on top of the baby during the night and kill her.) Men's compelling drive to provide can compromise their ability to see what needs doing (and sometimes even to enjoy what's happening) on the home front. There's no mental room for noticing the bottles need washing because the male brain is already in high gear calculating college tuition payments.

Stepping Up to the Plate

To their absolute and utter credit (and often to their own absolute and utter surprise), upon becoming Dads, men embrace their fatherhood in many wonderful ways. Many men described a "this is it" feeling, "it" being the big leagues, adulthood, the real deal. Gordon said, "I finally felt like I just might pull it off, being an adult: the kind of guy who provides a good standard of living for his family, as well as a good father to our boys. It feels really good, doing that." Provider Panic has its upside.

Guys Also Feel the Love ...

Like women, men, too, are rendered speechless by the enormity of the love they feel for their new babies. Some of them surprise both their wives and themselves with their newfound capacity for gentleness and sacrifice. They are delighted by their new role as Daddy, especially when the baby looks like them (which it invariably does). Quite a few told us they cried for the first time in their lives. Ross remembers the morning when he first felt a powerful connection to his daughter: "It had been a long, sleepless night, and as I was rocking her to sleep, it happened. She smiled at me for the first time. It was one of the greatest moments of my life."

Men's love for their newborns is of the low-burn variety, however, not the flaming vortex that engulfs their wives.

Without doubt they love their babies, but they just find them (dare we say it) a bit boring. We didn't hear of any men carrying baby blankets with them to work, or indeed finding it at all difficult to leave the baby for prolonged periods of time. Their bonding happens, but it just happens in a different way and on a different timetable.

> "I'm just as excited as Paula is about little Avery. I just get excited about different stuff. Paula notices the day-to-day incremental steps. I'm more into the big-picture milestones . . . I'll be excited about getting her a bike, playing ball. I can't relate to the baby stuff."
> —Ben, married 5 years, 1 kid

. . . And the Fear

Fears about Survival

An outgrowth of Provider Panic for many men is the "if something should happen to me" game. Our friend Jonathan, who has lived in Manhattan his entire life, described leaving the hospital after his son's birth and deciding to take a taxi home rather than the subway since it was late at night. "For the first time in my life, I worried about taking the subway. It suddenly seemed so dangerous. I couldn't let anything happen to me now that I had that tiny life dependent on me."

Some men—sometimes willingly, sometimes begrudgingly—also hand in their hang-gliding, bungee-jumping, extreme-skiing cards as they realize the incompatibility of fatherhood and potentially fatal pursuits.

Fears about Losing Their Freedom

> "Now that we have another baby, I feel somewhat trapped. If I want to do something on my own, I feel like I have to ask permission way in advance. I don't know why I even bother— more than likely she has some sort of family thing planned."
> —Gabe, married 6 years, 2 kids

"I used to play golf once a week. Now I'm lucky to play a couple
of times a year."
—*Doug, married 5 years, 1 kid*

Many new Dads fear that life, as they know it, is over. They are expected
to spend every spare moment with the baby and partake in only family-
friendly pursuits. There is little time left over for themselves. As much as
they love their babies, some worry that fatherhood amounts to a tread-
mill existence of work responsibilities, domestic responsibilities, and
baby responsibilities. This is particularly acute in the early months when
hanging out with a nonresponsive baby is about as much fun for them as
watching the grass grow.

How They Feel about Their Wives

"What happened to the woman I married? She's turned into a
complete control freak."
—*Vic, married 9 years, 1 kid*

"I feel like the old dog and my wife just got a new puppy."
—*Brent, married 7 years, 1 kid*

My Wife Is Nuts

Let us be clear that most men think that their wives walk on water during
this stage. They are amazed by their selflessness and patience and sheer
devotion. They say with absolute conviction that they could not do it
themselves, no matter how nurturing a man they may be. That said, all
men, it seems, at one time or another think that their wives go margin-
ally insane after having a baby. There are a number of versions of "my
wife is nuts," but they boil down to the following:

She is obsessed. She cannot stop thinking about the baby. She is consumed with unnecessary worry about the baby. She can't talk for three
minutes about something else before returning to the topic of the baby.

She is irrational. No matter what a fantastic job she is doing, she will
regularly question her ability. She rarely asks for help. When she does

expect him to help (e.g., asking him to get up to change the diaper in the middle of the night when she's nursing anyway), she can be downright unreasonable.

> "My wife wanted to do everything herself. One night she was trying to breastfeed our son and he wasn't latching on. He just kept screaming. I suggested that she give him a bottle of formula. It was as if I had told her to give the baby arsenic. The crying got so bad I just went and made him a bottle of formula and fed it to him. He went straight to sleep. Problem solved? No. Then she started crying because she thought she was an awful mother, and the fact that I had been able to shut him up made it even worse."
> —Chris, married 8 years, 2 kids

> "It's like a case of misery loves company. It's like if my wife felt miserable, I had to be miserable, too. If she was getting up with the baby every couple of hours, well so should I. Why couldn't one of us get a decent night's sleep? Why do both of us have to be wrecked?"
> —Anton, married 9 years, 2 kids

She has forgotten about me. This is closely related to men thinking their wives are obsessed, but to men, it is a stand-alone form of insanity.

> "In my darkest moments I wondered if all she really wanted was a sperm donor. And now that I had served that purpose, was I being summarily dismissed?"
> —Joel, married 10 years, 4 kids

She is completely consumed with the baby. It seems that all she wants is an errand boy, diaper dispatcher, and bottle washer. When he doesn't do those things right, she gets furious. "I thought she wanted me for my witty repartee, sensitive soul, and winning smile?" wonders many a Dad who has just been yelled at for his unseemly delay in finding the pacifier.

Breastfeeding compounds the problem. Few men will admit it, but none of them are happy to see their former playthings become Junior's exclusive domain. Most breasts remain off limits while Mom is breastfeeding. (For the record, having a feeder and a groper is quite honestly more than most women can bear.) Sex is nothing but a distant memory. For most men, the term "baby blues" takes on a whole new meaning.

Beware the Gatekeeper

Many men feel that their wives act as *Gatekeepers* to the house and the children. Moms open or slam the gate shut at their whim. Dads are relegated to the sidelines. Some men said that they felt disrespected and quite detached from the whole process. At best, they have an Assistant Mom role foisted upon them.

> "For three months she didn't let me take Ashley anywhere near the tub, then in month four, she bit my head off because I didn't know how to give her a bath."
> —*Harry, married 11 years, 2 kids*

SOLUTIONS FOR BOTH

> "I remember sitting on the floor of our baby's room, in tears as I talked to a friend on the phone. She promised me this stage would pass. I didn't believe her at the time, and I couldn't imagine how that could happen, but I clung to her words with a desperate hope for another few sleepless weeks, and sure enough, she was right."
> —*Leah, married 3 years, 1 kid*

The newborn stage is tough. The name of the game is survival. When you are going through it, it seems like it will never end. But it lasts just a few short months—less time than a semester in college—and things do get better. You won't have to get by on four hours of sleep for the rest of your life. Here are a few things we, and others, have learned (the hard way) that might help you ride out the storm together.

Perspective

It's not the time for a Relationship 101! Although there are plenty of arguments in the first couple of months, most can be attributed to hormones, sleep deprivation, and general baby shock. Some people panic during this period. We have a friend who, when their first child was five weeks old, told her husband that they needed counseling. What they needed was a good night's sleep. You are not a couple at this time. You are two people treading water. Until you're getting an eight-hour block of shuteye for two consecutive months, you shouldn't even *think* of analyzing your relationship. Neither of you are capable of coherent thought. By all means shout, tell each other how you feel, and/or hurl bottles at each other, but remember that the way you feel now will likely pass.

Call a time-out. Hindsight is a wonderful thing. One of the great advantages of having more than one child is that we can avoid some of the minefields we stepped in the first time around. On the eve of the arrival of their third child, Stacie and Ross called a time-out on their relationship for three months. They told each other, "OK, let's get our game faces on. Let's apologize in advance for all the crazy things we're going to say to each other. We'll take a time-out and know that our true selves will resurface in three months."

Humor

It's the first thing to go when we're stretched to the limit. But it *is* pretty funny—or at least it will be when it's all over. We have two choices when the baby pukes on our last clean T-shirt—laugh or cry. Given how much crying has likely taken place already, why not give laughter a shot? Some favorite funny moments people shared with us:

- "A few weeks after the baby was born, I ventured out to buy a pizza. I returned an hour later with no pizza and no idea why I'd left the house in the first place."

- "One time I fell asleep with the stove burners on while sterilizing bottles. I awoke God knows how much later to the smell of burning plastic and a hazy smoke filling the house. I grabbed the baby and ran to sit in the car while we waited for the fire department. The really funny part was when I did the same thing again two weeks later."

- "One night I dreamed the baby was in bed with us, but had fallen out. I awoke in a panic and started ripping the sheets off the bed looking for her until my husband wearily pointed out she was sound asleep in her crib in the other room."

Get Some Help!

"I had to have twins to learn to ask for help from friends."
—*Abby, married 5 years, 3 kids*

"Sell your wedding ring ... do whatever you have to do to get
some help."
—*Kimberly, married 12 years, 2 kids*

Bring on the village! Hired or otherwise, help is essential. Sure, the two of you can do this on your own, but why risk insanity or divorce if you have other options? We know that there are few men who will refuse an offer of help, so this suggestion is mostly for women. We must fight the irresistible urge and basic instinct to do it all ourselves. This isn't easy to do. It's not just that we love and want to protect our babies; we also want to prove to ourselves (and others) that we can do it. Guess what? We *can't* do it all on our own, and *we are not failures if we ask for help.* Furthermore, most women are delighted to be asked to help a friend with a new baby, because being asked is a vote of confidence, a sign that the new Mom considers the potential helper to be a true friend. When you think about it, *not* asking for help deprives our friends of an opportunity to show how much they care.

Preserve Your Couple-Dom

Once you've survived the first hellish three months and are gradually regaining what's left of your senses, call an end to the time-out and make some simple efforts to reconnect as a couple—as man and woman. Put a little distance between yourselves and the baby. Nothing radical—the three miles between the baby and the local pizza place usually suffices.

The first post-baby date is terrifying for all new parents, though. The babysitter gets a three-volume treatise on how to change, feed, and burp the baby, and emergency numbers are printed in an EXTRA LARGE font on the fridge. It takes at least three attempts to get Mom out the front door as she remembers yet another vital piece of information: "He really doesn't like the second song on that Baby Mozart CD, so just skip that one." You finally make it to the restaurant and put in a quick call to make sure everything's OK. Based on our extensive research, we've found that the non-baby conversation on these first dates lasts for approximately two minutes and thirty-six seconds. The dates themselves last only slightly longer, as both parents (or, most often, just Mom) are overcome with fear that the baby might be missing them. They drive home at breakneck speed to a baby who is, invariably, fast asleep, and has been since they left.

We've learned it is so important to pay attention to your adult relationship at this point, no matter how strongly the pull of parenthood distracts you. Try making it just *the two of you* a few times a month, even if it's just going to the gym or going for a walk together. If humanly possible, try to minimize the baby conversation. If you're like us, you'll vaguely remember that you had plenty to talk about before she was born. A couple of good non-baby subjects include the existence of God and which celebrity you'd most like to sleep with. For a complete list, see Chapter 6.

Play Nice

It's rough in the big leagues. Parenthood and new babies will try the patience of a saint. Last time we checked, none of us were married to one. Are you?

We all need to make allowances for our spouses and understand that it's difficult for each of us. If you think your partner looks more "beat up" than you, try stepping in and give him or her a night off. Do what you can to offer words of encouragement: "You're a great Mom/Dad. We'll get through this," instead of criticism: "Have you lost your mind? I can't believe you just put those clothes back on her when they have spit-up on them."—at least sometimes.

Someone Should Be Sleeping

We don't just mean the baby. With the best of intentions, many first-timers try to share the division of baby labor "equally." If only one person is required to feed the baby, why is the other awake at 3:00 A.M. just to change the diaper? Surely one well-rested parent is better than two barely coherent zombies? Misery does not love company in this instance. The well-rested one can rally the exhausted one: make dinner, crack a few jokes, and take the baby for an hour or two. It should go without saying that Dad can occasionally "take the baton" so that everyone (i.e., Mom) gets a night or two a week of sound sleep.

Cluck, Cluck. Put an end to Midnight Chicken! (And bring a halt to other forms of domestic dispute as well.) It's entirely straightforward: you have to have a system. It took Gordon and Julia one kid to figure this out, but it stopped their midnight shenanigans entirely by kid two. Dad does all feeds up till midnight, Mom (goes to bed early and) gets everything after. Or whatever suits your sleeping schedule (for the Cockrells and the Kadyan-O'Neills, Dad got the early A.M. shift because Mom is a night owl). Don't duke it out, *Divide and Conquer*.

The Yin and Yang in the Safety/Overprotectiveness Debate

When a couple finds themselves in a perpetual debate about whether the kids are safe enough/dressed warmly enough or whether the baby is old enough to ride a scooter, there are two things to consider. One, it's a natural tension that is actually good for the kids. The Yin Parent thinks "safety of the offspring," while the Yang Parent thinks "developing skills so the offspring can survive on his or her own." Two, we have to decide when something just isn't worth fighting about—to tolerate each other's instincts to some extent. Women will rarely back down if they think a child is sick or could get hurt. Don't mess with Mama Lion. But the lioness should also recognize that she can't lock the baby in a padded cell until he or she goes to college, and try to keep her overprotectiveness in check.

The Training Weekend: The Mother of All Solutions

This patent-pending, marriage-altering solution is guaranteed to bring you both some perspective and mutual understanding (and hopefully a few laughs as well) as you adjust to new parenthood. We call it the *Training Weekend*.

The Problem: "He Just Doesn't Get It!"

Think back to the chorus of women telling us their husbands were "clueless" about what caring for a baby entails.

> "When he comes home and tells me he's had a tough day, he
> thinks he's done. Doesn't he know that I, too, am exhausted and
> have an equal desire to park my ass on the couch?"
> —*Mary, married 5 years, 2 kids*

Most Moms bear the brunt of the baby care in the first few months. Some Dads instinctively know to start pitching in, but we heard plenty of stories about those who didn't:

- "Ray would come home and put his feet up and ask what was for dinner. Not once did he offer to take the baby out of my arms or see if maybe *he* could make dinner for a change."—*Nicole, married 5 years, 1 kid*
- "My husband actually said to me, 'What's the big deal about taking care of one baby? How hard can it be?' "—*Phoebe, married 12 years, 3 kids*

What's a woman at the end of her rope to do? Don't get mad. Get out of Dodge!

The Solution: Give Him a Training Weekend

Go away for the weekend and leave your husband alone with the baby for 48 hours. No sitters. No in-laws. No cavalry whatsoever. The point is to let him figure things out for himself. He doesn't get it because he hasn't done it!

Saturday   Sunday

The Training Weekend

The Benefits

The benefits of a Training Weekend are many and varied:

Mom gets a break. If Mama ain't happy, ain't nobody happy. So give yourself a little girl time or alone time. Everyone, including you, will benefit from your well-rested, recharged self.

> "I didn't know I needed it until I had it. Boy, did I need it!"
> —*Valerie, married 7 years, 2 kids*

Dad understands. By taking sole charge of all baby- and house-related duties for a weekend, a man will better understand his wife's challenges and frustrations. He will have the same sink-or-swim experience that she has. If he wants to take shortcuts by not feeding a full meal, or leaving dirty diapers all over the floor, for once, he will have to deal with the consequences. He learns because there's no other way out. Just a small glimpse into *this* "real world" will improve your communication level and your ability to work together as a team on the home front.

"I had a list of things I wanted to get done when I had the kids by myself, and I was lucky if half of it got done. I didn't shower and I didn't shave. I could barely hold things together. It gave me an enormous appreciation for what my wife does. This was eight years ago and I remember it like it was yesterday."
—*George, married 13 years, 2 kids*

"I had no idea taking care of a baby was so hard. How does she do this day in and day out? I was truly in awe of her when she got back."
—*Brandon, married 3 years, 1 kid*

Dad bonds with the baby. Dad will, possibly for the first time ever, connect with the baby on *his* terms. Once Mom is gone, guys can figure it out for themselves. They get to play by their own rules. This knowledge makes them more confident and competent fathers.

"It gives you a chance to get to know your kids better. It allows you to really fall in love with them."
—*Ian, married 7 years, 2 kids*

To All the Female Doubters Out There: Let Go of the Reins

To our surprise, when we suggested a Training Weekend, some women looked at us in horror as if we had asked them to donate their babies' kidneys. One of them even said, "Is that *safe*?" They also said:

- "My baby needs me; she can't survive without me."
- "My husband wouldn't know what to do. He wouldn't do anything right."
- "If I went away, it would be a Baby Einstein Extravaganza."
- "I would have to write out twenty-two pages of notes before I could get out the door. It just wouldn't be worth it."

The baby will survive! Your husband is, we assume, a highly functioning adult in full command of his faculties. (If he's not, OK, you have bigger problems and don't have to do the Training Weekend.) He can do this. The occasional Baby Einstein Extravaganza never hurt anyone. And if you have to write twenty-two pages of notes, so be it. Just do it.

The one legitimate objection we heard was that it's too hard to organize a girl trip. Most women just won't go away on trips and leave their families. It took Stacie *six months and over a hundred emails* to organize her college friends to go away on a girl trip. Another friend's first effort was aborted when one of the women wanted to bring her one-year-old along. By comparison, when men sense an opportunity for escape, they quickly organize themselves like flying geese in *Perfect V Formation* headed straight for the airport.

In Perfect V Formation

Don't let a logistical dilemma prevent a Training Weekend. Spend two days and nights on your own if that's the only alternative (sounds heavenly, actually). Yes, it is hard to leave your kids. Yes, you will miss them. But you will feel so much better when you get back. And, best of all, you will have a grateful and helpful husband greeting you at the door.

To All the Male Doubters Out There: You Can Do It!

"I'm not sure what the big deal is. I'm their father, for God's sake."

—*Lee, married 9 years, 3 kids*

Have you ever thought to yourself, "Aw, c'mon. What's she complaining about? It can't be that tough." Or maybe you're a little frightened at the prospect (we promise not to tell anyone) and you've thought, "It's unnatural, not to mention dangerous, to ask the JV squad to suit up for a playoff game, right?" Well, it's harder than you think, but it's also easier than you think. If you can change a diaper, and if you can feed the baby a bottle while you watch *SportsCenter*, you can do this.

True Story

Her Story

When our daughter was about four months old, Ross, who had told me he would be home at 7:00 P.M., rolled in the door two hours late. I was pretty ticked. I had had a day from hell and hadn't showered in three days. When he said to me, "Why is this so hard for you? She napped twice, so you had two breaks, right? What's your problem?" I knew there was no other recourse than for him to see for himself, so I planned a trip away.

His Story

Mainly, I was happy that Stacie was getting a break. I could tell she really needed one, and, honestly, I did think, "How hard can it be?" I thought she was making a big deal over nothing. Turns out I didn't need a Training Weekend; all I needed was one morning. I was dying. I just wanted it to be over. On that Sunday, she was supposed to get back at 2:00 P.M. I was counting the minutes. At 2:05 I called her cell phone. She said she was stuck in traffic and she'd be an hour late. I started yelling at her, "This is absolute bullshit. You told me you'd be home at 2:00!"

Her Story

It worked. Ross's attitude totally changed after that weekend. Now, he always lets me know his ETA. He makes no more insensitive cracks (well, hardly any). And I hear the words, "You're amazing and I don't know how you do it" (which is really all any mother wants to hear), a lot more often. He's really stepped up on the domestic front, too. He hits the house with a "what can I do?" attitude, and it just means the world to me.

His Story

Yeah, yeah, I get it now. I'll never forget how relieved I was to see her walk in the door. I was beat up. Now I know that's how she feels when she sees me. I have a lot of respect for her job now. I couldn't do it.

SOLUTIONS FOR WOMEN

He *Can* Do It (and He *Should* Do It)

"When the baby was born I wouldn't let my husband do anything. And when he did do something, I criticized him. My mom told me, 'You either let him do it his way or he will not help you.'"
—*Eva, married 8 years, 2 kids*

"They may not eat veggies when I'm gone, but I don't criticize him. If I do, I will break down his ability to relate to the kids."
—*Allison, married 7 years, 2 kids*

Most Dads can be pretty handy with babies. Yet how often do we complain (and the three of us have often done so ourselves) that our husbands are completely clueless? Are we contributing to that cluelessness? We don't deliberately set them up to fail, but do we equip them to succeed? For most of us, motherhood is a trial-and-error/baptism-by-fire education. We learn as we go. If we stand over our husband as he tries to identify the front end of a diaper, or make sure that he is holding the baby just so, how will *he* learn as *he* goes?

"I don't have any baby responsibilities. There is no division of
labor. She refuses to let anyone else care for Owen. Even me."
—*Doug, married 5 years, 1 kid*

Plenty of guys are happy to use their wives' controlling tendencies to escape their shared responsibilities. Don't give him that excuse. A few years down the road, when that baby is a toddler throwing a tantrum, and your husband tells you that you should deal with it because "you are so much better than me at this stuff," what will you say? If we never gave them an opportunity to hone their parenting skills, can we really blame them?

Turn to Other Women

Julia and Gordon moved when she was eight months pregnant with her second child. She didn't know a soul in their new town. But a couple of her new neighbors took her under their wings. They helped her find everything from a pediatrician to a preschool to an OB to deliver the baby. They kept her sane after the baby was born, too. She's often wondered how she would have survived without them.

It's one of the few bad things about being born an American. In some other cultures, newborns are the exclusive province of women. The new mother is put to bed after the baby is born. She is fed and pampered. The baby is brought to her for feedings and then taken away so that she can sleep and recover. A community of women tends to her and the baby. (We're not quite sure what the new father is doing—assembling the baby's highchair, perhaps. . . .) While plenty of us had lots of great help from mothers, sisters, in-laws, and friends, no one we know had this kind of gentle adjustment to motherhood. But wouldn't you agree that the wisdom, empathy, and kindness of other women are essential for all new mothers?

One of the reasons we think we should turn to our female friends and relatives is that our husbands, as men, even though they are heavily invested in their kids and our emotional needs, are not equipped to give us everything we need at this time. Only another mother can understand how thrilled, overwhelmed, and terrified we feel. Only another woman can talk to us about latch-on and nipple shields. (See, we just lost whatever male readers we had up to this point).

When Stacie and Julia had their first kids, they joined forces and helped each other out. They shared a sitter twice a week to keep the baby-sitting costs down and give the kids some playtime together. Even after the sitter went home, they'd often hang out together through the long afternoon "witching hours." They even kept each other's kids overnight so the other could get a break with her hubby.

We women have to be careful what we demand and expect of each other with new babies on the scene. Like the preschool teacher who asked Stacie to make a casserole for the class party *eight days* after she'd had her third baby. Like the friends who raise an eyebrow when they come over to your house for a playdate and things are a little untidy. Let's be sisters united in the cause, not sisters who sit in judgment of each other.

How Full Is Your Cup?

"I didn't start doing yoga again until I started getting migraines and my doctor said I had to."
　　—*Leslie, married 8 years, 3 kids*

"I gave myself over to motherhood until I realized, hey, I need to keep myself healthy if I'm going to be around to take care of my child. So I finally got my butt back to the gym."
　　—*Margaret, married 5 years, 1 kid*

We are, for the most part, thrilled by our new role, but the thrill diminishes if we don't take care of ourselves. Once we are out of the Twilight Zone, we need to reclaim our sense of self. We need to make time for some exercise and pursue something we enjoy, even if it's just time with our girlfriends. If we can't get motivated enough to do it for ourselves, we need to do it for our kids. A frazzled mother running on fumes is not a good mother.

SOLUTIONS FOR MEN

Now's Your Chance to Play Varsity

In talking to as many men as we did during the course of writing this book, we noticed a funny thing about men and new parenthood: on the one hand, you are totally committed to your family and you relish your new role of father. On the other hand, the realities of caring for a newborn just don't do much for you. To you, that little ten-pounder (a.k.a. The Blob) requires a heavy investment (feeding, burping, diapering, bathing) that gives very little payoff, at least initially (an occasional smile if you're lucky). A few minutes a day with the little football is usually sufficient, then you're more than happy to make the handoff back to Mom, Grandma, or, well, pretty much anyone else with a pulse who can dial 911 in an emergency.

In this chapter, we've talked a lot about how we women should be mindful of our instincts to control everything once we become mothers. Here is the logical outgrowth of that idea: *overcome your instinct to head for the sidelines until the game gets more interesting. Your team needs you*—especially during this critical newborn stage. Think of it as the fatherhood equivalent of all the time Tiger Woods spends practicing out in the rain. You don't get the reward if you don't put in the time.

Assuming you fall somewhere in the middle of the "hands-on" spectrum between the "everything but breastfeeding" brigade and the "proud to have never changed a diaper" crew, here's a handy set of New Dad plays we bet you can master:

Basic Competency List, or What Every Self-Respecting Dad Should Know How to Do

- Change a diaper

- Dispose of a diaper (properly)

- Bottle-feed the baby (includes preparing the bottle)

- Burp the baby

- Put the baby down for a nap

- Dress the baby (in weather and destination-appropriate garments)

- Put the baby in a car seat

- Put the baby in a stroller and push it around the local park

- Basic orienteering skills: know where to find the diapers, wipes, bottles, and formula (both in your own home and in the local grocery store)

No Excuses

Yeah, yeah—you don't know how to play the game ... the first baby you ever held was your own ... the baby doesn't really like you ... you might accidentally hurt it ... your wife is so much better at everything ... your wife won't let you do anything ... yadda, yadda, yadda. We've heard 'em all. Some of those excuses do have merit; a newborn baby can be quite terrifying. Ah, but you'll get no violins playing around here. Your wife really needs your help, even if she sometimes acts like she doesn't want it. What's more, your baby needs you. He needs your love and attention, too.

The payoff for you comes later. Don't worry, we'll get to that.

Why Your Participation Is Important

During the course of writing this book we saw so many women reduced to tears as they recalled how "disappointed" and "abandoned" they felt during the early newborn phase. Sometimes, the kids are in junior high and they *still* remember how hurt they were by a nonessential trip their husbands took, or how he behaved as if nothing had changed in his life, or how he never once offered to do a full night of feedings.

As much as fatherhood is a sacrifice, it's also an opportunity: it's your chance to be a hero. Women whose husbands had stepped up couldn't sing their praises loudly enough. "He was fantastic." "I was so lucky. He was with me every step of the way." You have an opportunity during this time to foster feelings of love and tenderness and pride in your wife. These are feelings that she will hold on to forever.

Team Think

It's a trade-off. As a father, you should consider your partner's and your kid's needs in your calculations. It's simply a quid pro quo. If you want to go to the game on Saturday afternoon, present it this way: "Hey, if we don't have anything going on, I'd love to go see the game ... Then (and this is important) quickly follow it up with, " ... and I'd be happy to keep the baby tomorrow while you go do your thing." Somehow, the balance idea doesn't always seem to make it into the request to get away. Without it, to many women, it feels like you're always just angling to get away at her expense. The trade-off shows you get it—that you view this baby thing as a joint effort.

Seeing and doing. Here are some suggestions to help you support your wife and show your undying dedication to your family:

The Situation	How to Be a Hero
Your wife was up five times last night.	Take the baby so she can catch a nap. Or offer to do a full night of feedings once a week.
Your wife looks kind of grubby and pale when you get home, which is daily.	Take your place on the assembly line and pitch in with those feedings, diaper changes, and baths.
Your wife was on baby duty all week without a break.	Offer to take over part of the weekend so she can get a breather and do something for herself.
Your buddies are going to a bar after work.	Go another time. Your wife needs you more than ever. Maybe she'll have the energy to make you a cocktail when you get home.

The Situation	How to Be a Hero
It's a perfect day for golf.	Is there any other sort of day? Barring an earthquake, the golf course will still be there in a few more weeks.
The game is on.	Tape/TiVo it and watch it later.
Your mother is honing in on the nest.	Run interference. Blood relatives and hormones don't always mix well.

Empathy ... Ick

Listening and understanding: Two words that really turn a man off. New Moms, however, need empathy in spades. Unfortunately it's not one of your strongest suits. To paraphrase John Gray, the author of *Men Are from Mars, Women Are from Venus,* men have natural impulses to solve problems, not listen to them.[2] When your wife is suffering from baby wipeout and complaining about her tough day, the urge to fix the problem is no doubt irresistible, but she just wants you to listen. (Note: by "fix the problem" we do not mean ship the baby off to the in-laws until he can feed himself.)

We know you want to help. We know you mean well. But it's just not helpful when you suggest that, maybe, the crying baby your wife has been rocking for the past hour is hungry. (She's probably already thought of that one, Sherlock.) It's not helpful when you tell your exhausted wife that she'd be less tired if she didn't check on the baby every thirty minutes. (She'd be less tired if you'd take a night shift once a week.) In her mind, your suggestions mean that she's not up to the task of figuring out her baby. *There is nothing that upsets a new Mom more than questioning her maternal abilities.* She just wants you to listen and offer understanding.

A Brief Lesson in Empathy

Your wife says: "I'm so tired. Taking care of this baby is really draining."

You say: Nothing. Look her in the eye. Nod your head in agreement. Make some sounds that indicate you're listening. Murmur reassuringly, "I know it must be hard. You're a great Mom."

That's pretty much it.

Gimme an "M"! Gimme an "O"! Gimme an "M"!: The Power of Praise

Another unnatural act we're going to suggest you perform: that of cheerleader. No one is tougher on herself than a new Mom. More than anything else your wife needs to hear "you're fantastic," "you're amazing at this," "(insert baby's name) is lucky to have you as a Mom." You need to be her one-man pep squad.

Cathy once turned up for her daughter's four-month checkup one day late—right time, wrong day—and called Mike from the parking lot, sobbing that she was a terrible mother. He said just the right thing, "Don't worry, you're doing great." When a new Mom has one of those moments, the "I can't do this" feelings can be overwhelming.

So many accomplished women told us that the most important praise they ever received was, "You're a great mother." We need to hear those words on an almost daily basis in the newborn stage. And we need to hear them from you. You are the only other person who loves this child as much as we do. At the end of the day, no one is better qualified to tell us that we're doing a good job.

Just Fake It

If empathy and cheerleading just aren't your thing, then it's time to pretend. We all have those times in life when we just suck it up and fake it. You don't like your boss at work because you think he's a complete idiot? You just put on your happy face for eight hours a day. Your mother-in-law comes through the door in all her glory and talks your ear off? You don that sincere look that says, "Hey, just fascinating." When you think your wife is behaving like a lunatic and you don't understand why she is so upset that she bought the wrong diaper size, just fake it. Look concerned, make soothing noises, and just tell her she's an amazing Mom.

The Payoff

Finally. What's in it for you? Thought we'd never get here, didn't you?

Number One: You get to be a hero. You don't actually have to do that much to look like a total champ.

Number Two: Your kid will be better off.

Number Three: When you make an effort to help your wife, and to understand where she is coming from, you will put her in an appreciative frame of mind. She'll likely be more open to understanding your needs, if you get our drift. Maybe not as soon as you would like, but hey, better late than never.

Some of this new father stuff will not come naturally to you, though you might be surprised at how much actually does. We mourn the passing of your old life with you. (We lost ours, too, you know. ...) Will you miss it? Absolutely. Will you learn to love your new one? Absolutely. And most men, no matter how much they complain, will say it's the best trade they ever made.

THREE

What's the Score?

The Post-Baby Battle of the Sexes

"I am always in the doghouse. That's the baseline. I walk in the door at the end of the day and say, 'Hi, Honey, I'm home. I'm sorry.'"
—*Chris, married 8 years, 2 kids*

"It's not very difficult to keep score: fifteen to me and zero to him."
—*Maggie, married 7 years, 3 kids*

So who has it tougher in your house? Who's working harder? Who's giving up the most? When we become parents, domestic responsibilities explode. Financial pressures increase. The pace is relentless. Not surprisingly, we start to argue about the division of labor in our homes. *Scorekeeping* is an endless tit-for-tat war between husband and wife—an eternal debate over that most fundamental of all philosophical questions: "Who's on bath duty tonight?"

There's more to this chapter, however, than who's doing what. It's about the collision of expectation and reality. It's about the state of modern marriage and whether the ideal of a true partnership can ever be attained. It's a snapshot of where we are as a generation and a society, and what we think about the roles of women and the roles of men. Every man and woman we spoke with got ticked off while talking about this subject. Women argued about the stalled progress of feminism. Men said things like, "More complaining. I've heard all this crap before!" Talk about hitting a raw nerve. Phew! At times we wondered if our collective gray matter was up to the task of writing about it.

Expectation vs. Reality

Scorekeeping is evidence of the modern-day battle of the sexes on the home front. Why, oh why, after all this time, and all this supposed progress, are we still duking it out? Most of us expected equality in our marriages, that our careers would be equally important, and that parenthood would be a joint venture. So why doesn't it feel equal to any of us?

Most women we know feel burdened with the lion's share of the household crap after kids arrive, and that is not easy to swallow. We wonder why our share of the domestic pie looks so much bigger than our husband's.

> "I don't remember signing a prenup that said that when we had kids, I would take care of them *and* all the household crap. I thought we were on the same team here."
> —*Mary, married 5 years, 2 kids*

Meanwhile, many men feel their home lives and scant free time are dominated by their wives' demands to take on more of the domestic and child-rearing burdens. They wonder why their contributions, at work and at home, just never seem to be enough.

> "The competition is on, so on! I feel like a second string JV player going up against Shaquille O'Neal. I am always thirty points behind and I will never catch up."
> —*Jack, married 7 years, 1 kid*

We've all wondered, "Is this it?" Is our married life going to be an ongoing debate about this stuff? We all struggle to reconcile our expectations with the reality of marriage and parenthood. This struggle serves as a backdrop, and adds tremendous fuel to the fire, of our division of labor scorekeeping.

Slam Dunk

How the Game Is Played

On any given weekend in thousands of homes across America, wives stand in front of their husbands listing all of the selfless acts they have performed in the last week: "I paid all the bills, bought a birthday present for *your* mother, read *Goodnight Moon* five times, took four six-year-olds to Chuck-E-Cheese ... and that was just Tuesday. ..."

The husbands return fire: "Excuse me, but did I not make the kids breakfast every morning last week, including the morning it made me late for my presentation, when I really should have gone in early? *And* I picked up the dry cleaning without being asked, *and* I did bath duty three times last week. What more do you want?"

A volley of personal accomplishments and sacrifices ensues. Not exactly what we thought life would be like when we eyed each other across the room all those years ago, is it? We both end up angry and defensive, each convinced that we have it tougher. Some people are habitual score-keepers. Some people just do it occasionally. But we all do it.

Sometimes our low-stakes spatting game escalates into all-out combat. Men wage a sort of guerrilla warfare, where accumulating positive points is always a hit-or-miss affair. Women draw upon a major arsenal of weaponry. Our bazookas hit the target again and again, but for reasons we will explore later in this chapter, we never quite seem to get what we want.

Both sides are convinced that they are right and will up the stakes to prove their point. Women, men tell us, will pull out a list of his "priors" lest there be any doubt as to who is in the wrong. Often men are not equipped to retaliate effectively. Our friend Brad says, "It's like I am trying to make my point with a peashooter and she has a missile launcher and is just wiping up the floor with me. I can't win." He says, "I got up with the kids on Tuesday." She responds, "Well, I got up with the kids every morning for the last three weeks, other than that one Tuesday." Faced with such superior weaponry, men choose to retreat, but they *do not* concede defeat.

The bottom line: nobody wins this war.

The Rules

The game of scorekeeping involves the trading back and forth of *Marriage Capital*, or "points," between husband and wife. Pay attention here, because the rules are exceedingly complex. Here's a short overview:

1. In most instances, according to husbands, it is the wife who determines how many points a specific activity scores. "Why doesn't checking the air in her tires count, but cleaning the kitchen does?"

> "I always thought that I would get points for yard work. I'm out there on a Saturday morning trimming the hedges, mowing the lawn, making it all look pretty, and I walk in and she says, 'Where the hell have you been?'"
> —*Jacob, married 7 years, 2 kids*

2. Men often think that they have scored major points ("Hey, I was up at the crack of dawn with the kids; I did all the grocery shopping this weekend"), but to their wives, activities that count as "doing his fair share" don't score any points at all.

3. In fact, a man may have points *deducted* because he *expects* major kudos for simply pulling his weight.

4. Positive points have a use-by date. If they are not used within recent memory of the point-scoring activity, they expire.

5. Negative points, however, last indefinitely. Women, we've been told, keep a detailed mental log of all infractions and omissions.

> "You get credit for a good deed, but it only lasts for about six months. You have to use it fast. But demerits, they last forever."
> —*Francisco, married 4 years, 2 kids*

6. In effect, there is no statute of limitations.

> "What do you mean you're going to the game? You only spent an hour with the kids last weekend! And when your parents were here last month, I was the one playing Scrabble with your mother until all hours. ..."
> —*Tracy, married 5 years, 2 kids*

7. Advanced-level play:

> "You can get multiple points if you actually forgo a golf game or whatever and tell your wife you want to spend time with her."
> —*Simon, married 3 years, 1 kid*

> "No way. My wife would call bullshit on that right away. She'd smell a rat."
> —*Vince, married 5 years, 2 kids*

Weekend Warriors

Welcome to the weekend, the Scorekeeping Super Bowl.

> "TGIF? That's a joke. Thank God it's Monday is more like it. I kiss my desk on Monday morning."
> —*Dev, married 7 years, 2 kids*

> "Peter and I argue over 'pacing.' He's not in any hurry, but I feel like I have to keep moving or the whole family will be buried in laundry, toys, dishes, and dust bunnies. I can't stop. And I can't take a break. If I take a break, then the baby will want to nurse by the time I'm ready to start working again and I will fall further behind. Meanwhile, he wants to relax on the weekend and sip his coffee. I want him to be up and cleaning the bathroom."
> —*Kelly, married 8 years, 3 kids*

Remember Saturday and Sunday? Forty-eight hours of R&R. You could stay in bed (together) until noon … or not. You could have brunch at your favorite little bistro. Take in a movie. Paint your toenails, paint his toenails. The options were endless. He did his stuff. You did your stuff. Then you did some couple stuff. Remember when the most taxing issue you had was "Hey, what'll we do this weekend?" Kids arrive, and that question becomes, "You're doing *what* this weekend?" The *what* being fishing, jogging, aerobics, a manicure, work, golf, or whatever activity it is that takes you away from kids and spouse for more than thirty minutes.

> "I really resent that he wants to take off for five hours to play golf on Saturday, then he expects me to be oh-so-grateful because he watches the kids while I go to yoga for an hour. Big friggin' deal."
> —*Jane, married 9 years, 2 kids*

At no other time is the transition from carefree couple to encumbered parents more apparent than on the weekend. There is no more "me time." Your errands and all the house maintenance still have to be done, but now at breakneck speed with small people hanging on your legs. A little personal time to pursue your favorite activities becomes the subject of intense negotiation.

Those women who work outside the house descend into the depths of domestic hell on the weekend. During the week they either don't notice, or have no choice but to ignore, the crap under the sofa, the pile of unwashed laundry and the almost-empty fridge. Saturday arrives and those clothes *must* be washed, the living room *must* be picked up, and the fridge *must* be filled. Needless to say, their husbands are not thrilled to be sucked into a maelstrom of cleaning, shopping, and child-minding. (For the record, we girls are not too thrilled about it either, but what's the alternative—domestic chaos and smelly, starving kids?)

Scorekeeping Confessions

The three of us have at one time or another been serious scorekeepers. We're not proud to admit it, but there you have it. We each had different styles and our own way of letting our husbands know the score. Notice we are using the past tense. That is somewhat aspirational, but we have improved enormously and we're still working on it. Meet the Silent Sulker, the Quarterly Exploder, and Exacto Woman:

The Silent Sulker

Never being one to let a good grudge go to waste, in addition to being a consummate conflict avoider, Julia subjected Gordon to what is perhaps the most dangerous form of scorekeeping: *perpetual double-secret probation.* In her mind, being "equal partners" meant he should see, should implicitly understand, what needed doing and do it without being told. Telling him, or asking him, to do a task seemed to be an admission that the housework and child care were ultimately *her* responsibility. As the dishes piled up in the sink and the baby played happily with a load in his pants, Julia would note the mounting evidence of Gordon's "unhelpfulness" on her mental log. She wanted him to be a mind reader. When, lo and behold, he wasn't, well, that was his fault, too. Instead of communicating her concerns, though, Julia would don her martyr's cloak and set about the tasks at hand with a sizable chip on her shoulder.

Gordon responded in kind, retreating to the couch or the yard, silently stewing. Perhaps this behavior speaks more to Julia's psychological makeup than simply her scorekeeping practices, but that's how it went down in her house.

The Quarterly Exploder

Cathy is a self-confessed control freak. If something needs to be done she would rather do it herself. Most of the time that suits her just fine. Most of the time. She waits until she's drowning before she screams for help. She doesn't notice she needs a break until she's neck-deep in quicksand. About once every two to three months Cathy has a meltdown, an "I am sick of this, you do nothing, the house is filthy, the yard is a joke, I need a haircut, and if you ask me one more time what's for dinner I will lose it" type of meltdown. Mike gives the "You are an amazing, fantastic, super wife and outstanding mother, and I am not worthy to have you wash my socks" response and then takes off with both kids for six hours. By the time he gets back, she feels great and thinks she has the best husband in the world. (Yeah, Stacie and Julia don't understand it either.) Then everything is fine for a few months until the next explosion.

Exacto Woman

Stacie's brain operates like a precise mathematical computer program, complete with detailed files, heavy-duty analysis, and at least a hundred gigabytes of memory. According to Ross, during an argument, she accesses *any and all relevant data*—times, places, names, *entire* conversations, you name it—then she proceeds to analyze every last detail.

During the early post-baby years, the scorekeeping battle was on. Ross, the Debate Club Champion met *Exacto Woman*. During arguments about Ross's poorly timed golf outings or how little he helped out with a birthday party, Stacie, thinking that he still didn't "get" the big picture, would access the real ammo: every infraction from the last six months. Ross would return fire with detailed rebuttals, complete with statistical percentages comparing the merits of their arguments. But how could you blame him? He had to put his best game face on for *Exacto Woman*. They were both guilty of trying to win rather than achieve mutual understanding.

Why Do We Keep Score?

After kids arrive, amateur scorekeepers turn pro, and those of us who never cared about how much, or how little, our spouse did around the house start to keep score. Why do we do it?

- **Validation.** We feel like our spouse either doesn't get how hard we are working, or gets it, but doesn't give us our propers. We need a little expression of understanding and appreciation.

- **Exhaustion.** Parenthood is like playing in heavy surf. The waves are relentless. We've eaten one too many mouthfuls of sand. We hope our spouse will lessen our burden. We're looking for some action.

- **Injustice!** Either we think we are pulling more weight than our spouse and are pretty ticked off about it, or we feel falsely accused of not doing our fair share.

- **Hardwiring.** Maternal instinct is powerful. "Doing it right" suddenly becomes more important to women. Men, however, just want it done.

- **Habit.** Don't we all get in a marital rut and stay there? When there is no letup in the back and forth, scorekeeping simply becomes the currency of our relationship. It's how we communicate about everything, dragging the baggage of all those earlier accusations and counter-accusations with us into each new conversation.

- **Fear?** Yes, fear. We think we're angry, but really, we're scared. An attorney (uh-oh) we know said:

    "Those fights are never about the trash. Anger is a secondary emotion, fear is the primary emotion. She is afraid that he doesn't value her contributions. She wants to know that she is not doing it all on her own. He is afraid that he will never make her happy, that no matter what he does, it will never be enough."

The thing is, it doesn't *feel* like he's afraid he can't make you happy when he moans about having to take the kids to Costco. It doesn't *feel* like she craves your validation when she complains that you washed the baby's clothes with your jeans. It just feels like you are both overworked, under-appreciated, and in need of a break. And you are.

I Win!

HOW WOMEN FEEL

A Special Word to the Opposition (Oops! We Mean Our Male Friends)

Guys, we know what you're thinking (because our husbands have already said it to us): "*How women feel about domestic crap? You must be joking. Could there possibly be a more boring topic that I could be less interested in?*" Before you hurl this book across the room and head for the couch, though, hear us out.

Are you sick of scorekeeping? Do you wish you had more free time? Do you want a little more credit for all the acts of domestic and professional heroism you perform week in and week out? We've got your side of the story covered in this chapter as well. The thing is, we've talked to hundreds of women. Many told us this issue is as important to them as sex is to you. (We know you've already read that chapter first, so don't pretend you haven't.) So now it's your turn. Read on and try to understand how your wife feels about the division of labor. C'mon. Fair's fair.

Why Do Women Keep Score?

"Despite my thirty years of research into the feminine soul, I have not been able to answer ... the great question that has never been answered: what does a woman want?"
—*Sigmund Freud*

All Dr. Freud really needed to do was spend a day with a mother of two preschoolers and he would have had his answer: we want a partner, not a helper on the domestic front. We want the gender equality we were raised to expect in our marriages and our parenting. And, not to be too demanding or anything, but we'd also like a little more validation from our husbands to go along with it.

Oooh! This Nerve Is Raw: Expectations about Equality

"We had our first kid and almost overnight I felt like I went from being an equal to being the lesser partner in my marriage."
—*Becky, married 8 years, 3 kids*

"Why am I the only one in the house who knows where the
pacifier, diaper wipes, and sippy cups are? Where the hell has he
been living for the last three years?"
—*Rachel, married 6 years, 2 kids*

In the course of writing this chapter we realized women tend to keep score more than their husbands. There are two very good reasons for this:

1. **We are blindsided.** No matter how much we love being Moms, it's difficult to reconcile the first thirty (or so) years of our lives, which we spend pursuing education, careers, travel, and all manner of personal and professional fulfillment, with the physical and emotional reality of domesticated motherhood.

2. **We wonder what happened to *That Whole 50:50 Thing*.** We expect equality in our marriages, and are surprised and disappointed (to put it mildly) when, after the kids arrive, the domestic and childrearing responsibilities, for the most part, fall squarely on our plates, whether we work or not. We feel like our husbands pull a *Domestic Bait and Switch*.

Our experiences growing up in the swell of the feminist-minded '70s and '80s did not prepare us for what we encountered when we became mothers. Most of us grew up in homes where, even if we saw Mom doing most of the household stuff, we were encouraged to excel academically and succeed professionally. The message we got from home and from society was that we could do anything we set our minds to—in school, in sports, in the workforce, in family life. Few, if any, of us (and we say this as a statement of fact, rather than one of judgment) were raised to place much value on the role of housekeeper. While many of us looked forward to one day becoming mothers, we were often surprised to learn that the housedrudgery is inextricably linked to the babies. "Oh, you mean you have to cook for them and clean up after them, too? Well that sucks."

What's more, the playing field with boys was, for the most part, totally level. We viewed ourselves as equal to men from a very early age. As a second grader, Stacie gave a third-grade boy a fat lip when he told her boys were better than girls, and that they should have different rules for flag football. Julia, at age nine, bought herself a T-shirt on a family trip to Washington D.C. that read, "A woman's place is in the House. And the Senate." Growing up, Cathy always asked for (and got) a biography of a trailblazing, force-to-be-reckoned-with type of woman in her Christmas stocking.

We'd spent our entire lives up to this point sharing basically the same experiences as men—in education and in seeking the challenge and reward of a profession. *These experiences shaped our expectations about marriage and parenting.* When the three of us met our husbands and got married, we felt like their equals, and our husbands viewed us as such (we asked them again, just to be sure). They liked it that we were independent and opinionated. (Don't they now rue the day?) Our marriages did feel like equal partnerships. We had attained the ideal.

But when we became parents, somehow, the ideal of equality came unraveled. Aside from the few exceptions who've achieved the nirvana of co-parenting, most women we talked to were bitterly disappointed that the post-child division of labor was not more equal in their marriages, and that the increased volume of work was not more obvious to their husbands. Women don't understand why the sharing thing is not working out the way they thought it would.

The Working Mother: Having It All?

"I expected to have it all. I didn't expect to be doing it all."
—*Debbie, married 8 years, 2 kids*

When a woman remains one half of a dual-income household after becoming a mother (which most do), she wonders why the parenting and housework "buck" stops with her. Most working mothers we spoke with feel, accurately or not, that they are the alpha parent and by default responsible for all things domestic. A far greater percentage of the work created by babies and preschoolers falls on their shoulders. They are ultimately responsible for the children's day-to-day needs—selecting day cares, making doctor's appointments, keeping the mental grocery list.

Working mothers feel that they have two full-time jobs: work and motherhood. The motherhood piece is often referred to as the "second shift." Shift! That's a euphemism. It's a round-the-clock, day-in-day-out job. Men, on the other hand, have one full-time job: work, and one part-time job: fatherhood. If the milk supply runs out at dinner, whose fault is it? Hers. She didn't notice it was running low, and she didn't stop at the store on her way home. To women that just seems patently unfair. When both spouses are working, why does the lion's share still lie with her?

Working mothers told us they feel enormously overburdened. Not only must they meet all of their professional and domestic responsibilities, they must also bear the weight of societal and their own personal expectations to "do it all" perfectly.

> "If I leave work at 4:00 P.M. to go to a soccer game, people wonder if my desire to be with my kids is compromising my professional responsibilities. If my husband leaves work at 4:00 P.M., people say, 'Oh, what a great Dad.'"
> —*Holly, married 11 years, 3 kids*

> "The expectations are so high. We are expected to outperform our fathers at work and outperform our mothers at home."
> —*Pam, married 3 years, 1 kid*

The Stay-at-Home Mother: Whiplash

Our friend Janice echoed the despair of many formerly equal-status women turned stay-at-home moms when she said, "It's like his job is more important than my job. In a way, it's like all this stuff is beneath him now. It's 'woman's work' and he can't be bothered. I don't think he respects me anymore, and that makes me feel awful."

When a woman decides to stay home after becoming a mother, she often experiences *Whiplash*—the sensation of hurtling back to the 1950s. When her husband, her supposed equal, moans about having to help, or is constantly looking for the nearest escape hatch every weekend while she is up to her ears in kids and slimy, wet things, it feels like he is the one setting the dial and pushing the button on the time machine.

Most of us are shocked by the Whiplash phenomenon. It can feel like our lives have diverged completely from our husbands'. We may cherish the role of Mother, but we often do not cherish the "mind-numbing monotony" of domestic minutiae. Women tell us that they start to feel their husbands take them for granted after they stay home.

> "Sometimes I feel like a stay-at-home slave."
> —Brandy, married 8 years, 2 kids

All of this leads us to the following thought, which, guys, we hope we're making crystal clear: once we have kids, we are still equals, we are *still* a team. *Women want a partner, not a helper.*

Your Fair Share Is Not a Favor

> "He feels like he is helping me, like he is doing me some huge favor. Doing his fair share does not mean he is helping me. It means he is doing his fair share."
> —Abby, married 5 years, 3 kids

> "My friend Jim just told me he had to 'babysit' his kids this weekend while his wife is away. I told him, 'It's not babysitting when they're your own kids, Jim. That's called 'parenting.'"
> —Carla, married 9 years, 2 kids

Many men, whether or not they believe that much of the domestic stuff is their wife's domain, think that if they pitch in, they are doing her a favor. Guys, what you see as a favor (and a points-scoring activity), we view as doing your fair share. This is "helper" behavior, not "partner" behavior. When you want special credit for "helping out" with the day-to-day minutiae that is parenthood, it drives us mad because this expectation of credit tells us you believe the minutiae is technically not your job. It is, by default, our job, and any assistance you are providing is a special gift to us. Pardon us for not swooning at your graciousness. Some of us may stay home. And some of us may be more than happy to do most of the "stuff," but the inference that none of it falls in your court unless we put it there is just a big ol' fat burr under our saddles.

Men's Accountability, or Lack Thereof

"My wife has the ultimate accountability for the kids, not me. It's as much her perception as it is mine. To me, that means I don't have to worry about something unless she tells me to do it."
—*Ken, married 6 years, 3 kids*

Plenty of guys we've talked to complained that their wives micromanage their time. Absolutely a fair point, and we'll get to it in a minute, but maybe, just maybe, there are some legitimate reasons why we're "always after you about something"—reasons that are not about our own control-freakish, über-mothering tendencies, but instead about the reality of domestic life, and what your actions (or, more accurately, lack thereof) imply about your attitude toward that life.

"He doesn't do anything until I ask him to, then when I ask him to, he acts so *put upon*, like I am imposing on him. I can't win."
—*Elizabeth, married 4 years, 1 kid*

"What's up with the high drama? Recently, I had to finish up a big report for work, so I asked Evan to take the kids for the day on Saturday, and of course we were low on diapers, so I would need him to make a quick stop at the store. You know what he said to me? 'Thanks for ruining my life.'"
—*Sarah, married 7 years, 2 kids*

Did-Enough Dads

"Why is it that whenever my husband changes a diaper, he just leaves it on the floor? He doesn't even roll it up and tape the ends together. If I'm gone for more than an hour, I find a little trail of them when I come home. Follow the Yellow Brick Road!"
—*Nina, married 8 years, 2 kids*

Guys are all about shortcuts. They're looking for the easy way out. A guy may do a job, but does he get the job done right? Kids are not bathed. Vegetables are not eaten. Clothes are not clean. Teeth are not brushed. Shortcuts drive women nuts because (a) we have to pick up where you left off, which means more work for us, and (b) we always have to be "in charge" because you will not assume full responsibility.

Our friend Karen complains that her husband uses up all the *Convenience Cards* (i.e., all the easy activities) when it's his turn to watch the kids: "They'll spend most of the morning watching TV, eat junk for lunch, and then, when he hands them back to me, they're hyped up on sugar, wearing dirty clothes, and begging for more *Blue's Clues*."

Top Ten Convenience Cards That Our Husbands Use

1. TV
2. DVDs
3. Skip baths and brushing teeth, because, hey, there's always tomorrow.
4. Fast food
5. Fruit Roll-Ups count as fruit, right?
6. How about juice, doesn't that work?
7. The kids can just wear their PJs all day. We're not really going anywhere.
8. Do we really have to fix her hair? Can't it just be messy this one day?
9. My turn to watch the kids? Dial 1-800-Grandma.
10. Bribe the kids with candy or ice cream to do things they should do anyway.

What's the big deal about shortcuts?

The big deal is that many of the things women think need to be done "right" are fundamental, essential parenting functions. Health! Nutrition! Hygiene! Safety! If standard operating procedure was that fruits and vegetables, toothbrushing, bathing, and mental stimulation were optional activities, imagine the generation of toothless, ratty-haired, pajama-wearing street urchins that would see us into our old age. Guys want all these things done, but they don't want to do them themselves.

> "I know my husband wants to be with the kids, but he just
> doesn't want to worry about whether their developmental and
> nutritional needs are being met. In essence, he wants to coach
> the team to victory, but he doesn't want to attend practice every
> week."
>   —*Jennifer, married 9 years, 3 kids*

Another reason it's a big deal is that we *really* do want to turn the mommy pager off occasionally. But if you call us during our away time to ask, "Is it possible that the baby might have a poopy diaper?" (true story—one of us actually got that call), we might as well have stayed where we were. If we genuinely worry about a diaper not getting changed for ten hours, or about the life and limbs of our kids while they are in your care (some women do: "As long as our two-year-old is within shouting distance, my husband thinks he is watching him. How the hell can I leave him in charge?" says our friend Amy), of course it's going to upset us that you don't do things "the right way."

And, yes, we'll admit it: sometimes, *sometimes*, we're just being control freaks.

They're Your Kids, Too

> "I feel like I am always shoving family time down his throat.
> On the weekends he's more concerned with doing his own stuff
> than he is in spending time with us. Sometimes, I'm not quite
> sure where we fit into his life."
>   —*Maggie, married 7 years, 3 kids*

Guys, what's up with the *Perma-Scowl* all weekend when you're hanging out with the family and helping with the kids? It is absolutely heartbreaking for a woman when she sees that her husband looks ready to bolt when she suggests they all go the park. It is profoundly dispiriting when, every weekend, it's the same old bad attitude from you. Our friend Tammy said, "I hate it when we're out doing something with the kids and I can see on his face that he doesn't want to be there." We want to know that you see your family as the headline event, not some sideshow you fit in between work and hockey. When you consistently make your extracurricular pursuits your default M.O., you're telling us exactly what your priorities are.

Men often respond to requests to give the baby a bath or whatever by saying that it's harder for them to look after the kids. To all men with the "She's so much better at it than me" line, we say, "Maybe if you spent more time with them, they wouldn't be so difficult." In fact, we suspect that "She's so much better at it than me" is code for "I don't want to deal with any of the domestic stuff if I can possibly get away with it."

We're on to You, Buddy

Passive Man, the antihero, lurks in the hearts of all men. Plenty of guys out there think that passivity pays off. They think they can still get points for making a halfhearted effort to get to the dirty dishes first, or raising their posterior ever so slightly off the chair when they hear the baby crying, and then trying to appear disappointed when they say, "Oh, guess you've got him this time?" This time? You're not fooling anyone, Buddy.

> "I drive home at about thirty miles an hour. I do whatever I can
> to delay the moment."
> —*Chris, married 8 years, 2 kids*

> "Yeah, I call my wife from the car to ask her if she needs me to
> pick something up from the store on my way home. It's a great
> stalling tactic. She hasn't figured it out yet."
> —*Dave, married 11 years, 2 kids*

I Am NOT Your Mother

> "I have three boys. A four-year-old, a two-year-old, and a
> thirty-six-year-old."
> —*Olga, married 9 years, 2 kids*

Oedipal complexes aside, we know that most of you did not want to marry your mother. Why is it then that you leave your underwear on the floor for us to pick up? Why is it that when we take out a snack for the kids you ask, *did you bring anything for me?* Why is it that you expect us to plan all social events and family holidays? Why is it that you don't know where to find your daughter's shoes when she has been walking for the last two years? When you don't engage domestically, it sends the message that you think Mommy will come take care of it. Not cool. It's hard enough parenting the actual children in the family, without also Mommying someone who's just acting like a child.

What's Your Definition of a Sick Day?

"I spent the other night on my hands and knees doubled over with a stomach bug. The next morning, I'm still green, trying to make lunches and wondering if I might pass out at the wheel during the school run, when Brad came in, grabbed his shake, kissed me on the head, and said, 'Hope you feel better today, Hon,' and then poof, he was gone. Gone. I just sat down and cried. Then I threw up again, loaded up the kids, and drove them to school. He had no idea of the day I was facing, and it never even *occurred* to him that he might try to help me out a little. I didn't need a pat on the head; I needed him to do the school run."
—*Bethany, married 6 years, 2 kids*

What happens when *you* get sick?

Her day: Without a signed hospital note, there's no such thing as sick leave for a stay-at-home Mom. When the factory whistle blows, she has to clock in for diaper changing, tantrum resolution, transport, and feeding duty, no matter what the thermometer reads. She can't even take the good drugs to knock herself out for a few hours. By the end of the day, you might as well put her on a stretcher and load her into the ambulance.

His Day: When Dad takes ill, however, his day looks a little different. He swills his Nyquil, tucks himself into bed, and maybe watches a little *The Price Is Right* before the drugs kick in. Then he calls it a day. If he feels up to it, he might catch up on his TiVo-ed favorites or work on his Fantasy Football trades while the wife replenishes his sick supplies.

Don't get us wrong; we don't begrudge a sick man a day in bed. We're all for it. It's just that we don't think this situation is fair, because a) we could use a shot of Nyquil and a day in bed, too, and b) it seems to us that men don't realize they have a role to play in keeping the factory running during a state of emergency.

His & Hers Sick Days

A Little Validation Means a Lot

"Honestly, I really need him to tell me more often that I am doing a great job, that what I am doing is important. He gets affirmation all the time at work; I don't."
—*Denise, married 10 years, 1 kid*

So many women said the same thing: "I just wish he'd tell me he appreciates what I do." A lot of us wonder, at times, if the work we put into home and family is largely unnoticed and unappreciated by you. You may think, as one guy put it, that domestic crap has no value, that the everyday keeping of home and hearth is not important. But it *is* important. Without it, what kind of family life would we have?

Why She Does What She Does

The Volume Problem

Most women believe that their husbands simply don't understand how much there is to do. What we consider mandatory, they view as optional.

Leave aside the huge number of "basics" (the cooking, the shopping, the cleaning) required for daily household functioning, disease prevention, and starvation avoidance—all of which must be performed during our lunch break or with a child hanging on our leg. There are also many long-term issues that require thought and preparation: health (nutrition, doctors, exercise, safety), education (schools, classes, learning styles), and development (socialization, behavior, values, family interaction).

The volume problem is why we're up at midnight researching the safest car seat online. It's why our friend Carolyn said, "I've been thinking about schools since Annie was six months old. I'm researching on the net, talking to other Moms, reading everything I can. Joe would wait until Annie is six *years* old before he realized she should even be in school. Then he'd probably just say 'Hey, there's a bus stop at the end of the road. Just leave her there.'" It's why we sometimes complain about feeling overwhelmed. It's a lot to think about. It's a lot to do.

Mommy Brain: What's It Like?

We've already talked about the Mommy Chip that runs, all day and all night, in our brains. As a result of this chip, the kids are always just a few steps away in our thoughts:

We're always thinking about the children. "I need to get that report finished by 3:00 P.M. Hmmm, that reminds me, doesn't Tim have a pediatrician appointment at 3:00 P.M. on Tuesday?" As we drive to work in the morning, we're mentally rummaging through the cupboards to see what we might have for dinner that evening. Men leave their parenting hat behind them when they walk out the door and don't pick it up again until they walk back in that night.

We always want to do our best for the children. Our intentions are perfectly honorable, though we admit we can get carried away in the pursuit of perfectionism. We have that voice in our heads that says, "If I don't get her to eat that lentil soup, she's going to be unhealthy and have bad eating habits her entire life. If I don't get her into that preschool, it will hurt her long-term chances to excel academically. If I don't arrange enough playdates, she's going to get cut out of the preschool social circle." Obviously, our husbands want what's best for our kids, too, but they don't understand the compulsion we feel to match, or at least be in the same ballpark as, the extreme mothering happening all around us.

We get stressed about doing it all for the children (and for you, and for ourselves). Men's answer to this is invariably, "Just chill out." Telling a mother who has child and work commitments to chill out is like telling a nuclear engineer not to worry about the leak in the reactor he has been sent in to fix. We know you mean to be helpful when you tell us to relax, but often that suggestion is infuriating. It kind of underlines that you just don't get it.

Men have no *Mommy Chip* and no *Guilt Circuit*. You, in light of this, often wonder why we create so much unnecessary work for ourselves. The answer is that to us, it's not unnecessary. It's called being a Mom.

Freud, Here's Your Answer ...

Guys, there's a reason we've laid all this out for you. We're not trying to lecture. We're not trying to say we have it any tougher.

We're just saying it *is* hard work. And it *has* to get done. We too often feel like you take it for granted or angle to get out of doing your fair share. What do women want? The same thing you do! A little more appreciation, and a little more time to park our tired asses on the couch. Those "Thank yous" and "You're a great moms" are pretty hard to come by. What we tend to hear instead is, "We're out of coffee," "Where are my shirts?" and "Can I go shoot hoops on Saturday instead of taking Sammy to the birthday party?" We want a partner in our family and home life. Not a helper. Not a Sleestak stalking ominously around the house. Your words, your positive attitude, and your willingness to roll up your sleeves show us how you really view your home and your family.

Some "Scientific" Research on This Topic

An MSNBC survey asked men and women whether or not they shared chores equally. 74 percent of men said that they shared chores equally with their wives. 51 percent of the women said their husbands shared chores equally.[1] Clearly, men overestimate their contributions, or, rather, they give themselves credit for doing things that their wives don't consider a contribution.

An interesting parallel is that, in our experience, women tend to overestimate how much sex they are having. Men, on the other hand, know exactly how long it has been since the last touchdown.

And while we're on the subject of sex … are ya gettin' any? Noted marriage researcher Dr. John Gottman reports that husbands who are more willing to share in domestic chores have a more active sex life.[2] It's a chicken and egg thing. We're not sure which comes first, the sex or the domestic help. The bottom line, however, appears to be that he who gives more, gets more. (Note to the men: *willing* is the operative word here. Emptying the dishwasher with a scowl on your face won't send us running to the bedroom.)

HOW MEN FEEL

Top Ten Things Your Husband Really Wants to Tell You (During a Scorekeeping Argument)

1. "I really don't enjoy playing with the baby for more than ten minutes."
2. "It's not fair that after a full day at the office, you expect me to hit the door at sixty miles per hour."
3. "You can't have your cake and eat it, too. Being Super Provider and Super Dad isn't easy."
4. "I just want a little free time without being made to feel guilty. I'll be a lot happier if you let me off the leash for a couple of hours on the weekend."
5. "I'm not stopping you—it's not my fault you haven't been to the gym in three months."
6. "Doing every last thing 'as a couple' or 'as a family' is emasculating."
7. "Stop micromanaging my relationship with the kids."

8. "Tell me what you want me to do! Make me a list and I will do it!"
9. "Why is it you see only the stuff I didn't do ... what about everything I did do?"
10. "What happened to my old life? I feel trapped in the trenches of domesticity."

Why Do Men Keep Score?

As we've said, in most relationships, women are the primary scorekeepers. But men play ball, too. In this section we'll try to unravel the reasons why. Here's what we think they are:

1. **To preserve parity.** Men feel like whatever they do, it is never enough.

2. **To maintain control over their lives.** Men express irritation that, often, their wives control (or attempt to control) their relationship with their kids, their home environment and, inadvertently, their free time.

3. **They need acknowledgment (just like their wives).** If the "Thank yous," the "You're working really hards," and the "You're a great Dads" are few and far between, they begin to wonder if their wives take them for granted.

Just as most women are stunned by, and rarely happy about, the domestic obligations associated with motherhood, men, at times, rail against the lack of freedom that accompanies fatherhood. Some men despair that fatherhood has reduced their life, outside of work, to one of relentless domesticity. It is this fear (that nagging "*is this it?*") that serves as a backdrop to much of male scorekeeping.

It's Never Enough!

"I get zero recognition for work. It doesn't matter how tough of a
day I've had. I get home and I have to be *on*."
—*Phil, married 7 years, 2 kids*

Welcome to the doghouse. Most men feel like, no matter what they do,
It's Never Enough. They make comments such as, "my contributions are
never appreciated," or "I am behind, and always will be, for the rest of
my entire life." Many think that their wives have superhuman expectations of them. Most say it is completely unfair for their wives to criticize
them for not helping enough at home when they make Herculean efforts
to excel at work. This sense of unfairness is especially acute among men
who are the primary, or only, income earners.

"You women want to have your cake and eat it, too. You can't
actively choose an aggressive alpha male because he's a good
provider and then expect him to be Mr. Mom at the same
time."
—*Harrison, married 8 years, 2 kids*

Another friend, Lee, said, "I cannot, cannot function at work when I'm
constantly down in the weeds scrubbing bottles and burping babies at
3:00 A.M." He may have a point. The three of us have all felt, at one time
or another, that our husbands don't do enough, despite the fact that they
all do a hell of a lot. There are several categories of *It's Never Enough*,
including:

1. A man does not get credit for what he does do, especially what he
   does at work.
2. When he *does* do something around the house, it's never right.
3. He has to guess what he is supposed to do.
4. When he doesn't do something, or he doesn't do it right, his wife
   holds it against him ... indefinitely.

The three of us will be the first to admit that we've been guilty of
some, if not all, of these infractions.

Work Counts for Nothing

> "Why does work count for nothing in her mind? Shouldn't there
> be some kind of percentage exchange going on here? If I am
> contributing eighty percent of the household income, shouldn't
> I just be responsible for twenty percent of the domestic stuff?"
> —*Vince, married 5 years, 2 kids*

Once children arrive, men feel the weight of the potential long-term consequences of every decision, whether it is seeking a promotion or selecting a college savings plan. The stakes are higher than they've ever been, especially if a man becomes the sole breadwinner. To him, it is a new world order. He is now shouldering 100 percent of the responsibility to provide enough money for the family. He starts to see it, as Vince does, as a percentage exchange, and he wonders why work is not included in his wife's fifty–fifty calculation. Women born any time in the last fifty years, however, expect their husband's share of the domestic workload to remain, if not exactly the same, at least in the same ballpark as it was before kids. Many men think this is totally unfair.

It is an ironic coincidence of timing, or the twisted sense of humor of an omnipotent deity, that the baby-making years occur just as the heat turns up on the work front. If, like many couples in our generation, you are marrying and having children in your thirties, you feel considerable pressure to make these years at work count, just as your responsibilities on the domestic front explode. (Women also feel this pressure. If they have taken a career break to focus on the kids, they fear they will never be able to catch up with their professional peers.)

> "This is all happening during the sweet spot of our careers. The
> stakes are really high at work. Your thirties are make or break
> time. You can't take your foot off the accelerator."
> —*Karl, married 12 years, 3 kids*

It's Never Good Enough

Guys, as we've said, are problem solvers. They see a situation, especially one in which their beloved is not happy, and they want to fix it. They will fix it in the most expedient manner possible, but they are not detail-oriented about it. Wife wants to sleep in? No problem. I can turn on the Baby Einstein and the kid will be happy and she can sack out. Baby needs changing? Change the diaper. Doesn't matter where I put the diaper after the changing part is over.

> "Here's an example of not good enough for you: last week, after I got up early and made the kids breakfast, I scrambled to shower and get dressed to make the 8:00 A.M. (i.e., late) train into work. I conscientiously threw away the dry-cleaning wrap from my dress shirt into the wastebasket in our bathroom. On my way out the door, my wife came at me with a scowl and said, 'I don't mean to be picky, but can you throw out all your dry-cleaning wraps in the downstairs garbage and not the one in our bathroom?' I mean, come on! Which garbage can is the right garbage can? Has it come to that?"
> —Robert, married 12 years, 2 kids

> "So I took both kids and went to Costco. Just sucked it right up and did it, just like I thought she wanted me to. Did I get even a 'thank you' when I got back? No. Instead, she went through the shopping list and sighed and told me I forgot the detergent and the plastic cups."
> —Frank, married 7 years, 2 kids

It's Never Good Enough

Guys asked us, we guess because we're women: why does she always want to micromanage everything? Why is doing it my way so terrible? What does she care if I take Matt and Andy to my parents while she's at the gym all morning? They wonder why they don't at least get partial credit for trying.

Men Answer Women's Number One Question (Well, One of Them)

Question: Why don't guys *see* the domestic crap the way we do?
Answer: They don't see it because they just don't care. They just don't care.

Do you remember his apartment when you were dating? Would you have *ever* taken a shower in there? Or, God forbid, used the moldy, festering towels that hadn't been washed in months? Today's husband is not a closet chauvinist. He has no interest in seeing his wife on her hands and knees scrubbing the floor. He's probably not even threatened by her earning power or self-sufficiency. He is fully prepared to step up and help out. But he doesn't like the routine running-of-the-household stuff and he never will. In his mind, it has no value and it should be avoided. If it cannot be avoided, it should be minimized. If possible, a shortcut should be used. He cares about getting it done, but not *how* it gets done.

Top Five Shortcuts Men Use

1. Change the diaper. Put soiled diaper on the floor or *on top* of the Diaper Genie, but not actually *in* the Diaper Genie.
2. Take the trash out. Don't replace the trash bag in the kitchen.
3. Never change the toilet paper roll. Use tissue from the tissue box instead.
4. Place dirty clothes *on top* of the dirty clothes hamper.
5. Dress the kid in the first thing you pull out of the drawer. Whether it "works" or not is not an issue.

The Moving Target

"When my wife is upset about something it doesn't matter what
I say, I just make her madder. I never seem to help the situation.
Whatever she's upset about changes on a daily basis. So every
day, I have to figure out what the 'issue du jour' is and avoid it."
—*John, married 11 years, 2 kids*

GET THE GROCERIES

"You got the wrong kind of milk."

TAKE AMY TO BIRTHDAY PARTY

"Why didn't you put her in her new dress?"

BRING HOME A PAYCHECK

"What's the big deal? You'd be working even if you didn't have a family."

Moving Targets

To a man, every single guy we've spoken to said something along the lines
of, "It seems that the hardest thing for women is to articulate what it is
they want us to do. We're just supposed to know what they want." And,
shockingly, when a guy can't read his wife's mind, he gets in trouble.

"We would help out more if our wives would tell us exactly what they want us to do. For example, last Sunday night the house was a total mess and I said to my wife, 'When this TV show is over we really need to clean up.' She said, 'You mean *I* need to clean up.' And I didn't—honestly—I meant that we both needed to do it. She got so annoyed with me and then told me about all the ways I had not helped her over the weekend. And I swear I had asked her so many times, 'What can I do to help?'"
    —José, married 7 years, 2 kids

As much as we want them to be, men are not mind readers. When they don't have targets, they get frustrated. When we expect them to just "see" the things we see, we are bound to be disappointed.

Prior Convictions and the Log of Evidence

"If a guy messes up and does his 'penance' that should be the end of it. It's not right to throw it back in our face six months later when we can hardly remember what it was all about anyway. Each individual incident should be dealt with separately. No mention of prior convictions."
    —James, married 9 years, 3 kids

Guys told us they feel there is no statute of limitations for their violations. What can we say? That statement is absolutely, totally, one hundred percent true. We can't seem to forgive, or forget. It's not one of our more attractive feminine virtues. (In our defense, though, we usually have to bring up the "priors" because our husbands are *Repeat Offenders*.) When we rehash old incidents, our husbands, quite naturally, get defensive and angry. They are less likely to want to talk about the issue at hand or be receptive to what we want to say.

Lack of Control

Most men feel as if they have little control over their environments. They are rarely the boss at work, and hardly ever the boss at home. As we described in Chapter 2, their wives act as *Gatekeepers* to the house and the children. Their wives plan weekends, select baby names, and evaluate vacation destinations. In many cases, their wives simply tell them where they need to be and when they need to be there. Lots of guys like it this way, but many others complain that their wives try to orchestrate their lives and fatherhoods.

They're My Kids, Too

"My parents were divorced, so I never spent much time living with my dad. I don't want that for my own kids, and I don't want it for myself, either. I want to be there with them, watching them grow, sharing their ups and downs. And I want to help my wife. I don't expect her to do everything."
—*Omar, married 10 years, 3 kids*

The overwhelming majority of men want to be active, hands-on fathers, but it's hard for a man (as it would be for anyone) to enjoy being a parent when his wife micromanages that relationship.

"I come home at night and it's a great way to let off steam, rolling around on the floor with the boys. But I don't do it anymore because she yells at me about getting them 'all riled up' before bedtime. Even when it's 'allowed,' like on Saturday morning, she's still kind of hovering over us. I can't wait till they're bigger. Then maybe she won't be so worried all the time."
—*Luke, married 7 years, 2 kids*

Men have commented to us that they "fall more in love" with their kids when they are left alone with them. As long as Mom is around, Dad is just the copilot.

It's My House, Too

Some men confided to us that they can feel like (unwelcome) guests in their own homes. It's their wife's way or the highway. What's the point of showing any initiative if you're always getting smacked down? As Doug says, "Why do I always have to raise my standards? Why can't she lower hers? Why is it when I clean the bathroom—and it looks totally clean to me—she gets mad and redoes it? Then I get no thanks for what I did do!"

> "Sometimes I just want to retreat to the basement and watch a game for a few hours. I feel like I need to get a signed permission slip from my wife to watch the Rose Bowl in peace. I repeat, the Rose Bowl!"
> —*Jack, married 7 years, 1 kid*

I Have a Life, Too (Don't I?)

> "I don't even bother to plan anything on the weekends anymore because my wife has already planned every minute—on Microsoft Outlook, no less."
> —*Joel, married 10 years, 4 kids*

Why do guys keep track of points? To trade them in for freedom. As much as they love their wives and kids, a lot of guys feel the leash tighten around their necks as their families grow. They keep score about how much free time they are losing. Lance put it this way, "To men, marriage equals 'I can't do the things I want to do anymore.'" Charlie said, "I want it to be a *quid pro quo* so I can get some freedom."

Men just want a little freedom from their responsibilities. "I want time away." "I just want a break." "My wife has never said to me, 'Go do your thing. I'll see you whenever.'"

Why Doesn't She Just Go?

Guys also find a particular element of female scorekeeping confusing and annoying: they are perfectly willing to give us free time in exchange for their own. But then we don't take advantage of the opportunity, and, exacerbating the problem, we turn around and: a) complain that we never get a break, and b) make our husbands feel guilty for taking their break. Understandably bewildered, they say, "She tells me she wants time to herself, but when I say go, she doesn't go. Why doesn't she just go?"

"If my wife hasn't spent enough points, I'll encourage her to
spend them so that I can redeem mine. I want her to max out
her points so I can use mine. I can't go play golf for five hours if
she hasn't had a break for days."
　　—*Nathan, married 6 years, 1 kid*

"I buy her spa time with an expiration date so she'll be forced to
use it."
　　—*Paul, married 9 years, 2 kids*

Stop the Complaining and Start the Validating

"Last week, I had to go on two business trips for work. It was
absolute hell, but she just seemed annoyed that I wasn't around
to help with the kids. Like I had some choice in the matter!
Doesn't she realize that I am working my ass off for everyone?"
　　—*Mark, married 11 years, 2 kids*

Just like women, men need validation. Just like women, men can feel
their efforts on the domestic and work fronts go unnoticed and unappreciated. When a guy hears his wife express some appreciation, he feels
like a million bucks. Who wouldn't? They are disheartened by martyr-ish
tendencies and too much complaining.

"I'm Married to a Martyr."

"A lot of the stress women feel is self-created. There's a lot of
keeping up with the Joneses."
　　—*Felix, married 6 years, 1 kid*

"My wife's maternal instincts whiplash the whole family. I feel
like I spend half my time depressurizing her. It's just too much."
　　—*Toby, married 9 years, 2 kids*

All of us girls have played the Martyr. We've all slaved away on our husband's behalf, and made damn well sure he knew about it. But a woman
getting bent out of shape about an incomplete shopping list, or driving ten
miles out of her way to get the special carpet cleaner, or staying up into

the wee hours to hand-make party favors is virtually incomprehensible to a guy. Then, when she starts keeping score with him because he doesn't adhere to the same meticulous (some might call it anal) standards, he considers it unnecessary, annoying, and largely ridiculous—"martyr-ish" was the word many of them used.

The Free Pass, and Other Grossly Inflammatory Comments

Several men told us they think their wife has a *Free Pass* when she stays home with the kids, even when they support her decision. They say, "She doesn't have to get up and go to work every day. Yeah, it's work and all, taking care of the kids, but the pressure to perform is not there, and she knows it." We swore we wouldn't reveal the identity of the guys who said this, because they all acknowledged that it is a grossly inflammatory comment, likely to elicit an "off with his head!" response.

Did he just say what I think he said? Yep. But wait, there's more ...

> "Women have been doing this for thousands of years. There have been centuries of human history where women have had a lot more children than we have, and they had to do a lot more work, churning the butter and washing clothes in the river. Why is she always complaining?"
> —*Bobby, married 7 years, 1 kid*

> "It's hard on my wife because she's an educated, competitive working woman. But now she wants to be the perfect Mom, too. I don't see how she's going to make both things work."
> —*Warren, married 5 years, 2 kids*

These comments are out there in the realm of guy talk, so we're including them in our discussion. To a great extent they reflect what lies at the root of some men's scorekeeping behavior; they think that their wife is complaining too much about a choice she made—a choice he doesn't have (or doesn't think he has).

When a guy hears his wife perpetually complaining, especially in light of the fact that she does have a choice, it makes him hugely frustrated that he can't make her happy. He can eventually (consciously or subconsciously) become less sympathetic because he is so annoyed. It can even become his rationalization for doing less, in a passive-aggressive kind of way. He just tunes her out, because she'll complain no matter what.

SOLUTIONS FOR BOTH

As the writer George Eliot once said, "What do we live for, if it is not to make life less difficult for each other?"

How Do We Rip Up the Scorecard?

"I'd love to stop the scorekeeping. With each year and each kid, we are pushing ourselves harder. Kids and careers take you to a level where neither of you wants to do (or can do) the work because it's just too much."
Sam, married 9 years, 2 kids

Whew, here we are, all these pages of moaning and groaning later. Almost makes you want to throw in the towel, doesn't it? But let's not just yet. Maybe there's some way we can all figure out how to go on living together....

What would it take to get you to ratchet down your own scorekeeping behavior? How much of it is *really* your spouse's fault? How much of it is your fault? What are you *really* looking for? Action? Validation? Equality? Here's another question to ask yourself (it's harder to answer than the others): what is your spouse looking for from you? We used that term *ratchet down* on purpose. Notice we didn't say *end it entirely*. Big distinction. It's important to acknowledge at the outset of this discussion that we can't stop scorekeeping entirely. We are all human and we can all get kinda bent out of shape from time to time about the dirty dishes in the sink.

Scorekeepers Anonymous

Like those recovering from substance addiction know: it's so easy to hit that bottle again. It's so easy to fall off the wagon, back into your old, sorry scorekeepin' ways. So we've formed a support group of three to keep ourselves straight. Here are the minutes from our last meeting:

Hi, I'm Julia, and I'm a recovering scorekeeper. Before I started working on this book, and understanding how much I was hurting my marriage with my silent sulking and mental evidence log, I kept score with Gordon about everything under the sun. He was the one who cried out, "It's never enough!" And he was right; it wasn't. I couldn't define the rules of the game, much less how anyone could ever win. I stopped the scorekeeping by dividing things up with him. We have an explicit understanding now of who does what. There's nothing to keep score about anymore. I've also figured out that as long as we build some free time into our weekend plan, we're both so much happier. I'm even getting pretty good at ignoring things that are not important. If our sons go to church dressed in football jerseys, so be it. At least I don't have fish in my bathtub like Cathy! (Yuck. Read on.)

Hi, I'm Cathy, and I'm a recovering scorekeeper. My scorekeeping binges were usually preceded by months of never asking for help, and never accepting Mike's offers to do the bills, call the plumber, or whatever. "I can do it" was my mantra. I was a certifiable combination of perfectionist and control freak. I believed that to get things done right, I had to do them myself. (Basically, I thought the world would be a better place if I ran it.) Furthermore I believed that I, as the mother, was supposed to do everything. But there was a fundamental flaw in my plan. It was just not possible for a working mother of two to get everything done. And it was not possible to try to do it without getting very angry at my husband, even though he was standing on the sidelines eager to help (or, more accurately, to find help). I stopped scorekeeping by letting go. I realized that someone else can pay the bills, plan vacations, and find a music class. I am a better Mom, wife, and all around nicer person when I share the burdens with Mike.

Hi, I'm Stacie, and I'm a recovering scorekeeper. In fact, the last time I was in a heated scorekeeping battle with Ross was eight months, two weeks, and five days ago, to be exact. As we wrote this book, I figured out how infuriating it was for Ross when I accessed my mental database of incriminating evidence—with *exact* precision. I realized I needed to forget all of his past misdemeanors and recognize that he was not trying to be a repeat offender. He really was putting his best foot forward. Now, whenever a scorekeeping argument starts brewing, the first thing we do is laugh at ourselves and call it what it is—a silly, waste-of-time game. When we stop and think about each other's point of view, the funny thing is, we usually figure out that we are both right, in a very "inexact" way.

We all need to think about how we can make the situation better, because we can't make it go away.

For Starters, Hand in Your Martyr Badge

"For to feel oneself a martyr, as everybody knows, is a
pleasurable thing."
    —*Erskine Childers*

Sorry. That thing's gotta go. We're all guilty of it: men with their high-drama highjinks, "You're ruining my life," and women with their high-octane harping, "You'd be happy to let me do it all on my own, wouldn't you?" We all feel overwhelmed. We all feel underappreciated and totally put-upon by our spouses. We've all played the martyr, and made the scorekeeping worse with the great shows of our suffering. It doesn't really get us anywhere, though, does it? *Our spouse gets annoyed by the inference that we are working harder than they are, and withholds the very appreciation and validation we are seeking.* No one wins.

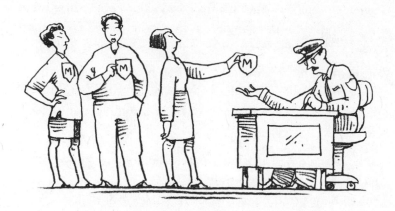

"C'mon, now. Hand it over."

Show Appreciation/Validate

There. That's better. Now for some good news. Universally, people told us they want empathy more than they want action. They are perfectly willing to do what they think is *more* than their fair share as long as they are getting a little appreciation for it—as long as their spouse says, "Thank you," or "You're doing a great job, and I appreciate it," rather than, "My life is so much harder than yours," or "Can't you see that I've got it tougher?"

What's the best way to motivate somebody? Positive reinforcement. Julia and Stacie learned this in business school. Cathy learned it in her legal consulting practice. Ac-cen-tu-ate the Pos-i-tive: "You were so helpful with the kids this morning," E-lim-in-ate the Neg-a-tive: "Why didn't you do the laundry tonight?" It's so much more effective. Even better if you go over the top a little bit—even if, deep down, you think it's something your spouse should've been doing anyway and they don't really deserve the accolades. When you let your partner know you appreciate what they've done, you'll motivate them to do it again. (P.S. this works with kids, too.)

> "I'm so focused on what Kevin *hasn't* done that I forget what he does do. And I know there are times I've neglected to tell him anything nice for weeks on end. Just as I'm talking to you about this, I remember his dad made some very nice comments about

him to me on the phone last week, and I didn't even bother to
tell him about it."
—*Janet, married 8 years, 3 kids*

Not sure how to start with this one? So mad that you can hardly for-
mulate a coherent sentence like, "Get off your sorry butt and help me
pick up these toys!" Here are some obvious-sounding, but underutilized
ideas to get you started:

1. *The Three A's*: Affirmation, Appreciation, and Acknowledgment.
   Just pick one and run with it.
2. Some sample (indeed, actual) *Nice Things to Say*:
   • "Gosh, I remember how hard it is to travel on business. You went
   up and back to New York in one day today. That's a bitch. Yes, you
   did that because you had to for work, but you also did it for me
   and the kids. Thank you."
   • "You are working and you keep the shit moving at home, too.
   Thank you for keeping it all together for us."
   • "The other day my husband told our daughter, 'Your Mom is wonderful. Do you know how wonderful she is? She takes such good
   care of all of us.' He's really good about saying things like that, and
   it means so much to me."

   Actually writing these down makes us feel kind of sappy, but just
   saying something like this to your spouse can make a big difference.
3. Think about the *101 Invisible Things* your spouse does on a regular
   basis, and point one of them out occasionally:
   • You did the dishes.
   • You put up with that putz at the office in an all-day meeting.
   • You did my laundry.
   • You changed the diaper.
   • You sat in traffic for an hour.
   • You got the boys dressed and fed before I got up this morning.
   • You get the picture ...

   Most of us wait until that invisible thing is *not* done to comment
   on it. We're all pretty familiar with where that gets us.
4. *Kumbayah*
   Sometimes we get so consumed with all the work that needs doing

that we can lose sight of the big picture. Once in a while we have to get our heads out of the laundry basket, the shopping list, the leaky faucet, the work deadline, and the state of the savings account long enough to appreciate all the good things we have.

Setting Expectations and Planning

The other most effective way to eliminate scorekeeping is simple, but none of us (and, for the record, none of our husbands) even thought about it until we started working on this book. *You have to have a set division of labor. Specific areas of responsibility.* This does away with score-keeping. Or at least it takes the sting out of it . . .

For example: Andrea's husband, Daniel, does all the cooking. Helen's husband, Phil, cleans up the kitchen after dinner as Helen gives their kids a bath and gets them to bed. Tom said that he and his wife Joanne have had very explicit discussions about how to divvy up the baby duties: he takes care of the baby from Saturday night to Sunday morning so she can sleep in. (FYI: Tom is the Baby-Einstein-on-repeat-play guy.)

Allison said, "We set expectations. Two mornings a week Bill gets up with the kids. It used to be me every single morning. He would never volunteer to do it, but we agreed on two mornings a week for him. Now, he does it and doesn't make a big deal out of it."

To do this right, you have to make a list and divide it up. Yeah, we know. We didn't want to do it either because it's boring and time con-suming. But it has several benefits, the most important of which being that *you can actually stop arguing about who is responsible for what.* If that's not reason enough for you, here are some more:

• It forces us to prioritize.

• It forces us to own up to our own scorekeeping behavior.

• It helps us to see that men are not useless and that women are not control-freak, life-dominating lunatics.

• It helps us eliminate unnecessary stress on our marriages by illustrat-ing the sheer physical volume of work we are both facing, together.

The Everything List

Make a list of everything, absolutely everything you can think of that must be done, sometimes every day, sometimes on the weekends, sometimes just occasionally (like every birthday and holiday).

Daily: work; children (up, dressed, nursed, fed, de-slimed after breakfast, hair brushed, teeth brushed, lunches and backpacks packed, notes, forms, etc.); drive children to school/day care; daily house maintenance (dishes, laundry, trash, etc.); lawn and garden care; prepare meals; nap management for small children and babies

Weekly: family activity and time management (includes birthday parties); adult social-life management (remember that?); grocery shopping/meal planning; after-school activities/playdate management and transportation; weekly/monthly/(biannual?) house cleaning (mopping, bathrooms, etc.)

Specials: extended family management (visits, calls, etc.); photo management; gift management: birthdays in your family (3–6 people), birthdays of extended family (6–20 people); correspondence management (birthday cards, thank-you notes, email); travel management; holidays (cards, decorations, gifts, activities, cooking); home projects (repair, maintenance, and generally making it look nice); volunteer for kids' schools

Ongoing Administration: bills; health care (appointments, insurance, etc.); education (school selection and evaluation)

Divide and Conquer

As one couple with five children told us: "We're each giving one-hundred percent here, each in our own way. We have to focus on the end result, not always keeping the score fifty–fifty."

Once you've made a list, you'll both clearly see the mountain of work that is always in front of you. The only way to get it all done is to *Divide and Conquer*.

Theresa said, "We have a good division of labor. If he doesn't do his part, it's his problem. If it's not that important, I wash my hands of it." Play on your strengths. If you love to cook, sign up for that. Retain control over things that are really important to you. If not washing the darks and whites together is tantamount to your happiness, don't let it go. Keep the laundry on your side of the list. Then relax and assume your spouse will take care of his or her fair share.

Let's Talk Fruit: Another Great Divide

In the course of writing this book, we discovered that when both spouses work, there is less scorekeeping.

An Apples-To-Apples Comparison
In general, we found that men whose wives work full-time pitch in more. Consequently, there is less scorekeeping. Our thesis is that these guys pitch in more because (a) they simply have to, because there are not enough hours in the day for their wives to work full-time and take care of everything on the home front, and (b) they have the shared experience of working outside the home (*an apples-to-apples comparison*), so they understand how tired/stressed their wives are at the end of the day, because, hey, they are, too.

An Apples-To-Oranges Comparison
On the other hand, there seems to be more scorekeeping in the at-home-mother households. What we found is that (a) most husbands have little understanding of how much their wives are doing (*think apples to oranges as you compare their days*), so they don't understand how tired she is, and are therefore less likely to pitch in, and (b) they think that their financial contribution drastically reduces (or negates) their domestic obligations. Faced with this, what's a wife to do but keep score?

Note: The most effective way to bridge this gap in understanding is the Training Weekend. You'll find the details in Chapter 2.

Here are some examples of how couples have adopted the Divide and Conquer team approach:

> "I am neat and he is clean. So I straighten up and unload the dishwasher and he cleans the bathroom. About three years ago, he decided to learn how to cook and now does most of the cooking. I do most of the laundry."
> —*Carla, married 9 years, 2 kids*

Brandon described a similar setup: "We both work, so we split up the day. I deal with Parker in the morning and Lisa is on in the evening. Consistency is key. You need to figure out who is good at what and divide the labor accordingly. I'm good at the macro stuff (fixing leaky taps) and she's good at the micro stuff (paying the bills), so we just divide it up that way."

Pass the Weekend Peace Pipe

So how do we stop the Warring on the Weekends? A pipe dream, you say? Possibly. But with proper planning (not necessarily in Microsoft Outlook) we can trade off responsibilities long enough to allow each of us to maintain a certain degree (albeit a shadow of its former self) of personal fulfillment. Again, it's a matter of priorities. It's just a trade-off, pure and simple. Give a little to get a little. No one should (ahem) be issuing instructions, and no one should (ahem) be angling to get out of his or her fair share. The trick is just to plan it in advance and prioritize. Weigh the errands, the kid's socializing, the stuff that has to get done, and your mutual desire for time alone. And, oh yeah, don't forget some time together.

Are You Housebroken?

Several people we've talked to, both men and women, said they'd occasionally like a little time to just be in the house, but not be on duty. The assumption is, or always seems to be, that if you are *there*, you should be working. We think we should all be allowed some downtime in the house, a House Break, for lack of a better term. You can't tell the other person how to spend those couple of hours. She can read a magazine if she wants. He can read the paper or watch TV. Either party is allowed to take a nap.

Quick, Call the Congress!

Imagine: A state-sanctioned division of labor prenup! Spanish legislators recently passed (unanimously!) a law requiring new husbands to agree to share fifty percent of housework, childcare, and eldercare with their wives or face legal sanctions in divorce court.[3] Margarita Uria, the MP who sponsored the new law, said, "Men have to learn to start taking more responsibility in the home and women have to help them do it." So it's up to you, guys, take the initiative now and self-regulate, or face the legislative consequences....

How and When to Measure

A bit of scorekeeping is inevitable in any division of labor discussion. There is a healthy give-and-take. Once we've meted out the chores between us, things should run a lot more smoothly. Should we ever start to feel that the scales are getting out of line, however, it's important to speak up. Don't be a Silent Sulker, be a Problem Solver.

Example:

- **Unproductive Conversation**: "I've been up since 6:38 this morning with the kids. And yesterday, I got up with them at 6:17. And the day before that at 6:20."

- **Productive Conversation**: "I'd really like to trade off mornings getting up with the kids." Or, "Two mornings a week I'd like it if you would get up and fix the kids breakfast."

Penalties for Flagrant Violations

What if you agree on a plan and then one spouse falls off the wagon? Say he or she doesn't touch a pan handle or a broom handle for a week, or makes a grossly inflammatory comment like "8:00 A.M. is not really sleeping in," when *you've* been up with the kids since 5:30 A.M. (another true story)—how should you handle it? Simply impose a previously-agreed-upon penalty. The offender will have to keep the kids another two hours during his or her "free time." This has a remarkable deterrent effect. And, in the unfortunate event such a penalty actually has to be imposed, it leaves a lasting impression on the delinquent party.

An SOS from Sick Bay

"I don't think my husband would notice I was sick until he had
to step over my dead body to get into the garage."
—*Amanda, married 9 years, 3 kids*

Girls, we hate to say it, but he probably won't a) notice how sick you are, and b) offer to pitch in unless you draw him a picture. (You did hand in that Martyr Badge, didn't you?) Speak up when your survival is in question. If you ask him to help and he doesn't respond appropriately, then it's time for a Training Weekend, preferably when he's pounding the ThermaFlu.

And guys, we have another exercise in empathy for you: the next time you've been up all night puking, just imagine having to pry yourself out of bed the next morning to make peanut butter sandwiches, change the kids into their bathing suits, and drive them to the Y for their swim lessons. Aaaaah, can you feel that pain?

"What am I supposed to do, take a day off work when my wife is
sick? That sounds great, but it will never happen."
—*Nick, married 7 years, 2 kids*

The next time your wife is facing a Day of the Living Dead, she'll think you're a complete gem if you can find the wherewithal to do any or all of the following, depending on the severity of her illness:

- Before you leave, dress, feed, and equip the kids for school.

- If you can, take them there.

- Go to work late, leave early, or come home during lunch.

- Call another living, breathing human being who might be able to come over and help her out for a while.

And if your wife is *physically imploding*, maybe it actually *is* time to burn one of your sick days in the name of love and general human decency?

SOLUTIONS FOR WOMEN

Do You *Really* Want Him to Be a Woman?

In writing this chapter, we spoke with many women whose husbands did a hell of a lot—e.g., regularly cooked dinner, gave baths, planned family vacations—yet they were still really unhappy with them. They said things like, "I want him to worry like I worry." "He should just know to ask how the baby's checkup went." "I wish he were more emotive." "Why can't he just see what needs to be done?" On occasion, the three of us have felt this way, too. Is it possible, however, that sometimes we want our husbands to be women?

Wanting men to do their fair share (and maybe, just maybe, to "see what needs to be done" and do it without being asked) is a perfectly reasonable request. Wanting men to respond on cue to every emotional nuance we feel is probably an unreasonable request, given the fact that they are, indeed, men. Perhaps there are some guys who are emotionally evolved enough to be a "best girlfriend" one minute, and a "manly man" the next, but we can't think of any at the moment. Don't take what we're saying the wrong way. We're not saying men are incapable of emoting, or that they aren't our "best friends," or that they don't care about the baby's checkup, because of course they are and they do. It's just to say that sometimes our expectations are either too high, or too unrealistic. Maybe calling a girlfriend about something on your mind is a way to help scale back on the scorekeeping. By all means, get mad at your husband for not cleaning up, but don't blame him for not having a Mommy Chip.

Open the Gate to Domestic Equality

Are You a Maternal Gatekeeper?

Are we keeping the door to domestic equality shut? Is it possible that our actions actually inhibit the collaborative efforts that we say we want? We complain that our husbands don't do enough, but then we micromanage their efforts and criticize their less-than-perfect performance. "I got so annoyed with my wife hovering over me when I would change a diaper. Leave me alone, Honey. I can handle it," said our friend Mark.

We forget that parenthood was a sink-or-swim learning experience for us as well. Few women would deliberately sabotage their husbands' parenting efforts, but perhaps we do it subconsciously. "You're not holding the bottle right." "That shirt you put on him is too small." He has to learn as he goes, too. If we always tell our husband how to do something, he will forever be in the *helper* role, a *"B Teamer."* He will never be an equal take-charge parent—that partner we've been telling him we want. (And that *is* what we want, isn't it?)

Let Him Be the Father He Wants to Be

Our maternal instincts also give us tendencies toward maternal chauvinism—"No one can care for that child like me." If we want our husbands to be more active fathers, we need to recognize and fight that tendency. Even Gloria Steinem, that most vocal of feminists, said, "We need to know not only that women can do what men can do, *but also that men can do what women can do.*"

They won't do it the way we do it, but they *can* do it. We've observed that women who are happier with their husband's parenting have learned to let go and let their husbands define how they father their kids. Our friend Denise said, "I still cringe when my husband roughhouses with the kids, but that is how he relates to them. I want to say, 'someone is going to get hurt,' but I bite my tongue. Someone always does end up crying, but they have a good time anyway."

Fish in the Bathtub

So how do we let them be the fathers they want to be? Here's an example. We use it because it is a regular occurrence in Mike and Cathy's house. If your husband wants to take your two-year-old daughter fishing, let him take her. Give him the sun lotion, but don't tell him how and where to apply it. Remind him he needs to take diapers, but don't pack them for him. Tell him that she might need a nap in the afternoon, but don't insist that he bring her home at a certain time. Let him discover for himself the dangers of overtiring a toddler. When they come home, who cares if their clothes are filthy? If he wants to put a couple of fish in the bathtub for her to look at, as Mike invariably does, so be it. Hey, what's a couple of fish in the tub when they had a fabulous time together?

Sure, it may feel like you've just let the Cat in the Hat into your house: things might get dirty and knees might be scratched while the kids are in his care. But we all know that could happen while they're with us, too. If we want our husbands to step up to the parenting plate, we need to get out of the way. We need to treat them like partners with whom we've gone into business—their input adds to the overall success of the organization, even if we see things differently. They won't act like partners if we treat them like assistants. When our husbands can connect with their kids on their terms, they'll want to be more involved. And we will all be one step closer to that co-parenting ideal.

Good Enough Is Good Enough and Shortcuts Are OK (Sometimes)

Many arguments about the division of labor arise because of differing standards. Women want things done just so. Men just want things done. Men despair that their wives never give them credit for what they do, but when 75 percent of a job remains unfinished, it's hard for us to get excited about the 25 percent they did do. We get annoyed because we have to pick up where they left off. It's just not good enough. Or is it?

Housekeeping and parenting are not exact sciences. Surely we have enough stress in our lives without demanding that everything in the house be just so. Maybe guys are on to something with their shortcuts? Maybe we can close the gap between how they see a chore and how we see a chore. We are not advocating domestic chaos. And personally, we don't think a "good enough is good enough" attitude should prevail when it comes to major stuff like our kids' diets or their safety. But what about the minor stuff? Do the dishes really have to be rinsed before they are put into the dishwasher? Do the kids' beds have to be made every day? The three of us have discovered that *lowering our standards feels really, really good*. Sometimes it's nice to say, "who the hell cares?"

Training Weekends: Continuing Education

If you think your husband is slipping a little in the appreciation and/or action departments, it might be time for some continuing education. Or, if the last time he had a Training Weekend was when your now walking/running, solid-eating, potty-trained child was barely able to sit up, he really doesn't understand what your life is like now, does he? (And if he's never had a Training Weekend, what are you waiting for?)

SOLUTIONS FOR MEN

We've come to realize that the only way for men to stop scorekeeping and to also stop enabling their wife's "bossy habit" is to understand why this issue is so important to her. Guys, in the next chapter we women will work really hard to understand why sex is so important to you. We'll think about it intellectually, logically, and even emotionally. Here's your opportunity to do some similar heavy lifting. Again, fair's fair.

Use Your Brain (The Big One)

Let's think about the roots of scorekeeping in a logical way. A + B = C (just the way you like it):

(A) Wife's Expectation of Equality

    +

(B) Husband's Failure to Understand (empathy) and Respond Accordingly (action)

(C) Unhappy, Resentful Wife who keeps score relentlessly and might just make your life miserable. Remember, like Jack said, she can play this game like Shaquille O'Neal and you are the sad-sack second-string JV benchwarmer.

Did you get the whole *"she wants a partner, not a helper"* thing? If not, reread the How Women Feel section of this chapter. Even better, ask your wife to explain it to you. Get to the heart of why she's annoyed that she has to shoulder, or thinks she has to shoulder, the lion's share of domestic responsibilities. There will be a quiz on Monday.

You got married (we're assuming) sometime well after 1955. Your wife was your equal partner in the marriage before you had kids. Why did you drop the ball once you became parents? To women that feels like a total *Domestic Bait-and-Switch*. We know you believe in your heart of hearts that your wife is your equal (if not your better half), but, when you act like all the boring household stuff is not your responsibility, or worse, you act like it is somehow *beneath* you, you are sending the following messages:

- that she is the lesser partner,

- that your job is more important than hers,

- that you don't respect her,

- that you place no value on what it takes to keep your family functioning.

None of which will go over very well with any woman we know. Your wife wants to see that your family is your first priority. She really needs to know that you are playing on the same team.

So, Better Get to Work

Empathy is all well and good, but it'll take you only so far. Actions speak louder than words. Time to grab your clubs and head out to the driving range in the monsoon, Tiger. Shed that *Passive Man* persona—you know, the guy who's always angling to get out of stuff or headed for the basement, and become a superhero instead. Look, up in the sky, it's a bird. It's a plane. It's *Helpful Man*!

As our friend Abby said, "My husband is always telling me to take a break . . . just leave the laundry . . . go take a nap. But how will the laundry then get done? Sure I could take a nap, but then I'll be up at 10:00 P.M. folding clothes. If *he'd* actually do it, then I *could* take a nap. What a revolutionary idea." Encouraging your wife to take a nap comes across as a half-assed attempt to share the load unless you actually back it up with an "I'll take care of that, Honey."

Passive Man vs. Helpful Man

Even if your wife stays home with the kids, that shouldn't mean she is automatically on duty every evening and every weekend. When the two of you make your work plan, she'll understand that you need your off-leash time, and you'll understand she needs your help. *And if it's been a while since your wife had a real break, send her packing—volunteer for weekend duty.*

Domestic Crap: Does It Have Any Value?

Hell yeah! Just imagine what your home would look like if no one did the domestic crap.

Squalor

Besides the fact that doing your share of the domestic crap is just the right thing to do, it might be possible that errand-running and baby-feeding have other intangible, but meaningful values. The actor John Leguizamo said in an interview:

> "When I'm not working, I have to be Dad. I have to be taking my kids to school, picking them up, taking them to the bathroom … But there's a closeness that happens when you do mundane things with your kids. It's like therapy. It's a Zen thing. I don't have to be doing important shit all the time—it's nice to be subservient to your child, up to a point."[4]

What other intangible values are there? Your presence makes your kids feel happy and secure. They just want to be with you. The time you spend with them now will influence how much time *they* want to be with *you* when they (and you) get older. The way you participate in your home life will influence what kind of parents (and partners) they'll become some-day. Oh yeah, and your wife will think you're amazing.

Other Little Gems to Think About ...

• Never use the "Royal We." As in, "*We* should think about feeding our kids more vegetables. *We* should really get them in bed by 8:00 P.M." If you want it done, do it yourself. They're your kids, too. If you suggest something and don't take action, you get major points deducted.

• Are you a *Repeat Offender*? Are you annoyed (even surprised) when your wife continues to call you out on your priors? Just an innocent question here, but were you paying attention the last time? Did you consider that maybe a minor behavioral adjustment on your part might help solve the problem? "Hmmm. Didn't she get mad at me before about wanting to play golf every day on our last vacation instead of spending time at the pool with the kids? Maybe I should play only every other day this year. ..."

• Superheroes always get the girl, right? *Helpful Man* has more sex than *Passive Man.* You score major points. Our studies prove it.

P.S. The Super-Secret, Sure-Fire Way Both of You Can End Scorekeeping

If all else fails, try Rock, Paper, Scissors. Works every time.

FOUR

The "Sex Life" of New Parents

Coitus Non-Existus

Same Story, Different Planets

Janet and Kevin have three young children. Janet stays home with the kids. Kevin's job requires him to travel a few times a month. Here's how they both described a recent evening at home:

Kevin: "I was thinking about Janet on the flight home. I've been traveling a lot lately and we haven't seen much of each other. And, of course, I'm wondering if she'll be in the mood later on—after all, it's been eight days, five hours, and twenty-eight minutes since we last had sex. When I got home, she gave me a big hug so I started feeling optimistic. But I hadn't even gotten my tie off when she starts laying into me with my 'assignments:' 'Can you get the kids bathed? Did you remember to call the bank? Did you pick up the dry cleaning?' She didn't even give me time to breathe. Who needs *that* crap? I should've flown directly on to Phoenix instead of coming home."

Janet: "I was so glad when Kevin got home. Finally, some relief! I thought that after he got the kids to bed we could sit down with a glass of wine. But what does he do? He rolls his eyes at me. I just needed some help. You'd think I'd asked him to rewire the house. And it's not like I went and put my feet up—I was cleaning up the kitchen and doing yet another load of laundry."

Kevin: "So I'm waiting there in bed. I was really glad to see her, you know? It's like 'Ah! My woman is here.' I'm imagining the stress of this crappy day on an airplane melting away as I reach over to touch her."

Janet: "Joey wet his new big boy underpants as soon as I got him into bed and the baby vomited on me—yet again—after his bedtime bottle. After cleaning up all that crap, I didn't even have the energy to change my puke-stained shirt. As I was finally sinking into bed, my radar went off. Kevin had that look in his eye and "it" started inching over from his side of the bed ... the paw! At that moment, here's what ran through my head: 'Does he think that's a turn-on? He does jack shit to help me out, then expects me to take care of him? We hadn't even had a conversation! What am I, a 7-Eleven? Open for business at his convenience? But if I say no, he'll get all bitchy. Maybe I could just lie here for five minutes, but God, I don't have another ounce of energy. Is that spit-up in my hair?'"

Kevin: "Well, what do you know? Bam! She lowers the boom right on my head. Second time in a week. I'm just this robot working stiff to her. She never wants to do it. I'm sick of this. I feel like I have a roommate, not a wife. What am I supposed to do? Rent Spank-a-Vision in my hotel room?"

Sound familiar? We've all been there.

The Most Important Chapter in This Book

How many times have you asked yourself, "How did this happen?" Sex used to be so natural and mutually satisfying. You both wanted it. You both got it. Why is it suddenly, now that there are babies in the house, a flashpoint for conflict and stress?

If you read nothing else in this book, read this chapter. *No one talks about this, but everyone goes through it: most couples experience a radical decline in the frequency and quality of their sex life during these early childhood years.* The problem is, where there is no sex, or where there is sex that is desperately asked for and grudgingly given, a marriage is reduced to a soulless domestic partnership. It's the pathway to true intimacy. It's the glue that keeps your marriage together. Without it, we can feel, as

Ethan Hawke says in the movie *Before Sunset*, "like we are running a small nursery with someone we used to date." When you are sharing your home, and your spouse, with small kids, sex may fall to the bottom of your to-do (or can-do) list, but in fact, you need it more than ever.

This sex issue took the three of us (and our husbands) completely by surprise, and it was, ultimately, the one that prompted us to write this book. We want everyone who reads this to understand: we don't have an agenda here. We don't fancy ourselves a three-headed reincarnation of Dr. Ruth. We just wanted to peel back all the layers of the onion and learn the truth. We're going to tell you what we heard from the hundreds of men and women we spoke with, and share some thoughts on what we can all do about this perplexing problem.

The Grand Canyon

Grand Canyon? Is it really that bad? Are men and women really standing on opposite sides of a gulf that wide and deep and foreboding? Well, maybe you're one of the lucky few for whom things are just humming along quite nicely, thank you, but, having talked to as many people as we have, we can assure you that you are decidedly *not* normal. After having children, women minimize the role of sex in their marriages. They experience a seismic shift in desire and ability. Men, however, still want sex, and the emotional outlet it provides, as often as possible. The wife's supply cannot meet her husband's demand. For most couples, it's an equation that just won't add up, no matter how they do the math.

Here's what two of our friends said that sums up the different male and female points of view:

> "In some ways this whole marriage thing is a fix. Your sex life is
> definitely over after you have kids. It feels like my wife pulled a
> bait-and-switch on me—like she was just pretending to like sex
> all that time just to get me to marry her. Since we had kids, we
> have sex about once every three months, and even then it feels
> like she's doing me a favor. I've tried to tell her so many times
> how much this is hurting me, but she always turns it around
> and makes it sound like I'm some kind of hound dog. I'm not
> a dog! I'm a normal guy. I do want and need sex with her. Why

is that so terrible? We've even been to a counselor about it, and she said she understood, but she doesn't, does she? I've pretty much given up. I don't want to cheat on her, but I sometimes wonder if I had the chance, what would I do?"

—*George, married 13 years, 2 kids*

"It's not that I don't want to be with my husband. It's not that at all. And I'm really not trying to hurt his feelings. That's the last thing I'd ever want to do. But the truth is, I couldn't care less about sex these days. I don't feel sexy; I feel fat. I don't want sex; I'm too damn tired. Spending the day with young children is about the least sexy thing there can be. I know deep down I should pay more attention to it, but I am physically and emotionally depleted at the end of the day. His demands for it feel almost childlike because he doesn't seem to care about my needs. I'm there, so I must be available, right? When it comes to sex, one, it's just not on my radar, and two, I feel vaguely taken for granted. I wish there was a female Viagra—a pill I could pop that would just get me in the mood."

—*Alicia, married 8 years, 2 kids*

He's using words like "fix" and "bait-and-switch" and "dog." He is full of frustration, hurt, and resignation. She's using words like "taken for granted" and "not on my radar." Grand Canyon? Great Divide? You tell us. All we know for sure is how it went down in our houses.

The three of us are average women with normal, healthy sexual appetites. Before we became moms we enjoyed sex; we were earnest students of the "how to drive your man wild" type articles in *Cosmopolitan*; we wanted sex almost as much as our husbands did, and were usually happy to oblige even when we didn't. But as mothers of small children, sex became less and less of a priority for us. Even after we had celebrated our babies' first birthdays, sex, once a weekly affair, still felt like a monthly chore, right up there with rearranging our sock drawers. We gave so much to our kids that there was nothing left to give our husbands. It wasn't deliberate. It just happened.

While we decamped to the other side of the canyon, our husbands were left behind, still wanting that emotional and physical connection with us and feeling deeply hurt by our repeated rejections. Only as we began working on this book and talking to other guys who weren't our husbands (i.e., those without a stake in the outcome of the discussion), we realized that this festering lack of intimacy was at the root of much of the discord in our marriages.

Was it *really* such a big deal to go from having sex once or twice a week to once or twice a month? Our friend Larry told us, "Just as in real estate the three most important things are location, location, location; in marriage, the three most important things for men are sex, sex, and sex." At first, we thought he was exaggerating, but turns out he wasn't at all.

To put this comment in perspective, we asked other male friends what their wives did for them that made them as happy as having sex. Their answer? "Nothing makes us as happy as having sex." Not a four-course dinner? "No." Not a weekend away with the guys? "No." Not a willingness to sit with them through some movie with lots of exploding robots and crashing cars? "Nope." Their response was unanimous: "This is the number one issue. One-thousandfold."

> "Nothing else matters. Nothing else matters. Nothing else matters. We have a great marriage. I'm a pretty easygoing guy. I can deal with finances. I can deal with problems. I can deal with 'issues.' I can't deal with no sex."
> —Harrison, married 8 years, 2 kids

But Why the Disconnect?

Especially on something so fundamental that it defines us as human beings, as creatures who mate for life? Is Mother Nature playing some kind of mean-spirited trick on us all? Wouldn't it just be better if men and women had the same sex drives throughout life? Well, apparently there is a good reason: it's the small matter of the propagation of the human race. Biology sets us up as mirror images of each other, as polar opposites, to promote the continuation of the species (*he* wants to spread his seed), and to maximize the survival of our existing offspring (*she* focuses on the baby). Robert Wright summarizes this idea in the first few chapters of his 1994 bestseller, *The Moral Animal*. Wright, borrowing language from biologist George Williams, describes male versus female genetic interests in terms of the sacrifice required for reproduction:

"For a male mammal, the necessary sacrifice to reproduce is
close to zero. [It] involves a negligible expenditure of energy
... on his part, and only a momentary lapse of attention from
matters of direct concern to his safety and well-being. For the
female, on the other hand, copulation may mean a commitment
to a prolonged burden (pregnancy, childbirth, and many years
of caring for her dependent offspring [sic]) and its attendant
stresses and dangers. Thus, it is in her genetic interest to
assume the burdens of reproduction only when circumstances
seem propitious."[1]

So there you have it. Men's bodies and daily lives are not affected by
the arrival of children the way women's are. They proliferate their genes
through sex. Women, alternatively, are compelled by nature to nurture
their young to the exclusion of all else. They ensure their genetic heritage
by caring for their offspring.

When you consider that our behaviors are ultimately derived from
millions of years of evolutionary biology, it does take *some* of the pressure off, doesn't it? So we can all relax. The root of the conflict lies in our
two competing biological drives. Our modern-day frustrations (known
in scientific circles as the *Hound-Dog/Ice-Queen Vortex*) are, more than
we will ever know, hardwired.

Guys, we've tried our best to get your version of the story right, and
we hope we do it justice in the pages ahead. Forgive us if we don't have
all the nuances down pat. As a demonstration of our commitment to ac-
curacy and sense of fair play, we're even going to let you go first. ...

HOW MEN FEEL. YES, FEEL.

"You get married because there are so many things you love and
like about that person. Sex with her is one of those things. You
don't expect that to just go away. You expect her to be there for
that. Surely that was part of the deal?"
      —*Larry, married 3 years, 1 kid*

"I feel like sex is the Holy Grail in marriage—you're always
searching for it."
      —*Mitchell, married 7 years, 3 kids*

What's the Big Deal? Why Sex Matters to Him

When we asked married men what sex with their wives means to them, the universal answer was "everything." But why? For the life of us, we couldn't understand. I mean, we women have always liked it, too, but really, why the big hubbub?

> "It's not just about the act of sex itself—what's important is the real, intimate contact. You are connecting on a whole different level with your wife."
> —*Brian, married 6 years, 2 kids*

> "When my wife has sex with me, she is letting me know that she appreciates me, that I'm a good person, and that she wants to be with me."
> —*Larry, married 3 years, 1 kid*

One friend, Paul, joked, "We're quite simple creatures, really. I know women want us to be these complicated, fascinating, emotional puzzles, but we're just not. It's really pretty formulaic." But as you can see from what Brian and Larry are saying, the reasons underlying a husband's need for sex are far from simple. If sex were really just a physical act for men, a necessary release and nothing more, they could quite literally take matters into their own hands. The physical need, however, is just the tip of the iceberg. Men told us they need to connect emotionally just as much as women do. They just do it differently. They connect through sex. When guys say they "need sex" what they are really saying is that they need "reassurance," "recognition," and "connection"—fundamental human needs that it's hard to fault them for having. David said, "When a wife lets her husband know she wants to have sex with him, he hears that he is loved, needed, and appreciated."

An April 2005 article in *Psychology Today* that talked about how modern women expect an unprecedented level of emotional intimacy from their husbands in order to consider their marriages "fulfilling" put it this way:

> "Sex is seriously underrated as a passport to (the) communicative country a lot of wives want to explore. While

some women seem to resent the fact that their husbands want them, and want to be wanted back, the very act (as opposed to talk) allows a lot of men to be more emotionally available. Men become vulnerable when they are sexually engaged. Maybe ... women could start to feel it as more a form of communication. Many women may see it as more work—but isn't that what they are asking of their men?"[2]

The Impact of No Sex and Rejection

"How did my wife react to becoming a mother? I can sum it up in one sentence: 'Honey, I forgot about you.' "
—*Gabe, married 6 years, 2 kids*

Most men we spoke to were blindsided by their wives' sudden loss of interest in sex, and they longed for the emotional intimacy they had once shared with her. They described feelings of loneliness, frustration, anger, and even resignation that the three of us found very surprising, and ultimately, revelatory.

They said they often felt abandoned and forgotten. They see their wives exhibit superhuman strength caring for their small children. No matter how exhausted she is, she will find the strength to read her child a bedtime story. She will get up, not once, but ten times during the night if the baby is crying and calling for her. You will never hear a mother say, "I am just too tired to feed this kid—let him go to bed hungry." But guys feel their wives, upon becoming mothers, let them go to bed hungry all the time. The "not tonights" start to add up.

Steve said, "Nothing says you don't matter like the back of your wife's head night after night. That same head will jump up when our toddler cries in the early hours of the morning. I'd need to set the bed on fire to get the same kind of attention." Brian realized his marriage had entered a new era when his wife, who was leaving for the gym, stopped to kiss their baby son who he was holding. "I didn't even get a peck on the cheek. No good-bye. She didn't even make eye contact with me. It's not like I'm jealous of my son, I just want a bit of recognition." Gordon said, "I feel like the *Bottom Head on the Family Totem Pole*. I'm standing there, supporting the weight of everyone else in this family, but my needs always come last.

Everyone and everything else gets attended to before I do, assuming I get any attention at all."

If you stop and think about it, it's easy to understand their resentment. They may not know how to communicate this pain in a language we understand, but the pain is there nonetheless.

Rejection: Why "No" Means So Much More Than No

"Sex is tied to a guy's sense of self-worth. When you're not having sex, your sense of self-esteem suffers. I feel resentful toward my wife when weeks go by without sex. I start to feel angry with her. I also start to think she doesn't find me attractive and doesn't like me."
—*Peter, married 8 years, 3 kids*

"I was out in a restaurant for dinner one time and I heard a group of women at the next table laughing and joking about how they always turn their husbands down and never put out anymore. First, it was like getting stabbed in the gut because it hit so close to home. Then, it made me feel so cynical. Is that really how women think about it?"
—*Seth, married 7 years, 2 kids*

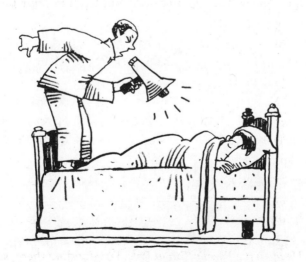

Attention! Attention!

Guys told us rejection is their worst fear. The cumulative effect of repeated rejection is "crushing." One of the ways men make sense of the world is by keeping score. It's why they like sports so much, because sports are quantifiable, because who won and who lost is black and white. They like to measure things. Sex is the yardstick by which they measure their wives' appreciation and need for them. When a woman says no to sex, in that "no," guys told us they hear that she does not want him, that she does not need him, and—if the no continues for months and months—that she does not love him. We didn't want to believe this, but men do count up the number of times they've been rejected by their wives. Ask your husband if you don't think it's true.

Consider the comments of our friend Thomas: "I read in a book that I shouldn't initiate sex and just wait for my wife to do it. So I don't initiate and neither does she. We go months without sex and I am miserable. It is humiliating and painful when you are rejected at your most vulnerable, when you're naked. And when that happens three times in a row, it's soul destroying."

Our male friends talked about the "wheels coming off" and "the sky falling down" when their wives rejected them. As women, we found it hard to relate to this anguish. We were not accustomed to hearing men talk in these terms. To be honest, a lot of us wouldn't mind taking a few months off from the whole thing. But how would we feel if our husbands didn't talk to us for a month? If they didn't ask us how we were feeling? If they simply ignored us? We would say the wheels were coming off our marriages and that the sky was falling down. We would find it, like Thomas does, "soul destroying."

"Oh, Alright Then" Is Not Better Than "No"

It's possible for a husband to feel the pain of rejection even if his wife has sex with him. Because sex is more than a physical act for men—his wife just lying back and thinking of England isn't quite the response he wants. He wants her to want to be with him. According to Patrick, "It's a bit of a mood killer when you hear a big sigh from the other side of the bed, 'Oh, alright then, if you really want to.'" Not exactly what makes a man's heart leap with joy. Recently, a woman on *Oprah* admitted that she watches television while her husband has sex with her. That's pretty appalling. It's a testament to the male sex drive that he is still willing to have sex with her under these circumstances! Women, imagine your husband taking you out to dinner and proceeding to read a book throughout the entire meal. Can you imagine how hurt you would be?

A Word About SGIs (Small Gestures of Intimacy)

"Men go through the whole week without touching anyone. Without any human contact other than a handshake. It's not unreasonable to look for some contact from the person you married!"
—*Frank, married 7 years, 2 kids*

Here's another issue we heard a lot about: when sex diminishes, *Small Gestures of Intimacy*, such as hugging and kissing, do, too. Why does this happen?

As a woman begins to lose interest in sex, she becomes very reluctant to kiss and hug her husband in case those gestures are interpreted as a sign that she wants to have sex. To her, a kiss and hug "hello" when he walks through the door may give him the impression that they are "on" for later.

For men, when sex diminishes, they get more desperate for physical affection, so they jump, literally, into action at the slightest show of interest. When the hugs and kisses don't lead them to their goal, over time, they resent the rejection and cut back on these small physical intimacies as well.

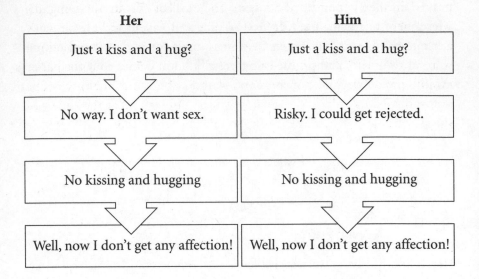

Communication, or Lack Thereof

Hitting a Moving Target

"I've never understood women, of course, 'cause I'm a guy. But I thought I knew my wife pretty well. I mean, we've been married awhile, right? But I can't understand what she wants. She's always changing the reason why we can't have sex. One week, it's because I've said something insensitive. The next week, she's just too tired. The week after that, she feels fat. And the week after that, well what do you know? I've said something insensitive again."

    —*Marcus, married 10 years, 2 kids*

"Trying to figure out what will get my wife in the mood is like playing Whac-A-Mole."

    —*Dan, married 9 years, 2 kids*

As we said before, men are goal oriented. A man's sense of self is defined through his ability to achieve results. They set targets for themselves and they shoot for them. Our male friends described the incredible frustration they feel when the target (i.e., more sex) is a moving one. Simply put, when men can't hit their targets, they feel like failures. After kids, we women start using the measliest of excuses to avoid sex. Or we make a list of conditions that are next to impossible for any reasonable man to meet. Women can be quite resourceful when it comes to ignoring, or avoiding, what they deep down don't want to deal with. The three of us know, because we all did it. What we didn't understand at the time was the serious blow we were delivering to our husbands' egos.

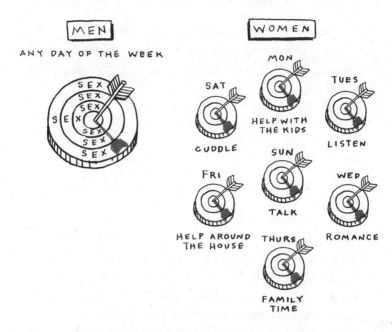

Moving Targets . . . Yet Again

The Audience Is Not Listening

"I was surprised when sex suddenly became a problem for us. I thought everybody liked it. I was also surprised how hard it was to talk to her about it. I'm not the most direct person to begin with, but I have been as direct as I have ever been with her on this subject, and still she doesn't understand. I feel even more vulnerable having put my feelings on the line like that."

—*Trevor, married 9 years, 2 kids*

The pain of rejection is doubled when men's efforts to communicate their needs fall on deaf ears. Many said that their wives don't take this issue seriously. Some guys described feeling hopeless. They feel resigned to a life of sexual deprivation, trapped in a marriage they committed to before someone changed the rules.

Hey Girls, Don't Believe Us? Think We're Exaggerating?

Read what guys have to say about their unmet sexual needs when they can say it anonymously. All this dialogue comes from a purported "sports fans" website that one of our "traitor" guy friends put us on to:

Topic: "Married Men Who Masturbate"

Bob: Do you make even a modicum of an effort to keep it secret? What I mean is, do you do it when your wife is away, or do you just go ahead and start wanking away in the bedroom knowing full and well (and not caring) that your wife could walk in at any minute?

Phil: I notice that we never run out of lotion at my house. ... We may not have any food, but there is always a full bottle of Jergens in the bathroom. I think she has it figured out.

Carl: Married guys, especially after shooting out a couple of kids, do it more than single men since we get less sex. I don't do it in front of her, but I also don't worry about her walking in or anything—she knows I do it. Heck, she supports it as it means it is less likely I will try to get some from her. This also seems like a good time for my standard Public Service Announcement to all the single men. "Do not ever get married and have kids; it is the worst thing you could ever do for your sex life. She is only pretending to be interested in sex so you will marry her and knock her up."

Mark: Carl ... I hope to hell that isn't true. Right now my fiancée is a horny little devil and loves to get it on. I would infer from your post that I should perhaps have her sign a legal document stating that she will attend to my sexual needs on a consistent basis, and consistent shall be defined by me. If this is a sham, all hell is gonna break loose!

Paul: Mark, better get a piece of paper and pen ready when you get home.

Brad: One time, my wife and I did it eight times on a Sunday before church. We weren't married then. I haven't seen her naked eight times in a month much less had sex with her.

Carl: Mark, listen to the voices of the wise elders. Learn from our mistakes.

Todd: Herein lies the little secret of marriage that no one talks about: you have to swear fidelity in public in front of God and everyone else, but she doesn't have to commit to taking responsibility for your natural desires as a male. When she has a kid or two, she barely even remembers that you exist. My sense is that approximately zero percent of women who have not been married before have any idea that this will require any effort on their part.

Ed: I think we should all collectively write a book entitled, *Married Men Who Masturbate*. It would be a best seller. Really.

Steve: Well, besides the kids, here is why I continue to stick around … Given the probabilities, I'd rather take my chances with the woman I have than risk getting something worse. I do get some at least once a week, generally, so it's not all that bad. …

Carl: Once a week? I'd give anything to get it once a week. You are living the dream, man.

Sean: Steve, man, do you have any idea what men like me would do to get it once a week? I'd strip down buck naked at work, and drive all the way across town on I–35 in 5:00 P.M. traffic in hundred-degree heat in a car with leather interior for a "shot."

Clay: My wife always says, "Sex is all you think about." Yes, she makes a solid point, but as soon as the average guy gets cut off—ME—it sure as hell becomes the only thing! Obviously you can add me to the list of extremely bitter married men who long for the days of strange women and wild sex. I honestly don't remember the last time I had sex that didn't begin with "Hurry up."

Ted: I feel for guys like Carl and the others. What kind of wife is that? As for the point of this thread, I probably 'reel in the marlin' at least once a week.

Sean: I've gotten so frustrated that it seems that I find myself getting more and more aggressive with flirting with female coworkers and friends. I'm trying to stay faithful, but at the same time, what am I being faithful to?

Mark: This thread is the scariest thing I've ever read. This keeps it real.

Scary indeed. Discount for a high level of testosterone-driven bravado and you can see the frustration underneath. They have nowhere to turn but total strangers. It's not like they're going to lean over to their old golfing buddy and say, "Hey, my wife and I haven't had sex in two months. Marriage sucks. At least I can choke the chicken when she starts snoring. Wow, nice drive! Beer? So, how's your marriage?"

HOW WOMEN FEEL (a.k.a. THE LAUNDRY LIST)

"I wish my husband knew how tired I am after dealing with the kids. Sex is the absolute last thing on my mind. Taking care of children is draining: the nursing, the carrying, the following them around so they don't kill themselves as they learn to walk, the tantrums, it goes on and on. I wish he knew what it felt like to be awakened night after night for months on end. I'm like a zombie. I'm so tired I'm afraid I'm going to forget to pick up a child at preschool. I'm barely functioning and he's standing there at the end of the day tapping his foot and looking at his watch."

—*Jennifer, married 9 years, 3 kids*

What's the Big Deal?
Why Sex *Doesn't* Matter to Her

The three of us have talked at length about our missing libidos. We know we wanted sex once upon a time. We know we had a good reason for buying that black push-up bra/corset/suspender thingy gathering dust in our closets. We still think our husbands are damned attractive men (not each other's—just our own). But we don't want to rip their clothes off when they come home. Since becoming mothers, not one of us has ever said to our husbands, "Darling, the kids wore me out today, what I really need is for you to shag me senseless this evening."

Where did it go, that sex drive? Honestly, we have no idea. *How does a girl get it back?* Hmmmmm. Hiring a full-time nanny, personal trainer, chef, benefits administrator, and possibly a plastic surgeon would be a good start. In all honesty, we never even thought about it until we were deep into the process of writing this book. Listening to men talk about what sex means to them at least prompted us to ask ourselves, and our friends, "*What happened?*"

After much discussion with many women, we've concluded that there are two categories of reasons *why* we don't want to have sex as much as we used to:

- The "New Reality" of Motherhood (what she can't control)

- It's Her Husband's Fault (don't worry, it's not really as bad as it sounds)

The "New Reality" of Motherhood

Nature Means Nurture

Guys, have you, like George at the beginning of the chapter, or some of those guys on the website, ever wondered whether your wife pulled a *Bait and Switch* on you? While you were dating, and before you had kids, she loved sex, right? Now that she's a mother, though, she seems to care less about it, or is even annoyed at you for still wanting it?

The three of us want all of you to understand that your wife is not re-

jecting you. As we said before, women are profoundly changed by motherhood. Those babies just consume us, often to a degree we never, ever
expected. We know that men's sex drive is biological, but women, too,
are creatures of nature, in case our raging hormones and unpredictable
instincts hadn't already proved it to you. Our biological drive tells us *not*
to reproduce when we are caring for our young. A woman's overwhelming urge is not for sex, but to protect and satisfy the needs of her babies.
An overwhelming urge for sex would mean she would likely get pregnant
with another baby before the previous one could survive without her.

ZZZZZZZZ

> "Yes, I'm too tired for sex. I'm too tired after the kids go to bed
> to even wash my face, let alone … And what about my books?
> What about me?!"
> —*Carla, married 9 years, 2 kids*

The constant refrain from our female friends is that they are too tired
to have sex. Tired. Tired. Tired. This is not just an excuse, guys. It is
simply the reality of caring for small children. Day after day. Night after
night. When you are in charge of the children, you are on the move all
day, schlepping kids, schlepping car seats, schlepping strollers, schlepping groceries. Either that, or you've worked all day, then schlepped the
groceries home, made the dinner, bathed the kids, wrestled them into
their pajamas, and read them their stories. Julia regularly falls asleep in
her five-year-old's bed during snuggle time. And *we know* that *you know*
it's true. We've seen you collapse after spending an afternoon on your
own with the kids. Ross compared the experience of handling three toddlers solo with having his fingernails pulled out. Cathy often finds Mike
passed out in the La-Z-Boy when he's charged with taking care of their
daughters. Gordon also *regularly* falls asleep in the toddler bed during
snuggle time.

Mommy Mode

It's not just about being too tired, though. For women, getting in the mood for sex is not so much a question of switching gears as switching identities. Going from *Mommy Mode* to lover mode doesn't happen with the flick of a switch. It is hard to feel sexy with a toddler hanging on your leg and that damn Barney song running incessantly through your head. We can't enjoy sex while we're in Mommy Mode. Our minds are so cluttered with work obligations, schedules, carpooling logistics, a toddler's troubling cough, and summer camp options that there is no *mental* room for sex. We're thinking about what to pack for the kids' lunches while our husbands are thinking about other things. And nothing kills the mood quite like a tiny voice at your bedroom door calling, "Mommy, where's my Build-a-Bear?"

The Physicality of Children

Besides the constant mental reminders of motherhood, there are the physical ones as well. From the moment of conception, and more so during the baby and toddler stages, a woman's body is no longer her own. This takes some getting used to, and it can be a significant deterrent to her desire for sex. Once we have a baby, we don't have our bodies to ourselves again until the children are well into elementary school. As Marianne put it, "The shower is my only haven. It's the only place where no one is touching me." Stacie has commented, "My body is the family jungle gym—my kids and my husband want to crawl all over me." With a grimace on her face, our friend Anne said:

> "OK, here's the truth, and it's going to sound gross, but that's kind of the point. I've got one kid chewing at my breasts. I have another one, who weighs thirty-two pounds, who wants to be held whenever he sees me. I have a ten-inch scar across my abdomen from two C-sections that throbs when I'm tired, which is always. And then I have this husband, who weighs 232 pounds, who wants to chew at my breasts and be held all night. I never have my body to myself."

Many women also commented that being touched by their children satisfied their basic need for physical contact, so sex with their husbands was not something they craved. When your kids are mauling you at every opportunity, you want your husband to keep his hands to himself at night.

The ICK Factor

Here's another thing women really want to explain to men, and since there's no ladylike way around it, we're just going to roll up our sleeves and get mucky.

Motherhood is a soggy business. Women are, for most of the years that our children are small, awash in a sea of bodily fluids and slimy baby food. We are exposed, daily, to the full battery of nature's most disgusting gross-out tricks that would give any good horror flick a run for its money: vomit, drool, poop, breast milk, snot, pee, you name it (if we haven't already). God forbid if you also own a pet. It's hard to feel sexy after just one hour in the *Trenches of Muck*. Even harder to get in the mood when we know that having sex with you tonight can land us right back in those trenches nine months from now.

After dealing with all that mess, we want to avoid another mess—yours. Let's say (just for kicks) that we have sex with you on Tuesday night. Then on Thursday, as we are cleaning the Gerber's Level 2 Turkey Dinner vomit off our shirt (which might also have breast milk stains on it) ... here comes that small reminder of our Tuesday session. It's just one more mess for us to clean up. It's a "gift that keeps on giving."

You Want to Have Sex with Meeeeee?

"I don't just have a double chin anymore. Now I have a double ass, too!"
—*Vicki, married 5 years, 2 kids*

"What happened to my breasts? They are two different sizes, they sag like shriveled-up grapes, and they point in different directions!"
—*Sally, married 4 years, 1 kid*

Despite the best efforts of marketers to tell us that motherhood is sexy, we know that is total B.S. Many of us never regain our pre-baby figures and consequently we feel less sexy and attractive. Body image is a huge issue for women. When we don't feel attractive, we don't want to get naked. To be honest, sometimes, we're truly amazed you still want to have sex with us.

It's His Fault:
What Her Husband Doesn't Understand

It's not that we women make a deliberate decision to cut back or even eliminate sex from our lives; it just drops off the radar. We're either too busy or too tired to care.

The Wifely Duty

"Let's see ... what to do today? Presentation for next week.
Towels to fold. What's for dinner? Make macaroni and cheese.
Make brownies for school bake sale. Jamie has a dentist
appointment at lunch. Playdate for Sarah. Hmmm. I know I'm
forgetting something ... "
—*Michelle, married 7 years, 2 kids*

The bottom line, guys, is that sex often feels like one more domestic burden. Sex is not something we do for ourselves. We do it for you. If we wanted to do something for ourselves, we would get a massage, watch a movie, or take a long, hot shower. Sex just isn't on our wish list. Actually, most of the time it doesn't even make it on our to-do list.

When we've spent the entire day working and taking care of others' needs, the last thing we want to do is attend to the "needs" of someone who is big enough to take care of himself. To Cathy, sex became just another box to check before she could get some time to herself. Julia thought, "Why is he being such a baby about this?" Stacie thought, "You're complaining about not having enough sex when I haven't *slept* in three months!" The "experts" tell us we shouldn't bring petty resentments into the bedroom. Easier said than done.

When a man's idea of "contributing" is to announce, from his prone position on the couch, that a diaper needs changing, we *so* don't feel like reporting for duty. Does the following sound familiar? You get home from work, spend about fifteen minutes with the kids, then watch TV in the den while we are on our knees cleaning up toys on the floor and washing the dishes. You engage in—maybe—a ten-minute conversation, and then, when its lights-out time, you ask if we are in the mood? If we've picked up your underpants on our way to bed, along with that dirty diaper in the hallway, are we in the mood? Hell no.

Run, Rabbit, Run!

Rabbits in a Cage

Mothers of small kids, whether they work or not, often feel that their sense of self is consumed by the roles of cook, chauffeur, cleaner, and toddler entertainer. When sex is added to the list of things that others demand from us, we start to resent it. We start to feel like a rabbit in a cage—a rabbit that is being pursued by an oversexed male rabbit. When a husband's idea of foreplay is to use openers like "Hey, it's been a while..." or to say nothing and just give us the *Ten O'Clock Shoulder Tap*, we want to run. We've already established that men feel close and connected to their wives *after* they have sex, but for women, the connection has to *precede* the act. When a husband doesn't engage in any form of intimacy, such as talking or cuddling, and simply expects to have sex, it makes a girl feel like an animal. You can't expect married sex to always be a wham-bam-thank-you-ma'am affair.

> "You know what I feel like when I get that intrusive hand on my thigh with not a word, not a hug, not a single acknowledgment that I am anything other than *convenient*? When he does that, it does not feel like a quiet act of intimacy, which I know is what he thinks it is. What it feels like is that he's plugging me into an electric marquee sign that blinks, 'Bad Wife. Bad Wife. Bad Wife,' over and over again. That hand screams at me that he feels neglected. But when he approaches sex that way, I feel neglected, too."
>
> —*Ellen, married 9 years, 2 kids*

The Ten O'clock Shoulder Tap

The Hourglass Effect

You also can't discount *The Hourglass Effect* that many women have described to us. If a woman says no to a request for sex, her husband makes it very clear that she needs to "make up for it" within a certain, usually twenty-four-hour, time period in order to prevent hurt feelings and grouchy behavior. As Katherine described it, "It's like the hourglass gets turned over from the minute I say no. The whole next day, I can hear the clock ticking. Tick. Tick. Tick. I have this sense of *obligation*. A fate I can't escape. I don't look forward to it, as you can imagine. I feel really resentful. I just try to relax and have a glass of wine before he comes home." Not exactly a strategy that will warm your wife up to a night of nooky. What it does do is leave her feeling colder than she did before.

The Hourglass Effect

I Want to Be Seduced: The Reverse Bait and Switch

When a man and woman start dating, and even after they are married, they put their best foot forward for each other. The woman makes a concerted effort to look great and listens rapturously to everything the man says. The man is extremely attentive, listens carefully, calls regularly, takes care when planning dates to make sure she will enjoy herself. But once the kids appear, the *Reverse Bait and Switch* can happen.

We women know we don't put out as much as we used to—but men, you don't put in as much as you once did either. There was a time when you wouldn't have dreamed of making a move without taking your wife out for dinner and making her laugh first. When you think that an ass grab or a shoulder tap are all that it takes to get sex, like Janet in our opening story, we feel like a 7-Eleven, open for business at your convenience.

We want to be wooed. We want to be pursued. That desire to feel attractive doesn't go away just because we've finally reeled in a man. We need you to show us you love us before you make a move—that you are looking for more than a warm body with a pulse. We just want a little romance, not a paw on the shoulder.

SOLUTIONS FOR BOTH

Don't Die With a Bowl Full of Jellybeans

"My accountant told me that before you have kids, put a jellybean in a jar every time you have sex. Then after you have kids, take out one jellybean every time you have sex. You will die with a bowl full of jellybeans."
—*Saul, married 5 years, 1 child*

Bridging the Gap

As bleak and insurmountable as the sexual abyss may seem at times—and we all know it can feel that way, to both the men who worry that their sex life is effectively over, and to the women who secretly wish that it was—*it is possible to emerge on the other side of these challenging preschool years with your sex life more or less intact.* For women, this means making a concentrated effort toward improving your sex life. For men, this means pitching in domestically, giving your wife some time to gear up, and bringing back a taste of the hunt.

"If you're telling me sex is what I have to do to keep my marriage intact, fine. I'm willing to listen. I love my husband and I want him to be happy and I want our relationship to be better. But there has to be more to it than either that old-fashioned 'wifely duty' way of thinking, or him just rolling over because I'm there in the bed. I was an independent, fully-evolved human being before we got married and had kids. It's not like that's just evaporated. I want to want sex again, but for myself as well as for him."

—*Laurie, married 9 years, 3 kids*

"Tell me what I have to do. Please! I don't know how to talk to her about it anymore. I don't know how to get her to listen. What can I do? Make me a list! I'm begging you. I'll do anything."

—*Anthony, married 8 years, 2 kids*

When to Talk and How to Talk

One of the goals of this book is to get you talking to each other. When and how you talk is just as important as what you talk about. Is there ever a right time for a husband to tell his wife that he is not getting enough, or for a wife to tell her husband that he is not doing enough? There is definitely a wrong time: 11:00 P.M. on a Tuesday when you've just argued about who should put the trash out, or 11:10 P.M. on a Tuesday when the husband's "paw" is firmly returned to his side of the bed. It should be somewhat obvious that this conversation should start on a date night, or a weekend away when you're feeling loving toward each other and the daily stresses are not weighing you down. If you're not sure how to start talking, hand this book to your spouse and say, "What do you think?"

One caveat here: if communication, or lack thereof, is so bad already, then forget about the talking and *take action immediately*. Men, try broadening your definition of foreplay, and women, try implementing the *Five-Minute Fix*. See below for details. After a few weeks you will likely find that your other half is a lot more receptive to whatever it is you want to say.

Tried and True and Easy to Do

There's also a whole host of little things that actually mean a lot. Some of them are absolutely free; others require a babysitter and a hotel room (not together).

1. Start Smoochin': Reestablish SGIs

Both men and women told us they missed the small gestures of intimacy like hugging and kissing that disappeared along with regular sex. Once we'd talked about it with our husbands and understood the reasons it had dissipated in our own relationships, we simply decided to hug and kiss every day. Preferably in front of the children. These hugs and kisses are given and received without any expectation for sex later on.

> "What guy with half a brain doesn't enjoy kissing? Why did we ever stop? And now I learn that kissing my wife without always expecting sex can score me big points and get me in the saddle more often? Talk about a no-brainer!"
> —*Randy, married 8 years, 3 kids*

2. Have a Date Night. Have a Date Night. Have a Date Night.

(We're trying some hypnotherapy here to get you to actually do this ...) How many times have you heard this advice? How often do you actually do it? You gotta do it! Couples who reported higher satisfaction with their post-baby sex lives were unanimous in their opinion that regular date nights kept them connected in an intimate, adult way more than anything else they did. As Kimberly put it, "The point is not which movie you see or where you go to eat. All that matters is that you have some alone time together." If sitters are too expensive, alternate nights with some friends who can watch your kids. We even heard tell of date nights that have occurred in the couple's own home. Two candles, one table-cloth, one bottle of wine, zero electronic gadgets turned on, and zero children awake officially add up to a date night. (Note: dinner itself can be takeout.)

3. Escape When You Can

> "Our kids are six and eight and I still have to get my wife a
> hundred miles away from them before she's even remotely into
> having sex with me."
> —*Evan, married 9 years, 2 kids*

The greater the physical and mental distance between you and the kids,
the better the sex. Getting away is not always easy, but it's worth the
effort. Take a couple of weekend vacations a year alone together. Get a
hotel room just for the night every once in a while. It's the best way for a
woman to get out of Mommy Mode and remember her "other self."

4. Put It in Your Planner

Let's face it. The days of spontaneous "take me now on the kitchen table"
sex are over. Those carefree Saturday mornings and Sunday afternoon
sessions are a thing of the past. If you want to have quality sex (i.e., where
both people are in the mood and in the right place at the same time) you
have to plan for it. Cathy has been scheduling "spontaneous sex" with
Mike for the last year and a half. He thinks it's a spur of the moment
thing (well, he did up until now) when in fact it's a carefully timed affair.

> "I've finally started planning sex. It's not particularly exciting,
> but it's better than the alternative, which is not having it at all.
> What guys don't understand is that when a woman has sex,
> she's inviting someone into her body. We like having a little
> time to get ready, just like we would if we were having someone
> over to the house for dinner."
> —*Joanne, married 6 years, 2 kids*

It's nice for us girls to have a little time to get ourselves in the zone. We
can plan to give the kids leftovers so we won't have to cook dinner. Guys,
you can plan to get home a little early to help get the kids to bed. During that drive home, you could even think of something nice to say to us
later.

Where the Rubber Meets the Road:
The Great Sex Negotiation

All niceties and kissy faces aside, at some point it's time to belly up to the bargaining table for some heavy-duty negotiating. Get your game face on. You might have thought you knew your spouse through and through, but wait until you sit across the table from each other and start trying to make two and two add up to ten.

How Much Sex Is Enough?

"Going for more than a week without sex is really, really tough."
—*Randy, married 8 years, 3 kids*

"Three or four times a year would be about right."
—*Kendra, married 8 years, 3 kids*

"After kids everything changes ... we're having sex about every three months. If I have sex, I know my quarterly estimated taxes must be due. And if its oral sex, I know it's time to renew my driver's license."
—*Ray Romano, comedian and father of 4*

Supply and Demand

How much sex do the married parents of small kids have? What's average? We asked our friends (you can do that sort of thing when you're writing a book). The women said "about once a week" and *the men* said "about once a month." Unless our friends are having sex with someone other than their husbands, they are unknowingly inflating the numbers. Our guess is that the men's answers are more accurate. After all, most men can tell you *to the hour* the last time they had sex. Women, on the other hand, are notoriously unreliable on the subject.

A couple of data points: a 2002 study by the National Opinion Research Center at the University of Chicago states that married couples say they have sex 68.5 times a year.[3] That's slightly more than once a week. But according to a June 2003 *Newsweek* article, psychologists estimate that fifteen to twenty percent of couples have sex no more than ten times a year.[4] Twice a week? Twice a month? Who cares? All that matters, obviously, is whether or not the two of you are happy with the amount of sex you're having. One man's feast is another man's famine. Are you happy? What about that person lying next to you in the bed?

Come to Terms

> "I'm scoring like a third-rate British soccer team—once every fifth Sunday."
> —*Peter, married 8 years, 3 kids*

How do you reconcile one person's desire for sex every other day with another's desire for it every other month? Most couples who'd run the numbers together told us they'd had a little tête-à-tête (the polite term for banging their heads together) about how often they would generally try to do it. They'd figured out a happy medium they could both live with.

> "I still think about sex all the time, and I wish we could do it more than we do, but at least I no longer have that nagging sense of dread not knowing when the next time will be, or getting shot down three times in a row. And my wife likes it better than when I was pestering her all the time."
> —*Greg, married 10 years, 3 kids*

Based on our extensive conversations on the subject, we've concluded that *sex about once a week is required for basic marriage maintenance.* Experience has taught us that anything less than that leads to maintenance problems. Things are going to break down. One day you have a sweet, obliging husband, the next he storms out of the house when you ask him to take a look at the water heater. Some men get plain bitchy and would give any premenstrual woman a run for her money. If the "long dry spell" continues, a man who feels he's been relegated to *Bottom Head on the Family Totem Pole* status will start to invest time and energy in other things: work, the golf course, the gym, beers with his buddies. And if the drought continues: the Internet, strip clubs ... other women.

But guys, by the same token, give your wife a break, would ya? Cut her some slack if you can see she's in a "state" or too tired to get undressed before she collapses into bed. Just let it be at that particular time, even if she promised you'd do it tonight after she said she was too tired last night. Don't pressure her with the threat of the Hourglass Effect. If, on the whole, she's making an effort to meet your needs, don't start tapping your foot and glancing at your watch (or looking elsewhere) the minute you get turned down.

SOLUTIONS FOR WOMEN

"I always thought my husband's desire for sex was pretty
extreme. I thought he was way out of line. But now I'm learning
he's not any different from any other guy."
—*Victoria, married 5 years, 2 kids*

When it comes to sex, women have been in the driver's seat most of their lives. For all the years a woman is single, she determines who she will sleep with, when she will sleep with him, and for how long. If she doesn't want to do it, that's that. If she thinks a guy's demand for sex is too high, she can just politely deposit him by the side of the road and move on. We aren't used to guys having much of a say, much less getting an actual vote, on the matter. Now that we're married, though, we asked ourselves, "*Do* our husbands have a vote?" Is it really "part of the deal" as Larry described it? After hearing what all those guys told us in the preceding section, we at least decided to consider their point of view.

> "We have a pretty predictable pattern at this point. If it has been too long, more than a week, he starts to get cranky and a little mean and I realize he needs sex. Every time I swear not to let it get to this point, but what can I say?"
> —*Samantha, married 7 years, 2 kids*

The Five-Minute Fix: Transform Your Marriage in Five Minutes a Week

Really. That's all it takes. We are talking about the much maligned and undervalued (by women, that is) blowjob. It can be a wife's best friend. It's just like all those other "shortcut" items you buy to save yourself a little time and sanity—the disposable toilet brush, the shredded cheese and precut carrots, the microwaveable dinners.

Seriously, think about it. (Think about what it means to you, if nothing else.) It takes five minutes and you will reap the benefits of those five minutes for days. You don't have to get undressed. Your body doesn't have to be invaded. You don't even have to talk. You can return to watching TV, reading your novel, or scouring the catalogs for the perfect holiday gifts for the kids' teachers in less time than it takes to utter the following sentence: "I really don't want to do this because I'm about as excited as a loaf of bread, and, by the way, you've been a colossal pain in the butt this week, and oh, speaking of bread reminds me, can you please remember to pick up a roasted chicken on your way home tomorrow because Danny has soccer practice and I won't be able to get to the store after work."

Think, too, about what it means to your husband. (Oh yeah, him.) He will be surprised and delighted. He will no longer feel rejected and demeaned. Instead of scowling and staking out a position on who will take out the trash after dinner, he will be keen and eager to help you, his Goddess-Wife, in any way he can.

> "God, that would *transform* my marriage!"
> —*Ron, married 5 years, 2 kids*

As sexual acts go, this one really requires very little effort. It's much less effort than trying to get your body and mind geared up for having real sex when you're not in the mood. *And the three of us promise, no, we swear, on the Universal Code of Sisterhood, we wouldn't suggest this if we hadn't seen it work.* A friend of ours told us about it, and believe us—we were not interested at first. In fact, "not interested" is putting it mildly. We were totally bummed out (not to mention skeptical). But, we tried it out, and, well, she was right. We were so amazed at the results that we developed the following cost/benefit analysis:

Cost	Benefit
Giving up five minutes of recreational activity such as phoning a girlfriend, reading a magazine, five minutes of sleep, five minutes of *Desperate Housewives* or *Oprah* or *Law & Order* or *American Idol*, etc.	Your husband will think you are a goddess, and treat you as such.
Giving up five minutes of chores: emptying the dishwasher, folding the laundry, chopping vegetables, paying bills, scrubbing the kitchen floor, etc.	He will look at you with love, lust, and admiration.
Some physical exertion.	He will be smiling for days.
Mild feelings of compromising yourself. These will pass.	He will think he is one lucky bastard and look down with superiority at all the poor slobs around him. He will change the next stinky diaper without being asked. You will buy yourself a couple of days, maybe even a week.

. . . Five Minutes Later

Get Out of Mommy Mode: Reclaim Your Sexuality

The whole blowjob thing is well and good. It works, but that's slightly beside the point. It's a stopgap. A Band-Aid. The real questions are a lot harder. Girls, don't we all deserve to have a good sex life? Shouldn't we aspire to have *great* sex rather than *marriage-maintenance* sex? Or at least to have *great* sex a few times a year?

- What makes you feel sexy these days?

- What would *really* put you in the mood?

The three of us asked ourselves these questions and couldn't answer them. We looked at each other blankly. We stared at the ceiling. The girl who used to feel that way seemed like an old friend we hadn't heard from in a long time. Men are not miracle workers. If we do nothing to maintain our sense of self and just surrender completely to being Mommies, how can we expect them to make us feel sexy and desirable? We all have to pull ourselves far enough out of the mommy vacuum to reclaim at least a portion of our sexual, vital selves.

We asked our friends what they do to get themselves in the mood. Here are some of their recommendations:

"We get a room in a hotel. The sex is great and the room service is even better."

"I read a dirty beach book or sometimes even *The Joy of Sex* (best done with a glass of wine) and earmark the pages for him to read."

"I wear sexy underwear all day. I splurge a little on this. If you're going to do this, don't cheap out, because by 6:00 P.M., you'll feel itchy, not sexy."

"Sometimes I go to bed naked. My husband likes the 'surprise' when he gets in bed, and it helps me get revved up faster."

"When I am in the changing room at the gym I take a good look at the other women. This is what real women look like. Not like the stick insects in magazines and on television. I realize that I look better than a lot of them."

"I like it when my husband acts like he really wants me— especially when we're out somewhere like the mall and he can't do anything about it. The gleam in his eye is a turn-on for me."

"When we go out to parties, I like to flirt (tastefully, of course) with the other men there. It reminds me of my old self. It's nice to get a little attention. It also reminds me why I like my husband so much."

"God, don't tell anyone, but we watch the dirty-movie channels in our bedroom late at night. Just a couple of minutes of that pretty much gets me raring to go, even if I wasn't in the mood before."

Strike While the Iron (Psst, That's You, Honey) Is Hot

"Sometimes I take the sexual initiative just because I know that he needs it. On average I would say half the time. Usually, if I give him the ball he runs with it."
—*Marianne, married 12 years, 5 kids*

How often have you initiated sex in the last six months? In the last six years? Most of us never do. But when *you* take the initiative, you have sex on your terms, when *you* want it. You feel less like a rabbit in a cage waiting for your husband to make his move. You feel more in control and your husband feels, well, great. It can have a hugely positive impact on your marriage.

It takes some practice when you've been out of the habit for a while. Capitalize on a stray thought in the middle of the day. Hang on to it for later. Call your husband at work to tell him you're suddenly feeling amorous. Take an extra sneak peek at that good-looking guy at the gym. Needless to say, your husband will be thrilled that you want him (him, not the guy in the gym) and wonder what he did to spark your interest. Just by thinking about sex differently—as an activity you once enjoyed and might again one day, as opposed to one more demand that's made on your time and your body, you might start to get more interested.

> "If I feel even the slightest inkling—I've learned to act on it."
> —*Janice, married 5 years, 1 kid*

Dull Women Have Immaculate Lives

Damn you, Martha Stewart! One of the reasons we have less time and energy for sex is because we let household minutiae and our kids' social calendars drain us. Lazy Moms have more sex. They've got more energy for it. We can spend too much time finding the perfect Christmas card in July (with everyone dressed in matching reindeer sweaters for the photo), or organizing our cupboards in smallest-to-largest containers, and neglect our relationships. We can get more concerned with the minutiae than with keeping our marriages humming. *When it comes to housekeeping, go for the "Gentleman's C."* You can eke out a perfectly respectable-looking household with much less effort than would appear to the outsider. Learn to leave it. Save yourself.

Dull Women Have Immaculate Lives. And really, who wants to be a dull woman? Given the choice between making a casserole and having sex, perhaps there are times when we could choose sex. We've learned that maintaining a closer relationship with our husbands generally trumps a clean kitchen floor.

If you feel wiped out at the end of the day, try leaving the house in chaos and just sit beside your husband and watch TV or take a bath. Because if you're already feeling tired—with each toy you pick up and T-shirt you fold, your annoyance with him is going to grow tenfold. By the time you get into bed you'll want to kick him, not kiss him. A few times a month, try to be a slacker housewife. If your husband complains, tell him why. We have yet to hear of a man who would choose an immaculate bathroom over sex.

Just Do It

"As far as I can tell, what men really expect from marriage is a constant supply of sex. I'm not sure that is a lot to ask especially considering that women need a bit more attention and the kids need to be driven all those places. I am trying to buck up and be open to sex more often."
—*Carla, married 9 years, 2 kids*

Otherwise known as "suit up and show up." In an ideal world, or at least in the world of soap-opera television and movie romance that we all grew up with, sex would always be preceded by overwhelming feelings of lust and love toward your husband and an irresistible urge to be swept away in a roiling sea of all-night passion with him. If such feelings were a prerequisite for sex we'd have sex about twice a year. But, hey, the stars don't always have to be in perfect alignment, the temperature in the room doesn't have to be a constant seventy-two degrees, the light doesn't have to fall just right through the gently breeze-blown curtains, our hair doesn't have to be washed, our stomachs don't have to be flat, and the children don't need to be at our mother's.

Important note! Speaking of flat stomachs and the whole body-image thing, most guys echoed the thoughts of our friend Tim who told us: "Even though I know Margot doesn't feel that great about her body, I still find her as attractive as ever."

When the three of us realized how important sex was to our husbands and the health of our marriages, we decided to occasionally "buck up," as

Carla put it. Even though we don't always want to, sometimes we just do it. It's a shame, really, that it can sometimes feel so chorelike, but unlike doing the laundry, it does have side benefits.

> "The more I do it, the more I want to do it. My youngest kid is almost three, and I'm starting to get some of my old sex drive back. In the meantime, I'm doing my best to just stay in the game."
> —Nora, married 10 years, 3 kids

How to Ask Him to Help

The three of us spent a lot of time being ticked off at our husbands for not pitching in as much as we thought they should. What we've learned is the following: guys need targets to hit. While you're having that little tête-à-tête about how much sex you're going to have, you can negotiate a little more help in return. Combine this discussion with a *specific* one about the division of labor and who will do what. When he has a set of goals he can reach, he's fine. He doesn't understand the "general expectation" way of thinking. When he has a list to check off, you'll get some help, and he'll feel good about hitting his targets.

SOLUTIONS FOR MEN

In talking to men, we've heard from guys who are just about as low as a man can get because of lack of sex. Guys, the three of us are trying to feel your pain. *We get it now, so you have to trust us. We can help you get more sex, but your handicap is going to suffer.* The bad news is that our pseudoscientific research did actually confirm your worst nightmare: there *are* guys out there having more sex than you. But keep the faith, because that same research also showed there are lots of things you can do to up your average.

We wish we could sum it all up for you in a neat little formula, but women are complicated (and therefore fascinating) creatures who require a little more effort than you may have thought you'd have to expend after you got married. We can't give you $a + b = c$, but we can give you a few long-term investment strategies to implement. We're not saying you will automatically get laid every night you do the dishes or take her out for a pizza, but you will create a more positive atmosphere, and hopefully, find a major payoff at the end.

• **Investment Strategy #1:** Try stepping up to the domestic responsibility plate in a big way. Not a puny way, but in a Babe Ruth kind of way. Big hits. Game after game after game. Women who reported they were more into sex said their husbands had put their arms around their share of the domestic burden and given it a big ol' man hug. We call it redefining foreplay. The women felt respected. They had time and energy and enthusiasm left over for such dedicated and thoughtful husbands.

• **Investment Strategy #2:** Women want their Mommy Brains turned off and their Womanly Brains turned on. *Romantic attention shouldn't just evaporate once you've bagged yourself that deer.*

Wait a minute before you start groaning and saying, "Great, more work—another day in the coal mine," consider this: focusing on sex is more work for your wife. Putting out, especially when she's not in the mood, requires serious effort on her part. Here's the effort you can expend for her. You say what you do around the house is *never enough*. We can relate! We feel what we do in the bedroom is *never enough* for you.

Since no one, not even your harping, nagging wife, wants to talk about domestic crap, let's save that one for later and start with the romance.

The R-Word

"The courtship ritual adds to your sex life. I consciously set things up for us to do so I can be with my wife, the woman I fell in love with, away from the nightly assembly line of caring for the kids. I know some people hated dating and were really happy to get married. But I liked dating. I think a lot of that stuff adds to our relationship. We go out. We laugh. We have fun. And what do you know, when we come home, we generally wind up having sex. You have to make time for each other."
—*Scott, married 8 years, 2 kids*

Remember on *Happy Days* when Fonzie couldn't ever say the word "sorry?" "I'm sssssz-z-z-z." After they are married, lots of guys retire the word "romance" from their active vocabulary. One woman, who gave up planning all the date nights, told us it took her husband *a year and a half* to notice they hadn't gone out. Just because she's landed you and had her babies, she still wants to know that you find her attractive and that she's worth a little effort.

When she's working hard, in the largely thankless and decidedly unsexy roles of "Mommy" and "Employee," she needs someone to remind her she is also "Honey" and "Gorgeous." We're not talking surprise trips to Paris here (though don't rule them out!), but when you plan simple, thoughtful, fun things for the two of you, she feels special and appreciated. But when you *don't* make any effort, you send the message that you just don't care about her anymore, or that your relationship and her happiness are not all that important to you. *She can feel rejected and neglected just the way you do.*

> "My wife has been telling me for four years now that she wants me to plan dates and think of things for us to do together. Why didn't I ever do it? I'm not sure. Just didn't seem to matter to me who did the planning. I guess she sees it differently. I used to do it all the time when we were dating and before we had the kids. And I was pretty good at it, too. I'm finally starting to realize this is important to her."
> —*Nick, married 7 years, 2 kids*

We Are Not a Math Equation

Help us help you. With you, it's as easy as pushing a button. A flash of thigh and a strategically placed hand and you are in the mood. With us, it's like manning the controls of a 747. We need your help to transition from Mommy to Mistress. The old strategies like lighting the occasional candle or playing a Van Morrison CD just won't cut it anymore. It takes a lot more than a stick of incense to put a woman who has spent a sizable portion of her day herding two-year-olds "in the mood." We need to be put on notice. We need to start sloughing off the mantle of motherhood literally and figuratively hours before the main act. Unfortunately, we need to be wooed and made ready. We need an hour to ourselves. When we have time to shave our legs, brush our teeth, and not worry about the bedlam outside the bedroom, we can more easily slip into lover mode.

A Cheat Sheet

A little rusty in the romance department, huh? Been a while since you took her out to dinner? Here are some genuinely romantic gestures guys have told us they've made with very productive results (hint, hint):

> "I take her on a date. Regularly. Not a married-with-children date, a real date like the ones in the early days when I laughed at everything she said, tried to get her drunk, and feigned interest in whatever book she was reading."

> "When it's been a while, I'll go rent a chick flick that I have no interest in watching, but I know she'll love it. Maybe it's just seeing all those hot actors, but I don't care because it usually has the intended effect on her."

> "I always write a card that's thoughtful ... men almost never do this and women love it."

> "A full foot massage might be the greatest gift a man can give a woman (at this point in her life). Under no circumstance should you suggest or ask for sex afterward."

> "Hire a massage therapist to come to your house as a surprise."

> "One day I woke up with the kids and left her a note that I took them for the day. She flipped."

> "Once on her birthday, I threw her a party with all her friends. She'll tell you she doesn't want it, but trust me, she'll really love it. But you must organize and clean up."

> "I book the sitter sometimes. I figured you don't need some special code to talk to one. An occasional (or regular if you can afford it) sitter is one of, if not the, highest payoff investments in a marriage. Once, I even did it just for her to have time to herself. That blew her away!"

"I tell her I think she's sexy. And she is. She's smart. She's beautiful. I still feel like a lucky guy. Sometimes, she gets a look on her face like she doesn't believe me, but I know she still likes me to say it. How do I know? Because actions speak louder than words, baby."

"We all need positive reinforcement, men especially. Fortunately for us, we generally get it in the office, at home, etc. Stay-at-home moms generally don't, which I hear can be devastating to their psyches. So I give her some. It makes her happy. And guess what? It's free to give and you get a great deal in return."

Stop the Tap!

We hear you knocking, but you can't come in. Guys told us they'd tried so hard to explain to their wives what sex means to them, but there is one form of communication they use that is highly ineffective. When you "ask" not with words, but with the *Ten O'Clock Shoulder Tap*, and you keep "asking," over and over again, it's just not going to get you anywhere. Women view that as a demanding gesture, not an unspoken expression of love and tenderness. Best to try to find some words for it, guys. Talk to her and ask with genuine interest how her day was. If you don't, you are reducing sex to a purely physical act. Women don't like sex to feel mechanical. (And they sure don't like it to feel like a command performance twenty-four hours after they said "not tonight" last night!) Your wife is an intelligent, interesting woman who's still worth the wooing.

"Just Do It" for Men

"We absolutely split the domestic burden fifty–fifty, because my wife works full-time, too. She tells me I can be the boss in the bedroom because I am also the boss in the kitchen. I do most of the cooking and most of the grocery shopping. I also do most of the cleaning. And I pick up the kids, and I take care of things when she is out of town on business trips. It's not a big deal. And you know why? Because we still have sex twice a week, that's why. But I also know from experience that if that balance slips beyond sixty–forty, so does the sex. Sometimes the balance slips in *her* favor and then I know what she means about being too tired to do it."

—*Greg, married 10 years, 3 kids*

Of all the couples we spoke to, the ones where the man did two or more major household tasks on a regular basis were having more sex. A lot more, in fact. What's more, the women were much more enthusiastic about it. Like our friend Susan, whose husband works from home and does much of the cooking for the family, *and* the school run every day, who reported, "Let's just say there's not a problem there, if you know what I mean." Hello? Does much of the cooking? Does the school run every day? Imagine that—she's got more energy and enthusiasm for sex. Of course, her husband is Swedish, but maybe those Swedes are on to something.

We've recommended that women embrace a "Just Do It" approach to sex. Being in the mood shouldn't always be a prerequisite for sex. By the same token, men should take the same approach to some of that afore-mentioned domestic crap that they've come to expect their wives to deal with. They're your kids, too. It's your house, too. Pitching in in the kitchen can pay off in the bedroom.

Redefine Foreplay

Foreplay is now all about lightening your wife's load. Conserve her en-ergy so that she has something left in the tank for you. Make the dinner. Bathe the kids. Get up in the night every now and then. We know these things are not as much fun as blowing on the nape of her neck, but trust us, they are much more effective. *It's the thought that counts.* Each time you take care of one of your wife's to-dos, *especially without being asked*, you make it easier for her to feel sexy. *The bottom line is: pitch in if you want her to put out.*

"How Is That Attitude Gonna Help You in the Bedroom, Buddy?"

When we suggest the New Definition of Foreplay to men as a strategy to land them in the sack more often, we can see them, even the ones who really do contribute in a substantial way, start to squirm and grimace. Some men pride themselves on how little they do around the house. One guy bragged that he's never changed a dirty diaper. Another guy told his wife, before they had kids, that he would never do any of the child care or housework, and they could have kids only if she agreed to that arrangement. Asking some men to do the dishes is like asking them to have a root canal. They balk. They whine. They start looking around for someone else to do it. And there are also men out there, who, when left on their own with the kids, complain about how hard it is, but then, when their wife comes home, tell her it was all a piece of cake.

We say to all these men, "How is that attitude gonna help you in the bedroom, buddy?" What's your end goal? Get over your big, bad manly self. If your wife is making a serious effort to meet you in the bedroom with her bells on, then you can make a serious effort to meet her in the kitchen with an oven mitt. Those guys that marry Mommy are often startled to find she's suddenly not that into taking care of *them* after she has children. Mommy's got a Brand New Baby, Honey. And Mommy's tired.

A Quick Word About Timing: Nighttime May Not Be the Right Time

Don't underestimate the importance of timing. The end of the day may be perfect for some women. For most, it isn't. They are spent, in every way, and the thought of revving up when they want to settle down is part of the reason they get turned off. Some women told us they are much more interested in sex first thing in the morning when they are not yet in Mommy Mode, before intrusive thoughts of the number of bananas in the house and permissions slips for field trips start making their way into her head. She might even be coming out of a particularly interesting dream. Try setting the alarm a half hour early. Others like a little Saturday afternoon delight when the kids are hanging out with the electronic babysitter. One friend even reported she likes her husband to wake her up in the middle of the night. (To each his own, but maybe ask your wife before you try this last approach. Interrupting her precious sleep might get you nothing but a fat lip.)

> "What's the bottom line? Remember how things were and how
> you treated one another in those first few months of dating.
> It's impossible to replicate (and hold down a job, and raise
> children, etc.) but not that hard to approximate."
> —*Josh, married 8 years, 3 kids*

Same Story, Same Planet

Here's how that scene with Kevin and Janet could have played out with a few minor rewrites:

Kevin: "I was thinking about Janet on the flight home. I've been traveling a lot lately and we haven't seen much of each other. And, of course, I'm wondering if she'll be in the mood later on— after all, it's been eight days, five hours, and twenty-eight minutes since we last had sex. When I got home, she gave me a big hug so I started feeling optimistic. But I hadn't even gotten my tie off when she starts laying into me with my 'assignments': 'Can you get the kids bathed? Did you remember to call the bank? Did you pick up the dry cleaning? Not the best 'welcome home' she could have given me, but she looked wiped out so I just herded the kids upstairs and got to it."

Janet: "I was so glad when Kevin got home. Finally, some relief! He took the kids upstairs to do Bed Bath & Beyond while I started cleaning up dinner. I heard them laughing and running around up there, and thought 'oh, screw the dishes,' and went to join in the fun."

Kevin: "So I'm playing with the kids and Janet comes in. She puts her arms around me and says, 'You're a fantastic Dad and I love you.' I felt like a million bucks. I had a crappy day at work. This is what makes it all worthwhile. Later I'm waiting in bed.

She finally arrives. It's like, 'Ah, my woman is here!' But she had something sticky in her hair."

Janet: "Joey wet his new big-boy underpants as soon as I got him into bed, and the baby vomited on me—yet again—after his bedtime bottle. After cleaning up all that crap, I didn't even have the energy to change my puke-stained shirt. I finally sink into bed and Kevin starts cracking up. He says, 'Hey Honey, you're beautiful—but what's that stuff in your hair?' I know its regurgitated formula, and I don't feel very beautiful, but I loved hearing him say that anyway. And I loved that he could help me laugh after a day like this. He reached over, but I stopped him before the launch sequence was activated. 'I know it's been a while. Can we please, please, please wait till morning? What time is your flight? OK, it's a date. Set the alarm.' I curled up next to him, which I have to admit I haven't done in a while, and it felt pretty good."

Kevin: "Well, it's not perfect, but hey, it's worth it. Wonder if I can bring her with me to Phoenix next time. No need for Spank-a-Vision. Ooh, or maybe she'd even watch it with me ... Bow chicka wow wow...."

FIVE

In-Laws and Outlaws

The Good, the Bad, and the Ugly

"Happiness is having a large, loving, caring, close-knit family in
another city."
—*George Burns*

How many people made the slightly ominous "when you marry, you
marry the family" comment to you before you got married? As the wedding planning took on a life of its own, you started to understand what
that meant, right? You thought deciding whether to seat Uncle Walter
next to Cousin Lola took the diplomatic skill of a U.N. Secretary General? Just wait and see what happens to the extended family dynamic
when you have a baby.

It's yet another paradox of parenthood. On the one hand, it propels
many of us back to our families. We can grow closer and relate better to
our parents. On the other, it demands that we step into adulthood once
and for all and make our new family our first priority. Usually, this is a
less-than-seamless transition.

This chapter is about how profoundly our family relationships are
altered by a baby and how, in turn, these changes impact our marriages.
Sometimes these changes are wonderful; sometimes they are far from it.

Things can change for the better. It can be a veritable Love Fest. Having kids gives us an opportunity to develop a closer relationship not only
with our own families, but also with the whole cast of characters who
have an important role to play in creating a happy, joyful childhood for
our kids. What child doesn't benefit from another set of hands applaud-

ing every tiny achievement, another lap to sit on, another teller of tales, another adult who loves and cherishes them?

> "My parents and I have become so close since I had my kids. We've always had a good relationship, but they mean even more to me now. We talk at least once a day and they have been there for me every step of the way. I am so deeply grateful to them, and I am so thankful they will be a loving, positive influence in my kids' lives."
> —*Hope, married 9 years, 2 kids*

> "I can't believe I'm saying this. After Ellie was born, I had a whole new appreciation for my mother-in-law."
> —*Bob, married 5 years, 1 kid*

Family Tug-of-War

Things can also change for the worse. As a couple we can find ourselves in a *Family Tug-of-War*, with opposing in-laws jockeying for prime position and grandparents who want to run the show. Even the best of us can end up with a tit-for-tat mindset—"the kids see more of your family than mine"—either because we want to keep the peace with our own parents, or we feel genuinely hard done by because our spouse has joined his or her family in pulling on the other end of that rope.

> "My wife wanted to live near her parents, so we moved. It's great having them so close by to help, but I can't quite figure out

where I fit into this whole equation. I've changed my job. I have no friends. We see her family almost every day and see mine only a couple of times a year. I'm not the head of the family. I'm just a sidekick to theirs."

—*William, married 8 years, 2 kids*

Back to the Caves ... Again

Before we discuss the impact of our extended families on our marriages, let's pause for a moment to ask ourselves *why do we act the way we do after a baby arrives*? Why are so many of us drawn back to our families? Why do many of our parents, siblings, in-laws, and other family members seem to lose it when the babies enter the picture?

As you may have guessed by now, whenever we can, we blame less-than-perfect behavior (ours or anyone else's) on biological hardwiring. As we've already noted, having children can send us hurtling right back to the caves. Guess who's waiting there for us? Our entire families. The root of much post-baby family tension lies within each individual's innate desire to maximize the survival and dominance of their own genetic legacy. That's a fancy way of saying that everyone wants to call dibs on the baby.

Think about it. What's the most frequently asked question upon the birth of a new baby (right after "How is everyone doing?")? Right. *"Who does the baby look like?"* It sounds innocent enough, but it is actually the most loaded of questions. Don't we all have the secret (or not-so-secret) desire to know he looks just like us? Cathy's husband is Indian, and she was thrilled when her daughter was born with a freckle-like birthmark on her bottom. It was as if, Cathy says, Kate came into the world with "Irish" stamped on her bum. All families play their own version of the "Is she an O'Neill or a Kadyan?" game. Our German friend, Carolyn, told us, "My mother-in-law says, 'I see a little brown in there. Her eyes are definitely going to be brown.' My daughter is two and her eyes are sky blue. She keeps thinking her Italian side of the gene pool is going to ultimately emerge victorious."

Hardwiring also influences the way we relate to our spouses and our families. As parents, we often turn to our families for guidance and emotional support. Many of us forge a deeper and more loving connection with our parents and siblings (and sometimes even our in-laws) at this time. We appreciate our parents in a whole new way and we love sharing our children's early years with them.

The downside, though, is that it can make us competitive with one another within the marriage. We want to make sure the kids are sufficiently exposed to *our* family, and that *our* family (a.k.a. our genes) has as great, if not a greater, influence than our spouse's. We also want the pecking order to be clear. We get more protective of our "turf"—our kids, our spouses, our way of doing things—and we'll fight like hell if that turf is threatened. And we get supremely annoyed if our spouse doesn't see it like we do.

Issues for the Couple
(What It All Means for the Two of You)

The subtle, and not so subtle, changes in the family dynamics can cause serious tension between husband and wife. In fact, *the main issue is not that you might have arguments with your parents or in-laws; it is that your extended families might cause arguments between the two of you.* Of course, as with all things in life, it's not what happens to you, it's how you react to it.

Almost every couple we spoke with had one or two ongoing disputes, and an unfortunate few were having divorce-level arguments. Most of the conflicts (and, yes, we admit, we've had more than a few ourselves) center around the following issues:

- The Pecking Order
- Interference
- Grandparent Qualifications
- Equal Access

The Pecking Order

"My wife is married to her mother. She talks to her first about all
major decisions, and then I am told what *we* have decided."
—*Duane, married 11 years, 3 kids*

On an intellectual level, we know that putting our spouse above all others is how it's supposed to work. (Hmmm. Wasn't that a marriage vow? It sounds awfully familiar.) We all want to know that we have top billing in our spouse's heart. In many ways, prioritizing our new family over our original one is the final step into adulthood. And, for most of us, it's a difficult step to take. Telling Mom and/or Dad to back off is not easy, no matter how much we did it (or wanted to do it) as teenagers.

"My mother has no boundaries. She wants to visit all the time
and doesn't understand that this interferes with our family time
on the weekends, which is all we have since I work full-time.
It's created a real issue between my husband and me. He tells
me, 'You've got to stand up to her more,' and I'm trying, but it's
hard."
—*Anita, married 9 years, 4 kids*

It's not just about knowing when to tell our parents to stuff it (respectfully). It's also about how we choose to spend our time, because when we become parents, time is our most precious commodity. How much time we spend with our respective families is a clear indication of who comes first. Our friend Hillary had this to say on the matter:

"My husband helps his dad manage his money, so he's often on
the phone with him all evening. Maybe I'm being unreasonable,
but I really resent that he spends that amount of time with his
dad when we have so little time together. What about me and
the girls?"

Of course there will be times in life when our parents will need and deserve our attention, especially as they age or if they become ill. But, in general, if we put our "old" family ahead of our "new" family, we are effectively telling our spouses, "You are not my number one priority. They are." Even though that is rarely the intention, it can have a devastating effect. There are few things more hurtful than thinking that the person with whom you share your life does not put you first.

Interference

Closely related to recognizing who comes first are the disagreements produced by a grandparent (or an entire bevy of relatives) with interventionist tendencies. Grandparents in particular feel a certain sense of ownership, a certain right of involvement that causes them to encroach on their kids' turf. They interfere and, God forbid, they volunteer opinions:

> "My mother-in-law didn't think that I sent out the thank-you notes for our daughter's first birthday party quick enough, so she decided she needed to do it herself. She handwrote them all, signed our daughter's name, put our return address on them, and drove the fifteen miles into our town so they would be postmarked from where we live—all of this without telling me. I found out when a friend mentioned it."
> —*Tina, married 8 years, 2 kids*

> "My parents are so critical of my decision to work full-time. My dad says, 'Your working is so hard on little Jamie. He tells me he really misses his Mommy.'"
> —*Kristin, married 6 years, 1 kid*

> "My father-in-law keeps emailing me articles about childhood obesity. He thinks our eleven-month-old is too fat. She is a chubby, adorable, healthy baby."
> —*Beatrice, married 9 years, 2 kids*

Live and let live is not every grandparent's motto. They generally do mean well when they offer advice, or just haul off and do what they think is best. The problem for the two of you to resolve is what happens when one of you agrees with the infringer and the other doesn't. Since most of us have a much higher tolerance for our own parents' "misbehaviors" than our spouse does, and vice versa, there are lots of opportunities for disagreement.

"Janet thinks that it is fantastic that her mother is so helpful. And she is great. But she doesn't know when to stop. She will call on Saturday morning and have a whole day planned, movie with the kids or whatever. It's hard to say no, but I just wish she'd back off, or at least ask us if we have any plans first."
—*Kevin, married 8 years, 3 kids*

It's also an issue when an in-law's presence influences how your spouse behaves:

"When his parents are here, I see a change in my husband. He gets tougher on the kids to make sure they are well-behaved. He's so much more easygoing when it's just us."
—*Melanie, married 9 years, 2 kids*

"When my mother-in-law comes to stay with us, Danny becomes a complete lazy ass. He lets her do his entire share of the parenting load. She washes the dishes, picks up the kids, does his laundry. It's like he's the lord of the manor. I know he loves having her clucking over him, but it drives me nuts. He's a Dad now and he needs to let go of being her little boy."
—*Mary, married 5 years, 2 kids*

Grandparent Qualifications

In some instances one spouse thinks that a grandparent is perfectly able to mind the kids, whereas the other spouse wouldn't leave a small animal in his or her care. When your grandparenting standards differ, arguments will inevitably follow.

"I think my in-laws lack judgment. It's a safety issue. My father-in-law lets the kids jump on the bed with the ceiling fan on and leaves knife handles hanging off the kitchen countertops. My husband doesn't see what I'm so upset about, so I get no back-up from him when I tell my father-in-law that those things are dangerous."
—*Helen, married 11 years, 3 kids*

The "What If" Question

The discussion about grandparent (and other family member) qualifications can become heated, if not explosive, when you talk about who should raise the kids in the unfortunate event of your untimely deaths.

> "My wife vetoed my parents because my dad has guns in the
> house and has a real relaxed 'boys will be boys' approach to
> everything. I don't want her parents raising them because her
> mom is a loud hippie type. Whenever we try to discuss this we
> end up fighting."
> —*James, married 9 years, 3 kids*

Equal Access

We all love and feel a sense of obligation to our families of origin. Our spouse feels the same love and responsibility toward his or hers. Finding the time to meet each spouse's desire to be with their family is a huge challenge. Sometimes we don't get the balance right at all:

Holiday Hell

> "Since we had kids, my wife insists that we spend Christmas
> with her family, and participate in their 'special' traditions,
> which consist of eating dinner at a bad Italian restaurant, going
> to church in a school gymnasium, then playing poker and
> drinking Scotch until midnight with my wife's brother-in-law's
> senile step-grandmother. It's great."
> —*Bruce, married 8 years, 2 kids*

Deciding where to spend vacations can be, uh, a problem. Everyone expects you to be with them. Precious holiday time is meted out, with an eye to keeping everyone happy. Most of us try to rotate visits. It sounds simple in theory, but the practice can get complicated.

> "We used to try to split the time between each family when we'd
> go home to Chicago, but that meant three days at her parents,
> and three days at my parents. It'll be time to 'move' and my

Mom will say, 'Oh, can't you just wait a couple of hours to see
Aunt So-and-So?' So then you're feeling sad, but also looking
at your watch and knowing that you're about to get in trouble
with your wife because now you're cutting in on her time with
her family. You get to the point where you don't want to go
anymore."
—*Thomas, married 11 years, 1 kid*

And if either set of your parents is divorced and there are step-sets to
factor into the planning, you might have to break down your calendar by
the hour in an effort to keep everyone happy.

"Since my parents are divorced, Ed and I have to make three
different stops every Christmas—Christmas Eve, Christmas
morning, Christmas night—to make sure we cover all the
bases."
—*Janice, married 5 years, 1 kid*

Grandparent Rivalry or The Clash of the Grannies

The equal access issue is exacerbated when grandparents compete. Of
course, most grandparents like each other tremendously, and build a
deep bond based on the love they share for the grandchildren. But some
see the other set(s) as "the opposition." In effect, they want to be the
Alpha Grandparents. They want to have more influence on the grandkids
than the other family does. As a result, some of them don't share very
well as they battle it out for star billing.

The Title Championship

Sometimes, the battle begins before the baby is even born. Our friend
Tina told us that her mother claimed exclusive rights to the title "Grandma" when the baby was still *in utero.* The paternal grandmother, she
most generously conceded, could be called "Granny or Nana" but only
she could be called "Grandma."

The Battle for Wall and Floor Space

Have you ever done a Grandparent Audit of your home? Tallied up how
many gifts each set has sent or counted the number of pictures featuring

each one of them? No, of course you haven't. You have better things to do with your time. But plenty of grandparents have. They know *exactly* how much wall and floor space they occupy. We have been told, firsthand, about grandmothers mailing Glamour Shots of themselves to their toddler grandchildren. Sandy told us that she returned home from work one day to find that her visiting mother-in-law had replaced some of her parents' photographs with framed pictures of herself. And it's not just about pictures of the grandparents. As George told us, "You have to make sure the grandparents have all the same pictures of the kids, or they'll be like, 'Hey, why do they have that picture that we don't have?'"

Clash of the Grannies

The picture rivalry is matched only by that time-honored tradition of *Gratuitous Grandparental Gift Giving.* "If my mom comes over and sees that Brad's Mom has bought the girls a Barbie, she's back the next day with outfits for each of them. It's ridiculous. The house can't hold any more of this crap," says our friend Kyra.

The Battle for Face Time

The gift and picture competitions are, for the most part, easily resolved. If grandparents want to blow their retirement money hiring photographers and buying toys, so be it. The battle for face time is much trickier:

> "What I can't stand is the 'fishing.' I hate it when my in-laws, who are divorced, start their fishing expeditions to see if their ex is getting to spend more time with our kids. It's another game of monkey-in-the-middle, and guess who always winds up being the monkey ... me!"
> —*Alicia, married 8 years, 2 kids*

Brace Yourselves: A Grandma Gone Haywire

> "My mother-in-law, Barbara, is so jealous when my mom spends time with our daughter. Barbara lives in town so she sees Kaitlyn all the time. My mom doesn't. When she visits, Barbara is over in a flash. She won't let her have a moment alone with her granddaughter. The last time my mom was here, I overheard Barbara saying, 'If she picks her up one more damn time ... ' Excuse me? Another time, my mom walked in the door to find Barbara with Kaitlyn in her lap, stroking her hair like she was petting a dog. It's all about ownership. Like she is marking her territory. My mother has just as much right as she does to see her granddaughter. I told my wife she better tell her mother to back off ... or I will."
> —*Bobby, married 7 years, 1 kid*

Exclusive Access

That little nightmare story does bring up a point, however, that applies to those of us who are slightly more rational. Every grandparent wants "their time" with the grandkids. It's an eminently reasonable and understandable desire. But some grandparents don't respect the other side's alone time, causing major headaches for the couple caught in the middle. Danielle told us how hard this has been to communicate to her in-laws. "It's not about not wanting to be with Colin's family at all. They're really great. It's just that my parents would simply like to have some time with the kids by themselves. I'm afraid to say anything because I think the Bakers will take it the wrong way."

HOW WOMEN FEEL

When women marry and start a family, we envision a loving, respectful adult relationship with our husbands, parents, in-laws, and extended family. For many of us, this is exactly how things unfold. We feel an overwhelming sense of gratitude and appreciation for their help and welcome the positive influence they have on our kids.

But, where there is trouble, there can be big trouble. Stacie once casually mentioned the subject of family roles during her son's Gymboree class. As "The Wheels on the Bus" played in the background, several Moms abandoned their children on the mini-slides and kiddie tunnels to share their war stories of nest invasion and turf infringement. This is a big issue for women. We think our friend Lisa nailed it when she said, "I just want to know that I am number one. I want to know that our family comes first. How can I say that without sounding like a bitch?"

The Lioness and the Law of the Jungle

We have already written about the powerful instincts that accompany motherhood—what we deem the *Lioness Effect*. Most women delight in introducing our new cubs to the rest of the pride. But the instincts to protect and nurture our babies also make us guarded, possessive, and, in an animal-kingdom kind of way, authoritarian. *Those babies are ours.* Nature has charged us, not anyone else, with their ultimate safety, care, and survival.

Law Number One: It's MY Baby

Women are perfectly willing to let everyone else in on the kiddie action as long as they understand that ultimately, we call the shots. It's not because we like bossing everyone else around (OK, some of us do). It's because the parenting buck stops with us and the father. We have the ultimate responsibility, so we should have the ultimate authority.

The Lionness Effect

Post-baby tensions are usually rooted in the new Mom's perception, warranted or not, that Grandma or Grandpa is stepping on her turf. No matter how much we love our families, we want them to recognize the pecking order. Most grandparents simply want to help (and, of course, hold the baby). Unfortunately their desire to help (and hold) often collides head-on with our desire to do everything ourselves. We can perceive the kindest offers of help as a threat to our authority.

The Turf Battle

Of course, some women have a genuine gripe. There are plenty of extended family members who overstep the mark. For example, our friend Gretchen's mother-in-law thought that all babies should be potty trained by age two. She would constantly harangue Gretchen about the fact that her three-year-old old was still in diapers. Expressing an opinion is one thing, lecturing is over the line. Encroachment on a woman's turf is rarely well-received.

> "My mother bought the bedding for the nursery. I really wanted
> to decorate the nursery myself. It's my baby bird, my nest. I
> don't want some other bird flying in here with foreign materials
> where I'm going to lay my egg!"
> —*Alma, married 7 years, 1 kid*

"My mother-in-law rearranged my entire kitchen. She even labeled my spices and put them in alphabetical order. Hello? My house? I guess I could move out and she could move in. Maybe that would be satisfactory."
—*Helen, married 11 years, 3 kids*

Law Number Two: I'm Number One

Every woman, at least the ones we spoke with, wants to feel that the nuclear family is her husband's top priority. Once we have kids, it is essential that men understand this. That need is especially acute when we have a newborn. Consequently, there are few things more upsetting for a woman than to see her husband choose to "keep the peace" with his parents rather than support her during the monumental transition to motherhood.

Brace Yourself: Another Horrifying Tale

"When I had my first baby, my parents waited outside the delivery room. I wanted them to see Isabelle immediately and I especially wanted to see my mother. But my mother-in-law was still a couple of hours from the hospital when the baby was born and my husband, Jason, decided that no one could see the baby until his mom got there. He made my parents wait. They were furious with him. I was so busy trying to nurse that I didn't realize what was happening. His mom arrived and they all came into the room together. Jason handed Isabelle to his mother first. My mom has never forgiven him and it took me a very long time to."
—*Candace, married 11 years, 2 kids*

Candace's story is an extreme one. Thankfully, men like Jason are rare. But we tell this cautionary tale to show the dangers of pecking-order blindness.

One thing that raises an eyebrow with women is when our husbands say, "Well, my mom did it this way." The implication is that we should do it that way, too. Suggesting that we should "mother" the way his mother did makes us feel as if our husbands don't recognize our authority. Our friend Melissa said, "John says things like, 'When I grew up, I was in day care. I ate candy. My mother always worked. And I turned out just fine.' Yeah, he did turn out fine, but that's not necessarily the way I want to do it with our kids."

It's also important to us that our *parents and in-laws* recognize that our marriages come first. Some women, like Anita, whose mother had no boundaries, talked about how their own mothers or fathers wanted to claim too much of their family's time. Others told us they felt their in-laws didn't recognize their importance in their son's lives. *"I'm his wife"* is something women often feel they have to communicate with all the delicacy of whacking them over the head with a two-by-four.

Lionesses at Play: the Female Dynamic

While there can be substantial tension on occasion between men in the family web, it seems, based on the comments we collected, that the majority of tension flares up between women and their mothers or mothers-in-law. Why is this? *Once a lioness, always a lioness.* The maternal instinct never dies. Grandmothers often feel qualified to comment on child care and household matters because that was once their domain. Just because their daughter or son is now a parent does not mean they stop being a mother to them.

> "The day we got home from the hospital, I asked my husband to go into the kitchen to get me a bottle of water. His mother glared at me and said, 'He's tired, too, you know.'"
> —*Jill, married 3 years, 1 kid*

Our Husband's Relationship with His Family

Stop Calling in the Cavalry

> "Spending time with Grandpa is not the same as spending time
> with Dad. I've argued with my husband about this. His father is
> not his proxy parent."
> —*Linda, married 4 years, 1 kid*

Some women complained that their husbands are too quick to pawn the
kids off on the grandparents. "My husband has his mother on speed dial.
If I leave him alone with the kids for more than an hour, his mom is over
here in a flash," says Charlotte. Some women think this is an abuse of the
grandparents. Others fear that it encourages over-involvement. Others
call it *just plain lazy.*

HOW MEN FEEL

> "The secret of a happy marriage? How about this: lots of
> blowjobs and no in-laws!"
> —*Alan, married 9 years, 3 kids*

> "My dad had two things to say about getting married: 'If you're
> buying a house, buy one as far away from her family as possible.
> Then, make sure she has a car that works so she can drive back
> and forth.'"
> —*Jay, married 10 years, 2 kids*

Help Is Help Is Help

Men are anxious to help their wives with the child care or, more accurately, *to find help* for their wives. They often don't realize that their
choice of help *is* the problem and are often oblivious to potential tensions. Our friend Tim told us, "I thought she was happy to have my mom
help with the cooking and washing up. I didn't know she was annoying
her so much." Most of the time, they can't really relate to the turf battle

going on between the women. A lot of the time, they don't even know it's going on until they are told, and their services as peacemakers/mediators are requested.

A Rock and a Hard Place

"I just want to keep everyone happy. Why can't everyone just be happy?"
—*Brian, married 6 years, 2 kids*

That role of mediator is not one that many men relish. Many guys told us that they feel like they are caught between a rock and a hard place. They want to facilitate their parents' wishes to spend time with the kids, but they don't want to upset a wife who finds the parents a "challenge." As the web of familial relations grows more tangled, men can be frustrated by the difficulty of negotiating every twist and turn.

"I am an only child and my father died a couple of years ago, so I feel a tremendous sense of responsibility toward my mom. When we had our first kid, my wife, Andrea, wanted Christmas at our house. My mother refused to come. She just insisted that we have Christmas at 'her table' the way we always have. We tried to compromise: breakfast at Mom's and then dinner at ours. All through breakfast Mom moaned about how she was going to be eating alone that night. Then on the way home, Andrea was furious with me that I didn't tell my mother to quit her complaining when she could easily eat with all of us."
—*Daniel, married 11 years, 3 kids*

It's a Control Thing (Whaddya Know?)

The Male Version of the Turf Battle

Where there is tension, however, it revolves around that timeless question: "Who's in charge here?" Just like women (perhaps even more so, given all that testosterone), guys need to know that they, too, are numero uno in the pecking order. Some men describe feeling virtually invisible, especially during the newborn stage as the women take over the house and start issuing directives. Like our friend David who said, "No one seemed all that interested in what *I* thought we should do with the baby."

Stepping on My Manhood

While Dad won't feel like his authority is threatened if Grandpa suggests that the boys need a haircut (Mom, on the other hand, wonders if he is suggesting that she has been negligent in the grooming department), there are certain areas over which men want to maintain control, or at least the consulting rights.

> "My mother-in-law bought our son his first bike, and that was just stepping on my manhood. There's just certain things a guy wants to do."
> —*Anton, married 9 years, 2 kids*

> "It's gotta be a man thing ... One of my brothers was going to teach Charlie how to play chess and my husband got furious. I said, 'What's wrong with that? You don't even know how to play chess!' Well, I tell you what, he went and learned chess, and then he taught our son how to play."
> —*Gwen, married 11 years, 3 kids*

It *is* a man thing ... We didn't understand it, but our husbands all nodded in agreement and knew exactly what these guys were saying. It seems guys have a clear vision of what a father should do, and the rest of us had best steer clear of those things. For some it's playing chess, for others it's going to the first baseball game or coaching the soccer team. Each man has his own list of things that he believes should be Dad's prerogative.

BONUS SECTION: HOW GRANDPARENTS FEEL

> "Everyone should just skip the whole parenting ordeal. Being a grandparent is where it's at."
> —*Stan, married 30 years, 3 kids, 5 grandkids*

We Just Love Those Kids

"The happiest day of my life was the day Kate was born, the day
I became a grandmother."
> —*Krishna, Cathy's mother-in-law, married 38 years, 2 kids,
> 2 grandkids*

"When your grandkids give you a hug, it's completely genuine—
you know it's for real. The love we have for our grandkids is
one of the purest kinds of love there is. There are no strings
attached."
> —*Lou and Julie, Julia's parents, married 42 years, 2 kids,
> 3 grandkids*

Wow! They do love those kids. Who knew that we (the three of us, and all
of you) are raising the smartest, most beautiful, most talented generation
in the history of the world? At least, that's what you'd think if you talked
to any grandparent about his or her grandchild. Our own parents and
in-laws are just nuts about our kids. There are no expectations (except
for the few grandparents who insist on instilling handshake/eye-contact
skills). There is only a love fest.

In addition to the crazy love, grandparents have the deep desire for
immortality, to leave a mark on their genetic legacy. As Megan's mother
said:

> "When you get older, and you see your grandkids and know that,
> God willing, they will keep living long after you are dead, you
> feel like they are the way you leave a footprint behind. You want
> to touch them in some way that you'll be remembered by. It
> becomes almost imperative."

Consequently, they want to spend time with the grandkids. They want to
pass on family traditions. (In Julia's family's case, "tradition" means an
obsession with University of Texas football.) They want to have as great
an influence as possible on the child's development.

Some grandparents told us that being a grandparent offers them the
chance they never got the first time around to spend quality time with
family:

"When you become parents and raise your family, you mostly
experience shock and can only occasionally appreciate the awe.
For ten years, I worked three jobs as I endured a shaky career as
an Eastern Airlines pilot. Back then, it was about survival and
preparing for two college tuitions. I didn't get to spend much
time with my family. I missed out on a lot. When you become
a grandparent, however, it's total awe. You get to see the whole
picture. I feel like I have a second chance."
  —*Richard, Stacie's father, married 41 years, 2 kids, 5
  grandkids*

The Granny Grab

The grand-maternal instinct, in particular, is a force to be reckoned with
(and sometimes vigilantly kept in check). Cathy's grandmother-in-law,
at age 83, got on a plane, for the first time in her life, and left India, also
for the first time in her life, so that she could see and hold her first great-
grandchild. So many people told us about their mothers or mothers-in-
law just "ripping" the baby right out of someone else's arms that we decided it was worth naming. We call it *The Granny Grab*—an involuntary,
uncontrollable impulse to snatch the baby. Grandmas grab first and ask
later. And may God help the man, woman, or beast who gets in the way.

We Really Do Just Want to Help

No grandparent we spoke with had fantasies of usurping the parents and
running the whole child-rearing show. They just want to help. They see
how hard we are working and want to ease the burden for us. Many of
them think, however, that their kids are overly sensitive and too quick to
take offense. Jocelyn said, "I told my daughter that I'd be happy to take
the baby for a couple of days so she could get some rest. She wouldn't hear
of it. Honestly, all I wanted to do was help her get some sleep."

Who's Being Overbearing Here?

Many grandparents we spoke with told us that they found their own kids far too controlling. Miriam told us, "When I babysit, I am given detailed instructions, right down to being told not to put a sweater on the baby when it's ninety-five degrees outside. They treat me like I'm an idiot." Others said that their kids' reluctance to give them any caregiving autonomy ("I am told exactly what to give Taylor for dinner.") makes them feel like hired help rather than a member of the family.

> "I feel like an interloper, not an in-law."
> —*Bonnie, married 37 years, 4 kids, 8 grandkids*

Many of them think their kids need to lighten up on the parenting front. In their opinion, we take ourselves *waaaay* too seriously. Yvonne and Donald said their daughter-in-law sent them a reading list so that they could prepare for their upcoming visit with the new baby. Yvonne and Donald are the parents of six. All six of their kids graduated from college and include an engineer, an attorney, and a physician.

Others are baffled as to why they are always in the doghouse. They are always violating some strict edict no one told them about. Betty said:

> "The last time I was visiting Sophie, I brought the most beautiful book of fairy tales—*Cinderella*, *Sleeping Beauty*, the classic stories. I was stiffly told that Sophie is not allowed any 'princess material'—that it would give her the wrong messages about men and women. You would think I had brought contraband into the house."

Grandparents can find themselves walking on eggshells, tiptoeing around their kids. As Edie told us, "I learned the hard way that I should only give advice if I am asked for it."

The Generation Gap

The immense difference between our lives and our parents' lives sometimes makes it difficult for us to relate to each other.

"I had my first child when I was twenty-one. My daughter had her first when she was thirty-one. She was so much more earnest about the whole thing. She read books, she went to yoga classes, she even researched preschools before the birth. We just got on with it. And most of the time, maybe because we were younger, we would listen to our own mothers. We accepted that we needed help. My daughter dismisses most of the suggestions I give her. I'm out of date. I haven't read the latest books."

—*Dorothy, married 42 years, 3 kids, 7 grandkids*

Greetings from the Doghouse

New Respect

Even if they do, at times, find us a tad controlling, grandparents told us of feeling an enormous sense of respect and pride as they watch their children become parents.

"What an extraordinary thing it is to see the baby *you* brought into the world holding the baby *they* brought into the world. To see your child take on the responsibility of parenthood, and to remember what it was like when you took it on, just fills you with the desire to love and support them any way you can."

—*Lloyd, married 38 years, 2 kids, 6 grandkids*

This sense of respect can also extend (sometimes for the first time) to the daughter- or son-in-law. Yet again, hardwiring plays a part. Grandparents recognize that both parents are critical to their grandchild's (a.k.a. their genetic legacy) success, and they respond accordingly.

No Respect

A small but unhappy minority of grandparents told us they felt used. They suit up and show up to help with the kids, but get little in the way of thanks or appreciation. Said one grandfather, Ken, "Lizzie and Mack just assume we'll be there when they need us, which we will be. But Margaret and I feel taken for granted. A simple expression of gratitude on their part would be nice." Another grandfather, Ralph, said it was worse than just being taken for granted, "My daughter-in-law's parents get the red-carpet treatment because they live out of town. I live nearby, and I'm nothing but a workhorse. I get a call when my son needs help loading lumber in his truck, not to be invited to a ball game with the kids."

SOLUTIONS FOR BOTH

Once we have kids we learn that it's not just about us anymore. No matter how much our extended families might drive us crazy, they also enrich our lives and our kids' lives immeasurably. Ultimately, it's up to the "new grown-ups" (yikes! that's us) to keep extended family relationships and expectations in check. Keeping things running smoothly is in everyone's best interest: ours, our kids', and our respective families'. Easier said than done, we know. The three of us put together the following *BPYM Family Management Plan* to help us all with the "doing" part. We hope it will give us a framework for ironing out some of the kinks in our post-baby family dynamics.

The *BPYM Family Management Plan*

"We're trying to create a new policy, or the 'perfect symbiotic relationship,' that will be good for everyone. The plan is that my mom will have an overnight with the kids once every couple

of months. She gets her one-on-one time, and my husband and
I get a break together."
　　　—*Anita, married 9 years, 4 kids*

I. Establish the Pecking Order

When we put our spouse first, everything else falls into place.

　　If lack of recognition is the root of most family management arguments, the solution is straightforward: make it clear to all concerned
(sometimes that includes yourself) that your spouse and your nuclear
family, without exception, come first.

The Pecking Order

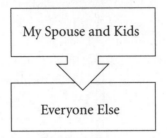

　　Most of the time, it's not necessary to hand out org charts. Ideally,
our priorities will be obvious from our behavior. Sometimes, however,
a heavier hand is required, and telling Mom or Dad to "back off" is the
only option.

> "My mother came to stay with us when our first baby was
> born. She started complaining that my husband was not doing
> enough with the baby. I told her that she was not to criticize
> my husband and that if she said or did anything to undermine
> my marriage she would have to leave. That was probably a bit
> strong, but I was hormonal. Anyway, that was five years ago and
> she has never said a bad word about Drew since."
> 　　—*Michelle, married 7 years, 2 kids*

If you are a Mama's Boy or a Daddy's Girl (or a Daddy's Boy/Mama's
Girl), it's time to *Cut the Cord*. Actually, the time to sever it was about ten
or fifteen years ago, but better late than never. In case there is any doubt,
the cutting ceremony is long overdue if:

- You can't make a move without consulting one or both of your parents.

- You make the aforementioned move after consulting your parents, but you don't ask your spouse what he or she thinks.

- You take a "my-way-or-the-highway" approach to implementing your family traditions.

- More than ten percent of your sentences begin with "My mom/dad always says ... "

- You make unfavorable spouse/parent comparisons (e.g., "My father worked on the yard every Saturday, why can't you do it once a month?" or "My mother always made lasagna on Sundays.")

Cut the Cord

Another way to resolve any pecking-order issues is to ask yourself the following question: "*What is best for our kids?*" In all but a few cases, you can answer that question with another one: "*What is best for this marriage?*" In Julia's case, putting her family first meant moving across the country for Gordon's job, even though it put 1,500 miles between her and her much-loved parents. There were lots of tears and gnashing of teeth on the way (and for quite some time afterward), but asking the right question made the answer obvious, even if it was painful.

No one relishes telling Mom and Dad what to do and/or doing something (or in Julia's case, moving somewhere) that will make them sad. We are still their children no matter how many kids and gray hairs we have. But if we don't establish the pecking order with each of our families, sometimes the results aren't pretty. In an effort to try to keep everyone happy, no one will be. Least of all you.

2. Good Fences Make Good In-Laws: Boundaries

> "I have spontaneous in-laws, but I am not into the unplanned.
> We'd just be hanging out on the couch, when suddenly my in-laws would show up unannounced. Not good. I like them a lot, but I want to know when they are coming."
> —Suzanne, married 10 years, 3 kids

Life is just easier for everyone when we know what behavior is acceptable and unacceptable, so it's important to set expectations and boundaries. This requires a) that we agree on appropriate boundaries, and b) that we communicate those boundaries to our respective families.

For example, when Suzanne told her husband she didn't like the surprise visits, he told his parents that they needed to call before they came over. Suzanne reports that there have been no further unanticipated drop-bys.

3. Run Interference

We have to get each other's backs. *If our family is the offending party, it is our mess to clean up.* If we don't deal with it, we are inflicting that relationship management burden on our spouse, who is the wrong person for the job.

> "I have a great relationship with my in-laws and that is largely thanks to my husband. If they ever upset me, he deals with it immediately and he does it in a way that makes it sound like he is the one who is annoyed, not me."
> —Emily, married 5 years, 1 kid

It's not fair to send our spouse into our own battleground. We can all tell our own families where to stuff something. Our parents have to love and accept us even when we upset and offend them. Odds are they're used to it by now anyway. But we cannot speak our minds to our in-laws in the same way. We might mortally offend them by saying, "no cookies after 6:00 P.M.," and the relationship might never recover.

4. Start Your Own Traditions

As our new families grow, we need to establish our own traditions. This is part charting new territory: "We're going to have Christmas at our house from now on," and part balancing act: "Next year, your parents will come and the year after that, mine will." It's also important to accommodate some of what's most important to your spouse about their own family's legacy. For example, Julia includes mastering the art of cooking sauerkraut (one of Gordon's family favorites) among her (long-term) life goals.

Zen and the Art of Family Maintenance: Tolerance and Respect

"Have children while your parents are still young enough to take care of them."
—Rita Rudner, comedian

It's all part of the great family balancing act. Even as we create new families, we each rely on our own old families for support and guidance. We all need to make room in our lives for our spouse's family. They are part of our family and our kids are part of them. They're not the enemy. OK, if they are inconsiderate, incompetent, or insane, they are the enemy. But for most of us, having them in our lives is a blessing. They are among the small handful of people who love our children as much as we do. They're not perfect, but who is?

"You accept your own family's idiosyncrasies. You grew up with them. You learned how to deal with them over time. You have context for all their oddities. In-laws just suddenly appear. You

have no framework for their weirdness. You just have to accept their issues the same way you accept your own family's."
—*Lisa, married 5 years, 1 kid*

"My parents are really involved and helpful. I expected the same from my in-laws. When I finally realized it wasn't fair to expect the same thing from them, things got easier. They are different people. I've learned to work with them. Now I arrange special activities to create more relaxed 'grandparent time' for them instead of looking to them to babysit. I don't expect them to help the way my parents do."
—*Melanie, married 9 years, 2 kids*

Appreciation

Even though being a grandparent is its own reward, all grandparents (and for that matter, everyone else) like to be told that they are appreciated. After she had her first daughter, Stacie sent her parents a Valentine's card with the note *I get it* written inside. Even if we're all not as thoughtful as Stacie (or we would be, if we could only find the time to write cards), at some level we all do "get it" for the very first time, and should make a point of saying so.

Don't Forget the Siblings

Our brothers and sisters also have an important role to play in our lives after we have kids. The hardwired part of this was for survival purposes, so we could help take care of each other in the event the parents didn't survive. Today we form a support network for each other and each other's kids. Limiting, or even excluding, our spouse's siblings from their life can hurt everyone. Sheila described the impact of one spouse hijacking the other's family life:

"My brother and I are eighteen months apart. We were so close growing up. We even went to the same college. But he married a woman who cut off our relationship. I've basically mourned the loss of my brother. Now there is a hole in my life, and probably in his, too."

Keep an Eye on the Road Ahead

Chances are that one day, many years from now, we too will be grand-parents. How else will our kids learn that grandparents are important if we don't teach them that? How can we expect them to be empathetic and responsible individuals who treat their elders with respect if we don't act that way ourselves? Our friend Katie, who has two little boys, insists that her husband call his mother every Sunday night. "He would be quite happy to communicate through me and call her once a month. I don't want my sons to see that. I want them to see that a mother should always be a priority in her child's life."

Tough Questions, Tough Love

Is There a Conflict-Free Way to Approach the "What-If" Question?

In short, no. Unless the identity of the potential guardians is a no-brainer, this is one tough issue to resolve. All we can do, friends, is ask ourselves the right question: *What is best for the kids?*

Flagrant Violators

If we have clearly set boundaries, issued warnings, and handed out the org chart and we *still* have a repeat offender in the family, we can try calling a time-out. We can take a three-month break from the person. If he or she doesn't get it, then that's his or her problem. There's too much at stake to let a family member's bad behavior affect your own family, especially your kids.

Locked Horns

What if we can't come to an acceptable arrangement? What if the Zen thing just doesn't cut it and one of us finds the other's family utterly intolerable?
Two possible strategies:
  1. *Divide and Conquer.* When it makes sense, consider giving your spouse a break while you take the kids to visit your

relatives. He or she could always use the personal time.

2. *Points and Rewards.* When the preceding strategy is impossible (like say, when you have to fly across the country for Thanksgiving), the spouse who is sucking it up is entitled to a mutually agreed-upon reward, whether it be a weekend to themselves or an unmentionable sexual favor.

Pecking-Order Blindness

If your spouse, after repeated attempts to show him or her this chapter and get him or her to understand how you feel, still continues to put his or her family before you and the kids—it's probably time to call the Maytag Man and get some professional help.

SOLUTIONS FOR WOMEN

Lighten Up, Frances

"Women have to learn to give up control when the in-laws are involved and just let them help. Yes, your kids will eat the wrong foods, and no, they won't follow your rules, but it's OK to leave them for the weekend and get a break with your husband."
—*Kimberly, married 12 years, 2 kids*

We girls tend to be more territorial than our husbands when it comes to the kids and the home. It seems that our Mom antennae are acutely attuned to notice the slightest criticism, or infringement on our turf. Our hardwiring to "be the mother" can mean that we dismiss or refuse offers of desperately needed help.

If your parents and in-laws are good people, the chances are that what you perceive as criticism and interference is, for the most part, an attempt to help. Beware of mistaking "experience sharing" for judgmental meddling. The three of us all did it with our mothers and/or mothers-in-law when we had our first babies, for which we'd now like to apologize publicly. Your mother-in-law innocently says, "All my babies slept on their tummies," and you roll your eyes and think, "She's saying that I shouldn't put my baby to sleep on his back. She leaves ... when?" If family members do, in fact, overstep their bounds, it's entirely possible that they are totally unaware of it. Try giving them the benefit of the doubt. Try to assume they mean well and see what happens.

> "I went into labor unexpectedly, so my mother brought my things up to the hospital. She just kept hanging around in the delivery room, and after several glances between me and my husband, I finally had to gently ask her to wait outside. *She didn't know she was imposing. Sometimes they don't necessarily know.*"
> —*Robin, married 3 years, 1 kid*

It's OK to accept some offers of help. There's room for everyone in your nest. Letting Grandma step in does not detract from your abilities or your supremacy as the Queen Bee.

Have a Little Fun, Would Ya?

Occasionally, it's also OK to let our standards slip. No need to be a 24/7 control freak. If our in-laws/parents are watching the kids and bedtime slides from 8:00 P.M. to 9:00 P.M., so be it. If Grandma's thing is to take the kids out for ice cream, let her do it sometimes. If Grandpa wants to dig for worms in the backyard and everyone gets filthy in the process, throw them in the bath and try not to throw a fit. A little ice cream and a little dirt might even be good for us, too. Let's just sit back, put our feet up, and let them enjoy each other.

Sometimes the Lioness Has to Roar

Of course, there may be times when an out-of-line relative violates our newfound goodwill and tolerance, and/or the lioness in us rears her head for one reason or another, especially when the health and safety of the cubs is in question. (Interestingly, some women who bite their tongue for years in the face of an overbearing relative find they suddenly have a voice after they have a baby.) Sometimes, the roaring is completely justified. But other times, the lioness might overreact and respond badly to a perceived infringement on her turf. What happens then?

- If it's minor, try ignoring it and, if at all possible, laugh about it.

- Instigate a respectful communication between all offending (and offended) family members that hopefully mends the fence.

SOLUTIONS FOR MEN

Be Our Wingman

Guys, when there is tension in the family, or your mother is doing her 'thing,' we need you to be our wingman; we need you to *run interference*. Even where there is no tension and all family members get on like a house on fire, we still need you to *engage*.

Communication

It's that damn C-word again … but we think we really are onto something here—a revolutionary new idea—talking. Specifically, here's what to talk to your wife about:

Define "reasonable." How much time do you think is fair and reasonable to spend with her family? (Note: not how much time you *want* to spend, but what you think is a decent compromise.) If you don't want the kids to spend so much time with your in-laws, that's fair enough, but realize that you will likely need to step in to give her the break that she got from leaving them with the grandparents. If you're not willing to do that, then scale back on the control thing. You can't have your cake and eat it, too.

Dad's domain. If there are things that are important for you, and *only you*, to do with your kids, let your wife (she will then tell her parents) and your parents know what they are. Stake out your territory. No one wants to step on your manhood. And even if a family member does, your wife will run interference for you all day long to support you spending quality time with the kids on their bikes, on the playing field, or at the chessboard.

Stay in the Game

There's no substitute for the real thing. And the real thing is *you*. No matter how fabulous your dad is he's not *your* kids' dad. You can't just enlist your parents to take care of the kids every other weekend, and tell yourself that grandparent time is all the quality family time the kids need. They need you, too.

Call your mother. Several wives recounted their frustration that they were the ones who ended up managing all of the birthday, anniversary, and Hallmark-related holiday responsibilities. Your wife doesn't want to be the Gatekeeper to your family as well as her own. Keeping up with everyone is a lot of work and shouldn't be a one-person job.

> "Every Mother's Day, I'm the one making sure the kids call his mother. It's the same thing for his parents' birthdays. How did all that end up on my plate?"
> —*Ruth, married 11 years, 2 kids*

It's not just about how your wife feels, though. No matter how much your parents and siblings love your wife, she is not your replacement. They want to continue to have a direct relationship with you, too.

BONUS SECTION: SOLUTIONS FOR GRANDPARENTS

Grandparents, we want to be clear: now that we are parents ourselves, we worship the ground you walk on. Despite all the huffing and puffing that's just taken place in the previous pages, at our core, we are thankful for your loving presence in all our lives—especially after you put up with the likes of us all these years.

As you can tell, though, from what you've just read, the family wires sometimes get a little crossed. We realize that's not unique to our generation. Our parents had challenges with their in-laws, and our grandparents had them, too. Chances are *you* can recount a tale or two about how someone came barging into your fledgling nest. So we hope you understand where we're coming from.

You might ask yourself, "Could that be me? Am I the dreaded in-law? Am I the village idiot?" More than likely, that's not the case at all. Remember, we're all just figuring this out as we go. Regardless, below is a summary of what couples have told us they'd like you to know. We've also included some examples of things you can do that will catapult you to Rock Star Grandparent Status and have your children begging for you to come over.

How to Be a Rock Star: Doing What's Best for *Their* Family

> "I'm really lucky. My parents just get it. They've never put
> pressure on me to organize our vacations around them. They
> just say, 'Let us know what you want to do and we'll fit in
> around your plans.' And they do. Every time."
> —*Emily, married 6 years, 1 kid*

Cheer Us On ... From the Sidelines

The parents' marriage is the linchpin of the family. When the couple thrives, the whole family thrives. If your behavior is causing tension between the couple, you are hurting them and, possibly, your grandkids, too.

> "I've got a great mother-in-law. She supports our marriage above
> her own desire to be with us. She tells my wife, 'You need to be
> with your husband. We'll see you however we see you.'"
> —*Frank, married 7 years, 2 kids*

Your Help Is Manna from Heaven

Maybe this is obvious, but just in case it isn't, more than anything else, parents of young kids need hands-on help. As Moms of preschoolers, we can tell you there's nothing more wonderful that hearing the words, "Hi, I'm here. How can I help?"

> "My father-in-law is so easygoing and totally helpful. Whenever
> he's in the house he has a kid in his arms. He's always changing
> a diaper, or kicking a ball or feeding someone. He never stops. I
> wish I had some of that energy!"
> —*Sabrina, married 7 years, 2 kids*

Follow the Leader

We value your help and support so much. We honestly don't mean to make you feel like you have to walk on eggshells. But there are times when it can feel like you don't respect our role as the ultimate authority. You seem to be pulling an Alexander Haig-like "I'm in charge here"— mistakenly usurping power that isn't really yours. An innocent comment about whether the children are enrolled in too many activities can get under our skin, perhaps more than it should. The best strategy is simply to bite your tongue and go with the flow (or you might bet booed off the stage).

> "I love it that my in-laws just check in with me before they
> do things. They ask what kinds of toys our kids might want
> for their birthdays, or what books might be appropriate to
> get them. When I know they respect me, it makes the trust
> automatic."
> —*Tonya, married 10 years, 3 kids*

Some grandparents drive their kids to distraction with their desire to "be alone" with the grandkids. That's an easy one to solve. As long as you show your understanding of, and commitment to, the parents' wishes, we are more than happy to hand over the kiddos. You'll likely get your hands on them a little more often than you bargained for!

You're Already a Champion in Our Hearts

Grandparenting is not an Olympic sport. They don't give out gold medals because you gave the grandkids a bigger birthday present than the other ones did. The best grandparent is a present one, not a present-wielding one. Relax. The kids have plenty of love to go around.

And Please, Leave the Fishing Gear at Home. We know exactly what you're up to when you ask where a particular gift came from or how often another grandparent calls. For those of you with competitive leanings, remember, "the opposition" has as much right to love and be loved by those kids as you do. Step back and let them have their turn. Each set is entitled to their Exclusive Access. Fair's fair!

> "My parents live in the same town as us. My in-laws live in another state. Whenever they come to stay, my mom stays away so that they can have their time with the kids. She talks about Bill and Mary (my husband's parents) to the kids all the time. And both sets will invite the other to their homes for holiday celebrations so that everyone can enjoy the kids together."
> —*Renee, married 8 years, 2 kids*

Avoid "Vessel Syndrome"

Quite a few people commented that their own parents seem to overlook them entirely once the grandkids arrive. We are delighted that you are so enthralled with the kids, but, hey, don't forget about us, OK? We need you, too. Gary said, "I'm so low on the list, my own parents don't even ask how I'm doing anymore."

> "My mom adores the kids, but she is still concerned about me, too. She always asks if I'm getting enough sleep, getting out to exercise, etc. I may be the mom now, but it's still really nice to know that she is there for me."
> —*Valerie, married 7 years, 2 kids*

Several women felt like they were little more than a means to an end (i.e., the grandkids) when they were pregnant. Our friend Hillary commented, "I felt like I was nothing more than a vessel to produce her grandchildren. A uterus. She would call on an almost daily basis to ask about what I had eaten." Pregnant Moms have feelings, too, ya know.

Can't We All Just Get Along?

Who are the real children in your family and who is just acting like a child? Sometimes it's hard to tell with all the shenanigans that go on. Let's all just share the pails and shovels and play nice with each other in the family sandbox.

SIX

Ramping Up and Giving In

More Kids, More Chaos

"I'd gotten all four kids dressed in their party clothes, and we were actually on time for the birthday party. I felt like SuperMom. Then, I looked up to see Ashley on the slide. I'd forgotten her underpants. So much for having it all under control."
— *Marilyn, married 11 years, 4 kids*

"Evolution of a father: with the first kid, Ross still played golf most weekends. With the second, he was home helping out. With the third, one day *he* told *me* we were running low on kitty litter. I told him that was a turn-on."
— *Stacie, married 9 years, 3 kids*

What Are You *Thinking*?

Hey, I know! Let's have another one! Just when you start to get the hang of the whole parenting thing, you go and have another baby. *How hard can it be?* you ask yourselves. *We've already made the biggest transition—becoming parents in the first place. What difference will another one make?*

What difference will another one make? Can you guess what we're going to say?

Don't have any more kids because it's just too hard and you'll ruin your marriage? No.

Your life is so totally over? No. (Well, maybe.)

Having more children presents us with yet another paradox in that on one hand, it means more work to do and less time for each other and ourselves, but, on the other, it can pave the way to a new equilibrium between husband and wife as we embrace the chaos and learn to work together as a team? Bingo.

Of course it gets harder. With each child, the love and joy in our homes increases a thousandfold, but so does the general mayhem. There's more noise, more chaos, more work to do. By necessity, we take time away from each other to care for our kids. "Your time" gets folded into "family time," and we can begin to lose the sense of being a couple.

But as it gets harder, somehow it gets easier, too. We realize that the struggle to get back to our pre-baby "normal selves" is futile. This noisy, chaotic life is where it's at. We step up and embrace it, and we surrender to the madness. Both parents get caught in the full-court kid press. We share more of the labor and more of the joy with each other. This leveling of the parenting field can put our marriage on a much more even keel.

A Caveat for Those with One Child

It is not our intention to suggest anywhere in this chapter that a family with one child is not a complete one or that there is no work involved. Even though we keep saying "more kids," don't touch that dial! Most of the ideas and solutions in this chapter will apply to you, too.

Incremental Impact:
The Step-Function of Lifestyle Complexity

With one child (who is getting older and more self-sufficient by the moment), most couples are able to maintain some semblance of their former lives: the parents outnumber the kids, family members compete for babysitting privileges, one child is portable, the house/apartment is big enough to accommodate all the paraphernalia, more often than not we're sleeping again, we might even find we have enough energy for sex and enough mental capacity to remember Valentine's Day. Once more children arrive, however, we wonder what all the fuss was about and recall those early days of *and baby makes three* with the fondest of feelings.

Life gets more complex with each child. It looks something like this:

Number of Kids	1	2
Parental Defense Method	Tag team	Man to Man
Grandparent Participation Level	Overwhelming	Halved
Free Time	30% of former life	Goes to zero
Minutes Required to Leave the House	5	10
Number of Appointments per Year (doctor/dentist etc.)	6	12
Number of Birthday Parties per Month = X (X also equals the number of times your ass is in Toys"R"Us buying a gift before hightailing it to Chuck E. Cheese)	X	2X
Number of Names of Kids' Friends' Parents to Remember (Assume A = preschool class size, B = neighborhood friends, and C = other friends)	2(A + B + C)	$2(A + B + C)^x$
Sibling Rivalry Decibel Level	0	3
Gallons of Milk per Week	2	4
Table Size at a Restaurant	Table for 2, plus a high chair	Table for 4
Travel Considerations	3 plane tickets, 1 hotel room, 1 cab, mid-size rental car	4 plane tickets, 1 hotel room, 1 cab, full-size rental car
Weekend Getaways	Once a quarter	Twice a year

3	4	5 or More (yes, they are out there)
Zone	Prayer	Brute Force
They'll take one kid at a time.	They'll take one kid at a time.	They'll take one kid at a time.
Ha!	N/A	Negative—you even dream about working.
20	Who knows? You've lost your watch.	Half a day
18	36	Unless your spouse is a medical professional, you consider leaving them to marry one.
3X	4X	You start hearing the Happy Birthday song in your sleep.
$2(A + B + C)^y$	$2[(A + B)^x (C^{\,y})]^n$	When you see anyone, you just nod your head and act like you know them.
11 (like in *This is Spinal Tap*)	You need a hearing aid.	You turn off your hearing aid.
6	8	You consider investing in dairy stocks.
You have to wait for a bigger table.	You have to wait for a bigger table.	You don't go out.
5 plane tickets, 1 very cramped hotel room, 2 cabs, mini-van rental	6 plane tickets, 2 hotel rooms, 2 cabs ... time to rent a bus	You are broke, having spent all your money on the previous vacation.
Bribery required	Weddings and funerals only	Not ever

Going from One to Two: You Never Stop Moving

In hindsight, taking care of one child was a hobby. Most people told us they'd found the transition from one to two kids a painfully difficult one. Everything suddenly turned into a production: getting everyone dressed and out the door is hellacious; juggling nap, feeding, and playtime schedules requires both parents to be "on" all the time; and downtime simply evaporates.

> "Going from one to two was less about culture shock, because you'd been there before. It was more about the dissolution of whatever organization you had before, the complete disappearance of any rest time/alone time, and the thinning out of communication between you and your spouse. I felt sort of robbed of my last vestiges of sanity, or of my resources to create sanity, when number two came around."
> —*Margot, married 7 years, 2 kids*

> "We're both on all the time. Two kids require two sets of hands. One of us feeds the baby, while the other entertains the toddler. At some point, that toddler gives up her long afternoon nap and wants to replace it with an all-afternoon Candy Land tournament."
> —*Tina, married 8 years, 2 kids*

(Authors' Note: A notable minority of people, like Julia, found the ramp-up an easier and more agreeable experience than they expected. Is spacing a factor? Julia's first was three when she had her second. Stacie and Cathy each had barely coherent toddlers when they had a second. Our main takeaway is that it is the two-in-diapers deal that really rocks your world.)

Going from Two to Three: Welcome to the Jungle

"Ha!" said those of you with three or more kids as you read that last section. *You have no idea what the words "painful transition" really mean until you add a third.* Three is a whole different deal, a jungle-island, *Lord of the Flies*-type of anarchy that comes from being outnumbered by a wild band of tiny people. Stacie and Ross, who have three kids under five, say they feel like Jane and Tarzan, swinging from vine to vine through

Code-Red Chaos

their house putting out fires: the teething newborn needs comforting, the two-year-old's artwork needs washing off the wall, and the four-year-old needs help on the potty. You can't imagine it until you're living it. Life with three is *Code Red Chaos*, and it also comes with a healthy dose of social exile, just for good measure.

> "When I only had two kids, I thought people with three or more
> seemed out of control. One of my friends was always talking
> about piling her three kids in the car and driving around just so
> she could relax. Now that I have three kids, let's just say I buy a
> lot of gas."
> —*Suzanne, married 10 years, 3 kids*

> "My husband and I constantly hurl diapers, pacifiers, blankies,
> and sippy cups across the house and up and down the steps. For
> us, parenting has become an extreme sport."
> —*Diane, married 9 years, 3 kids*

Going for Broke: To Infinity and Beyond ...

At this point, none of us have been brave (?) enough to go for four or more, so we were not qualified to do anything but ask the experts, "What's it like?" Typically, they smile stoically and say, "It's chaos, but it's wonderful. We wouldn't have it any other way," as they pry a toy car from their toddler's mouth, grab the baby away from the electric socket, and yell at the other two to stop fighting. Wonderful indeed.

> "I am one of four children, and I distinctly remember going to school without underpants."
> —*Cathy, married 7 years, 2 kids*

> "Whenever I tell people how many kids I have—I have six—I get one of two reactions. People either look at me like I am some sort of a crazy religious fanatic or like I have split the atom. They want to know how we do it, what kind of car we drive, whether or not I work, the ages of each kid. It's hilarious."
> —*Maura, married 15 years, 6 kids*

Life in the Family Circus

The more kids you have, the bigger the production. You need more food in the fridge, more diapers changed, more bottles washed, not to mention more brain cells to keep up with the kids, naps, and crap.

> "Just last week, I forgot about our daughter's soccer game and missed the deadline to turn in the preschool registration forms. When I try to explain myself to people, they all look at me like I'm just a train wreck."
> —*Annalisa, married 12 years, 4 kids*

> "With three, every hour is accounted for—you even schedule play time with your youngest. You need a spreadsheet three pages long to make sure everyone gets where they need to be on time. I used to be a Nazi about kids napping in their own beds. I can't do that anymore."
> —*Marie, married 9 years, 3 kids*

Two in Diapers

"I will never forget the days of sitting on the cold bathroom
floor trying to bathe Peter while nursing Ally at the same time.
Nothing can prepare you for that."
—*Naomi, married 5 years, 2 kids*

The sheer volume of work is especially painful for couples who, having
waited until their thirties to have their first child, have the second one
very quickly afterward. That describes about sixty percent of our friends
and two of us. If a first baby is a hand grenade thrown at a marriage, then
a newborn and a toddler are a full-frontal assault, complete with machine
guns, heat-seeking missiles, and stealth bombers.

"One night, I came home and my wife was still in her pajamas,
with a baby in one arm and a toddler in the other, crying
hysterically, 'Why did we ever get married and why did we ever
have kids?'"
—*Dan, married 9 years, 2 kids*

Multiples: The Instant Village

They are a growing facet of modern-day America, and some of them
will scoff at you when you complain that you have two, or fewer, kids in
diapers. Julia and Gordon recently counted. They know thirteen couples
with twins and five with triplets.

"Only one thought keeps me together when I have a bad day:
full-day kindergarten."
—*Veronica, married 9 years, 4 kids (3 of whom are triplets)*

"When the twins arrived, it was a long time before I could even
hold a conversation. Any adult thought in my head during their
toddler years was put on hold. I was in a permanent state of
exhaustion."
—*Sonja, married 9 years, 4 kids (twins plus 2 more!)*

"It's like a little army, a little boot camp. My husband makes the
lunches, pours the cereal bowls, and sets out clothes for school

the next day. I do seven loads of laundry a day. They all need
school clothes, play clothes, and their sports clothes, Cloroxed
and ready to go."
—*Marianne, married 12 years, 5 kids*

Hey, Where'd Everybody Go?

It's a cruel irony that as the workload and chaos increase, and your need
for help escalates, the resources dry up (well, the free resources dry up
anyway). The once overbearing grandparent presence in our lives comes
to a screeching halt. No one wants to watch two kids because it's just too
hard. Our friend Kim, who has three kids, concurred:

> "We went away for a day and a night and my parents stayed over
> to watch the kids. When we got home, they were sitting on the
> sofa *in their coats* and couldn't wait to get out of the house.
> They've never offered to do an overnight again."

Social Ostracism

Stacie and Ross noticed that their social life took a nosedive once their
third child arrived. Stacie said, "Your friends don't want your chaos in
their house, so they don't invite you over anymore. The phone just stops
ringing."

Although your Rolodex expands considerably with each child (a
three-year-old's social calendar can be astounding), you're not getting
out quite as much as you once did, both as a family and with each other.
You can venture out of the house with relative ease when you have two.
Not so easy when the kids outnumber the parents.

> "When I was very pregnant with my fourth, I was trying to
> navigate the stroller through the store while chasing my twins
> around. The twenty-five-year-old, size-zero salesgirl gave me
> *that look*, like she couldn't wait for us to clear out of there. I
> thought to myself, 'Just you wait, honey, you'll get yours.'"
> —*Selena, married 11 years, 4 kids*

Free Time: What About Me?

"When we had our daughter, I still had a couple of nights a week to myself. Once we had our son, that was over. The last traces of my freedom were gone."
        —*Robert, married 12 years, 2 kids*

"Book Club now feels like an enormous luxury that I can rarely afford. I work full-time, so any free time I don't spend with my kids feels like an extra that needs to be cut."
        —*Melanie, married 9 years, 2 kids*

When you have one child, one parent parents while the other does his or her own thing. With the additional demands of more children, it gets harder to carve out any "me time." Not having time to recharge and feed your sense of self is, for many, the real challenge of adjusting to having more kids:

"A girlfriend of mine just e-mailed me the other day and said she's grouchy and forgetful and just plain pissed right now because her baby has stopped napping at the same time as her three-year-old. I told her that looking back, I really had to *grieve* for the loss of that last little piece of freedom. Personal time is like a pursuit for the Fountain of Youth, or the Seven Cities of Gold. It's like winning the lottery. If I get it, I feel lucky."
        —*Ellen, married 9 years, 2 kids*

Losing these "joie de vivre" activities can also spell trouble for our marriages. Without them, we get emotionally and physically drained. What is left over, we usually give to our kids first. When our internal reserves are low, our threshold for dealing with our spouse's annoying quirks also gets dangerously low. At times, we circle each other like wolves, ready to fight over the scraps of free time that do exist.

"I really wanted to go for a jog last Saturday. I feel like I'm getting old and fat. I told my wife I'd be back in an hour and she glared at me. 'When do I get to go for a jog?' she said. I didn't go jogging, and we were both ticked off at each other. Nobody wins."

—*Edward, married 10 years, 3 kids*

Couple Time: What About Us?

The couple usually takes another hit when a new child arrives. Of course we get a tremendous sense of satisfaction from the mini-empire we are building together, but the time and energy required to work, maintain the house, and care for the brood means that our spouse winds up with little more than our leftovers.

> "I look at how we celebrate our anniversary as a yardstick. We used to plan a weekend away. After Jake, it became one night away. Then just dinner out. By the time Parker was born, we just exchanged cards we had bought the day of with a note we'd scribbled in the parking lot."
>
> —*Andrew, married 9 years, 2 kids*

> "I can't even keep up with my husband's schedule anymore. Last week, I was expecting him home at the usual time. Come to find out, he was in Boston on business."
>
> —*Ellen, married 9 years, 2 kids*

Our friend Sarah commented that it was the communication between her and her husband that was really affected after they had their second child:

> "Since all free time was cut out, and we are more tired at the end of the day, we either veg out, try to catch up on things, or go to sleep. Always separately. The last thing we want to do is communicate about the very things that are wearing us into the ground."

We all know that communication is key, but just having a conversation becomes a challenge after adding another kid or two. Even if we're both in the same room, it's hard to hear each other over the din.

When we do get to talk, ninety percent of the time we talk about the kids. While those conversations are necessary, when we relate to each other *only* as whoever's parents, it becomes pretty hard to keep the spark alive. A discussion about the best preschool program for your "high-energy" two-year-old doesn't exactly rev anybody up for a night in the sack.

And of course, sex can come to a grinding (sorry) halt when everyone is tired. We have not personally met, or heard, of any couple who has more sex after each child. Do let us know if you're out there. Actually, on second thought, don't. Too depressing.

Surrendering to the Madness

"Resistance is futile. You will be assimilated."
    –*The Borg* in Star Trek

When faced with more kids we have one of two choices: surrender or die fighting.

Having more than one child forces most of us, especially men, to make our family our number one priority. With one child, you don't necessarily have to do that. You can finesse it. You get caught between who you were and who you have to be. We spend our twenties and thirties developing a big sense of self. With more kids, the identity we built up as Mr. Super Lawyer or Ms. Big-Shot Mover and Shaker has to shrink to accommodate the new roles of Mom or Dad.

Surrendering is something most of us are not very good at. We're fighters, aren't we? Our surrender is usually preceded by a great struggle: we fight and complain and feel hard done by. We moan, "What happened to my (circle all that apply): waistline, downtime, gym routine (or, if we're feeling really sorry for ourselves), life?" Eventually, however, the overwhelming majority of us yield to parenthood. The signs are everywhere:

- We buy a minivan (some men, if finances allow, buy a convertible or a motorcycle to offset the effect of the minivan).

- We join Sam's Club or Costco at the Executive Level.

- There is so much kiddie crap all over the house, we think it breeds at night.

- We move, or are thinking about moving, to the suburbs.

- We (women) get our hair cut ... short.

- We (men) start to lose our hair.

- We gain fifteen pounds because we can't get to the gym.

- We develop a slight stoop from carrying thirty-pound children.

- We buy time-management and life-balance books, but never read them. We are still hopeful that someone, somewhere has got this all figured out.

> "I was mad at the world for a while after we had our kids. But, as I told my friend whose kids stopped napping at the same time, you inevitably slip into a comfort zone with the very things that made you uncomfortable, and you just plain get used to it. Now I cherish the moments when I'm given time alone with just one of my children. Not that I don't *wish* for them to nap at the same time."
> —*Ellen, married 9 years, 2 kids*

Team Think: Grown-ups versus Rugrats

> "It's 'All Hands on Deck' because it *has* to be."
> —*Cindy, married 9 years, 3 kids*

> "I feel like with each child our marriage got stronger, the bond got deeper, we understood each other better."
> —*Ruth, married 11 years, 2 kids*

For most of us, as our families grow, it becomes apparent pretty quickly that, like it or not, the two of us will be obliged to work together if we are going to keep everything afloat. If the game is *Grown-ups versus Rugrats*, we need each other in order to win. It's too much for one person to handle. Two interesting phenomena occur simultaneously, both of which precipitate our learning to operate as a well-oiled machine: *Dad Steps Up and Mom Chills Out.*

What's the old adage? *The first child makes a man a parent. The sec-*

ond one makes him a father. Many men we spoke with agreed that it was the second or third kids that drafted them into full-fledged fatherhood. "When we just had one kid, I was like the reserve unit called in occasionally for backup duty. But with three, man, I am on active duty big time," said our former-Marine-friend Sean. At this point, men are simply obliged by the level of work to get involved. Their participation is a given.

When things start busting at the seams, Mom quickly realizes she needs to relax her parenting standards (matching outfits are no longer required). She may also decide that her husband, clueless as he once may have seemed, is perfectly able to feed, bathe, and dress the kids. "I just couldn't do it all on my own anymore," said our hard-charging attorney-friend Gail.

Needless to say, we're not always moving in synchronized harmony (if ever) and there are times when we think we're pulling more weight than our teammate. It takes some players longer than others to get with the program, but eventually, we start to see some of the signs that we're working as a team:

> "As I look back, I can't remember when things changed or even talking about it, but now we have an understanding that when the kids are awake both parents are on deck. So, when one of us is making dinner, the other is doing homework/baths/kicking the ball in the backyard."
> —*Anton, married 9 years, 2 kids*

Fun with Family Math

The Numbers Game
Just *talking* about the possibility of more children can cause marital arguments. Many of us have ongoing "how-many-should we-have" debates. According to a poll on *babycenter.com*, 21 percent of couples are not in agreement about the ideal size of their family ("Yeah, she can have another one, but it just won't be with me!"), and another 43 percent "think" they agree.[1]

Some couples turn the numbers game into an intricate math equation, with each new variable (kid) requiring an economic analysis that would make Alan Greenspan proud. All for a question that requires a seemingly simple numerical answer.

> "We are debating having a third. There are days when we look at each other and say, 'This is a two-kid day.'"
> —*Ramon, married 10 years, 2 kids*

Recalculating
Many couples reduce their ideal number of offspring with each new baby. For example, when they got married, Mike told Cathy he wanted six kids. After the first, the number was cut to five, and after the second, he concluded that three would be just fine, thank you very much.

The Spacing Game
What do you do if one half of the couple wants to compress diaper duty into the shortest possible time span and the other wants to space the kids three years apart?

> "Each year we wait to have that third kid, means another year tacked onto the time it takes to raise our family. At this rate, we're going to be attending PTA meetings when we're sixty!"
> —*Dennis, married 10 years, 2 kids*

The Crying Game: How the Debate Is Settled
It's a zero sum game. Someone's going to lose.

Short-Term Impact Analysis:

> "Even though I didn't want another baby, the lure of having lots of sex was enough to convince me."
> —*Alan, married 9 years, 3 kids*

Long-Term Impact Analysis:

> "He only wanted two and he won. I think there are a few subjects where the no's always get to win. This was one of them. It took me a few weeks to reconcile to the fact that we would not have three. However, when I thought about how

tough things could be if we had three and he wasn't 100 percent
committed to it, it became a no-brainer."
  —*Vivian, married 6 years, 2 kids*

Ninety-nine percent of the time, the woman gets the swing
vote. And really, until men get pregnant and breastfeed, that
seems fair to us. Several couples, however, told us they'd used
a high-stakes bartering system to come to final terms. Laura
told her husband that she would have a third as long as she
never, ever had to cook dinner again. Bill extracted a promise
of weekly sex from his wife in exchange for a fourth.

  Oh, yeah, and be careful what you wish for. We know quite
a few couples who, upon going for that second or third, got
pregnant with twins ...

While more kids drag more chaos, work, and financial pressure into our
lives, they also instantly give us more clarity and direction. That second
one, especially, quickly forces us to close the book on our past life and
quit trying to "get things back to the way they were before we had kids."
We accept our new reality. And we are all the better for it.

Bonus Section:
A Family Vacation Is *Not* a Vacation

Ahhh, the family vacation. Fun in the sun? Absolutely. A little R and R?
Not quite. A family vacation is not a vacation. It's a *Schlep-Fest*. We work
just as hard, if not harder, than when we're at home; doing it in a different place. Often, we return home exhausted, minus the beloved blankie a
child can't sleep without, and sometimes, barely on speaking terms with
our spouse. Why?

> "The five-minute quickie never worked out, or the wife spent
> half the day looking all over Downtown Disney for her toddler's
> lost tennis shoe because it was such a cute pair. Or both."
>   —*(Ok, we'll admit it. That was one of us.)*

Remember the days when your vacation would start when you got on
the airplane (or even when you got to the airport)? Shoes off, magazine

open, head back … relax. Now, getting there is the most traumatic part of the trip.

Snooty Flight Attendants

When you fly with small kids no one wants to know you, least of all the flight attendants. On her maiden voyage alone with a baby, Julia struggled to collapse the stroller with one hand while holding the baby in the other. (She's a pro now, what with all the practice one gets in the security line these days.) Three flight attendants stood watching her, arms folded across their chests. "I asked them if they could help and they told me, most patronizingly, that they were not permitted to hold babies. I don't know why that stopped them from collapsing the stroller. The line was getting so backed up that finally, *the captain* of the plane abandoned the cockpit and came out to hold Theo. Surely he should have been figuring out how to get that thing off the ground, not letting a baby pull off his glasses. I was mortified. And furious."

Appalled Passengers

Cathy flew to Ireland last Christmas with a toddler and a baby. Alone. (She is quick to point out that it was one of the most stupid things she's ever done.) "I could smell the fear when I got on the plane. Everyone was terrified that they'd be pressed into babysitting duties at 30,000 feet. They all got furiously interested in their books and the contents of their carry-on. When we landed in Dublin ten hours later (after, I admit, almost continuous whining/crying from my two seats), I was approached by a man who asked me when I would be flying back. He wanted to make sure he wasn't on the same flight."

On another flight, Stacie's ten-month-old cried at the top of her lungs for an hour. She responded to the "if-looks-could-kill" daggers she was getting by lifting her screaming baby up in the air and announcing, "I've tried everything: bottle, food, pacifier, books … I've given it my best shot." She then apologized and sat back down.

The Airport Bathroom Stall

When Stacie was seven months pregnant she traveled solo with her three-year-old and one-year-old. Yes, she was that insane. She'll never forget her experience in that 3×3 bathroom stall: "My oldest said that she had to go, but she was too scared of the 'loud toilet that flushes by itself.' Boarding was about to start, so I got desperate. While holding my twenty-five-pound one-year-old, very pregnant mind you, I sat on the back of that evil toilet and placed her in front of me and encouraged her to go. But she was just too scared. No one was around, so I lifted her up to go in the sink. Of course a few women walked in and caught me in the act. Yes, I had reached a new low. But I didn't care. I was not going to board a two-hour flight and deal with a three-year-old who had wet her pants!"

A Plea to the Flying Public

When you fly alone with kids, one of two things happens. Either you decide that the human race is doomed, or your faith in humanity is restored.

A woman traveling alone with her kids is often made to feel like she is the lowest form of life on the planet. People sigh loudly and wring their hands behind you because they have to wait an additional two minutes to board the plane, or they sit stone-faced beside you as your adorable toddler waves at them and attempts to grab their watch. We know it's annoying. We were on your side not too long ago.

We have also been moved almost to tears by the milk of human kindness shown us by the countless strangers who've offered to carry a bag, hold a baby, or even play peek-a-boo over the seat for an hour with a toddler. We have all depended on the kindness of strangers, and we are more grateful than you can imagine.

So please, if you can't find it in your heart (or you are physically unable) to offer to carry a bag or collapse a stroller (honestly, no one expects you to hold a baby), just be patient. Maybe offer a weak smile of sympathy. That's not too much to ask, is it?

HOW WOMEN FEEL

> "As you have more kids, reality sets in. This is real life and you
>   have to make it work for your family."
>   —*Melanie, married 9 years, 2 kids*

Who knew our hearts held enough love to go around for all these kids? Who knew we had such reserves of strength and inner fortitude to care for them all (and our husbands, and maybe even ourselves)? We women sometimes surprise ourselves. Just when we think we can't possibly get up one more time in the night, or that there's no way we'll *ever* make it through the day at work without falling asleep and drooling all over our desks, somehow we do manage. It may not be pretty, but we manage. The question just becomes, "OK. Wow. How am I going to make all this work?"

The Big Chill

> "I have definitely mellowed out in a lot of ways. I've had to let go
>   and realize that so much is out of my hands and I need to just
>   go with the flow."
>   —*Leslie, married 8 years, 3 kids*

> "I read about all those moms who are depressed. I don't have
>   time to get depressed—I'm too busy surviving. I don't even
>   have time to think about getting depressed."
>   —*Erin, married 11 years, 3 kids*

One way we make it all work is that we do, indeed, mellow out. The actual care and feeding of subsequent kids is ten times easier than the first. Unless, like Kelly, we get the "if I had had the second one first I would have never had another child" colicky baby later in the lineup, we breathe a sigh of relief knowing that the child will survive in our care and we relax. We let our standards slip a bit. Note the following stories as evidence:

> Stacie: "I was oh-so-particular about when my first had a bottle
>   and how many ounces she consumed. With the second and

third, whenever they cried, they got some formula. I figured if they were hungry, I'd hear about it."

Julia: "After the little one did his first faceplant into the coffee table, I calmly drove him to the ER for stitches like it was nothing more than an extra-long trip to the dry cleaners. Granted, the bleeding was minimal, but it just didn't undo me. Of course I felt terrible for him, but, had it been my first, I would have beaten myself up about it for a week afterward."

Cathy: "My sister called one day when the baby was three months old and asked, with mock horror, if she heard TV sounds in the background. I had, of course, at one time stated emphatically that my kids would have no TV until they were three. I had to admit that the two-year-old was watching *Finding Nemo*—for the second time that day."

Sometimes, we even relax enough to enjoy ourselves ...

"I feel like I enjoyed my second's baby stage more. With my first, I was always saying, 'I can't wait until he's crawling. I can't wait until he's walking.' With my second I just relished every stage because I knew it wouldn't last long."
—*Allison, married 7 years, 2 kids*

The Romantic Stage

When we have our second child many of us look back and romanticize the early days. We don't remember the grenades. Stacie stopped swinging from the vines long enough to reflect on what she calls *The Romantic Stage*:

"Having just one kid—in hindsight, it feels like a movie scene: you're there on the beach with the sun setting as your baby discovers her first seashell. You and your husband smile at each other and reflect on the moment. With two or more, it's a different scene altogether: Jaclyn heads toward the ocean as James and (little) Ross head for the dunes and we are tag-teaming the near-constant application of sunscreen and building of sand castles and changing of diapers. You don't notice any sunsets. You have to really pay attention to catch 'the moments.'"

When it is just the three of you, no one is distracted—there is time, energy, and sufficient mental capacity to retain all those special moments. Add another kid or two, and it all becomes a big blur. The romantic stage is special. The romantic stage is fleeting. In an instant, it is gone.

Less-Than-Chilled

Even though we relax our mommy standards (*Surely sucking on the tooth-paste cap qualifies as teeth brushing?*), we want to make sure that nothing falls through the cracks. We respond to the many-kids-induced-chaos by trying to control it. We buy clothes for the fall at the beginning of the summer, we stockpile diapers and baby food like Armageddon is just around the corner, we schedule appointments months in advance, and we beat ourselves up when we don't manage to do all or any of the above.

> "Our second is six months old and I feel like I am barely keeping it all together. Things keep slipping through the cracks: missed appointments, unfinished naps, the older one wearing dirty clothes to preschool, and the baby not getting bathed for five nights in a row. The first was a huge adjustment, obviously, but the second has upended the careful arrangement I had laid out. Now, everything just feels so ... sloppy."
> —*Bethany, married 6 years, 2 kids*

The Great Balancing Act

> "I think juggling being a mother, wife, and professional is something that changes from week to week. Some weeks all is in order. Other weeks, it's just nuts."
> —*Gwen, married 11 years, 3 kids*

All mothers, whether they work outside the home or not, are in perpetual motion. If we work, we spend our lunch break running errands so we won't get completely steamrolled at the weekend; if we stay at home, we don't get a lunch break. It's a juggling act extraordinaire. We have to keep a bowling ball (the kid), an orange (the husband), and a baseball bat (running the office and/or managing the home front) in the air, all while riding a unicycle through a ring of fire and looking fabulous while we're doing it.

The Mom Pie

> "Everyone wants a piece of the Mama."
> —*Vicki, married 5 years, 2 kids*

When we have more kids, each little person gets a smaller piece of *The Mom Pie*. As our banker-friend Michelle said, "It's kind of like a dilution effect in an investment if new investors are brought in." (Thanks, Michelle.) Then, of course, our *Guilt Circuit* goes into overdrive. "I'm not spending enough time with William. Megan was crying when I left for work this morning. They're not eating enough vegetables."

And, of course, there's that big person lurking around the house looking for his piece of pie, too. One Sunday morning, Cathy, who had both kids yelling "Mama" and waving their arms at her, said to Mike, "Jeez, I need to split myself in two." "No," he said, "in three."

Everyone Wants a Piece of The Mom Pie

After a long day at the circus, there are two choices in front of us: sex and sleep. Do we even need to finish this sentence? We tell ourselves that things will get better when all the kids are sleeping through the night, or in preschool, or maybe fifth grade, and then we'll have time for our husbands again.

Something's Gotta Give

With so much more to do, something's gotta give. For the overwhelming majority of us that something is our free time, our hobbies, and sometimes even our girlfriends. When we have more kids, it's fitting in all the other stuff—professional aspirations, friendships, hobbies, exercise, and marriage—that becomes so difficult.

Most working moms want to maximize their "mommy time" and consequently give up all their free time. When they are off, they rarely hand the kids over to Dad to catch a break.

> "I work full-time and I feel like that counts as my 'me time.'
> When I've worked all day, I just can't justify going to a Pilates
> class or something at night. I am away from my kids enough as
> it is."
> —Hillary, married 7 years, 2 kids

Some stay-at-home moms feel a sense of isolation after having more kids. They're on entertainment duty solo all day long, but the alternative—getting everyone mobilized and out of the house for a playdate—is sometimes even more daunting. "Packing up to take two kids out? It takes a roller bag just to go out for pancakes," said Renee. When they don't get that adult stimulation, they feel like the walls are closing in on them. But if they pay a sitter to give themselves a little break, many wonder, "How can I justify paying someone else to do my job when I'm not bringing in any income?" There are no easy answers.

> "I hardly ever talk to my girlfriends anymore. I only chat briefly
> with the other moms at school pickup. They're nice, but I don't
> know them that well. I just never have any time anymore."
> —Sara, married 5 years, 2 kids

Reconsidering Career Choices

"When I was pregnant with my third, I thought, 'Time to quit
my job and leave all this crap behind.'"
—*Colleen, married 7 years, 3 kids*

The increased workload and the desire to find more "mommy time" leads
many women to rethink their work schedules. Some studies say that as
many as fifty percent of full-time working mothers change to part-time
or take a leave of absence when they have a second child.[2]

The decision to stay at home or work part-time is easy for some, but
agonizing for others.

> "I just didn't see how I could continue with the way things were
> after having my second kid. I had a really demanding job as an
> attorney, and my husband was traveling all the time for work.
> No one was really taking care of the home front, and the kids
> were going from day care to nannies and then back to day care.
> So we decided it made sense for me to stay at home. It was a
> hard choice for me. Work is a huge part of who I am. I think I
> was really depressed for a while and I know I took it out on my
> husband."
> —*Mary, married 5 years, 2 kids*

How We Feel About Our Husbands

Seeing our husbands really wrap their arms around fatherhood, we can't
help but feel that all is right with the world. It gives us the deepest sense
of happiness and well-being. When our kids are playing together, and we
exchange a "hey, look what we did" smile with our husbands; we can't
imagine being any happier. And when he is playing with all the kids . . .
well, we are just fit to burst.

> Julia: "Gordon is wallowing in fatherhood like a pig in mud.
> He hauls the boys off to the nursery to buy plants and spends
> all Saturday with them in the yard. He's teaching Theo to ride
> his bike and Henry how to stack his blocks. He handles bath
> and bedtime like a total pro. Here I am writing this book, but I
> don't have the words to explain how happy it makes me to feel

us cohere as a family, to feel like he's content with his family life, too."

Stacie: "Taking care of three kids under the age of five is no picnic. At the end of a tough weekend, Ross looks forward to his next business trip to escape the mayhem. But once he hits 35,000 feet, he can't wait to get back to Jaclyn, James, and little Ross. When he comes home, he runs through the kitchen to greet the rowdy fan club. They treat him like a true rock star. Sometimes, I actually tear up."

Cathy: "A couple of weekends ago we left the girls overnight with my in-laws. On Sunday morning, Mike told me, 'Let's go get them. I really want to spend some time with them.' It made me ridiculously happy that he wanted to do that—not go fishing, or sleep in, or watch TV, or catch up on work—just be with them."

Not surprisingly, though, we still want the same things that we have always wanted from our husbands: help and acknowledgement.

Help and Acknowledgement, etc., etc.

"The other day, Eric said, 'The thought of going to the grocery store with both of them is pretty daunting. It's no big deal taking just one.' I said to him, 'Do you remember when Emily was just born and I said to you, 'How am I going to do this?' and your reply was, 'Women have been doing this for thousands of years, you'll figure it out.' Do you remember that? *Now* do you understand what I was talking about?' And he said, 'Oh huh, yeah, I guess so.'"
　　—*Brandy, married 8 years, 2 kids*

We keep harping on this, harpies that we are. (Sorry, guys, are we starting to sound like the teacher on *Charlie Brown*?) It's really the only way that a true parenting partnership is achieved: *You don't get it until you do it.*

The Penny Finally Drops

Hurrah!

Some women said that as their family grew, their husbands *finally* "got it."

> "When we had the second I was amazed at how my husband helped me out. I feel like with the first one he gave fifty percent, but then with the second he gave ninety percent. His commitment and involvement really went up with the second kid."
>
> —*Marilyn, married 11 years, 4 kids*

Others didn't so much "get it" as they had "it" thrust upon them.

> "It wasn't like Tom just saw the second kid and said, 'By golly, I'd better roll up my sleeves around here.' I think it was when I started bouncing checks that he realized I had too many balls in the air."
>
> —*Joanne, married 6 years, 2 kids*

Will the Penny Ever Drop?

Other women complained that their husbands still don't get it, and never will.

> "For the first year after the second kid, my husband just lay on the couch and went into a funk. He constantly complained about how busy we were and how tired we were. *We?* I repeat, he lay on the couch and went into a funk. He didn't do jack squat."
>
> —*Cheryl, married 12 years, 2 kids*

> "My husband actually said the following: 'Why don't you appreciate the fact that I try to make your life easier? Don't you appreciate that I make the money so you can buy nice things and stay at home with the kids? You don't have to work.' Believe me, he didn't get laid for about a month."
>
> —*Rebecca, married 11 years, 3 kids*

Yes, our husbands "got it," but, of course, there was still lots of room for improvement. At the top of the list of annoying husband behaviors were their increasingly dramatic bids for freedom.

The Great Escapees

Even as our husbands ratcheted up their participation on the home front with each additional child, they also stepped up their escape attempts, becoming increasingly extreme in their desperation to fly the coop. Think Steve McQueen in *The Great Escape* trying to leap the fence into Switzerland on his motorbike.

Only in talking about this section did we realize that each of our own husbands had drastically stepped up a hobby or declared a lifelong time-consuming passion we never knew they had:

- Mike took up fishing during the last months of Cathy's second pregnancy. (Apparently, it is not possible to fish for less than five hours at a stretch.)

- Gordon announced that he intended to enter an amateur cycling event in the Alps, coincidental to the birth of Julia's second. (He'd always been a cyclist, but suddenly, that Alpine climb became an imperative).

- Ross trained every morning for months and ran a marathon during Stacie's second pregnancy.

And we're not the only ones:

> "A few weeks after we had our third child, my husband told me
> that he was going to start campaigning for John Kerry, manning
> phone centers and registering voters. I thought he had totally
> lost it. I was like, 'Who needs you more? Me or John Kerry?'"
> —*Maggie, married 7 years, 3 kids*

When women face the challenge of losing their free time, they say, "Something's gotta give." When men confront it, they say, "There's got to be a way out of here." We're scaling back while you're adding turbo-charged Iron Man activities to your schedule. Is that really fair?

The Great Escapees

What's understandable to a woman: missing your freedom and a perfectly reasonable desire to hit certain milestones before you turn forty. We can relate. When you step up to the plate as the Famn Damily gets bigger, we truly are motivated to make sure you get let off the leash as often as possible. What's incomprehensible to a woman is when you propose a weekly solo activity that takes you away for hours at a time. That makes it very hard for us to be magnanimous and say, "Go have fun."

What Am I? The Warden?

There's another little problem with these escape attempts: we end up playing the warden. We don't always want to be the bad guy. We get annoyed when you say things like, "John's wife still lets him play golf every Saturday, why can't I?" or "Hey, the guys are getting together for a little poker tonight. Can I have a hall pass?" What are we, the school principals handing out hall passes and demerits? Should we schedule homeroom and snack time in addition to recess, too?

We want you to act like a partner in this growing enterprise, and use your sound, manly reason to choose how and when to spend your free time. We're really not interested in being your ball and chain.

HOW MEN FEEL

"Now it's official. I'm one of those sorry bastards in the airport hauling two kids in the double stroller, the baby in the backpack, and fifteen pieces of luggage. I am the pack mule."
—*Dean, married 8 years, 3 kids*

"Two kids have Negative Covariance. They're like magnets with opposing forces. When one is happy, the other is sad. When one is crying, the other wants to play. When one is hungry, the other won't eat. When one is charging off to the right, the other one charges off to the left. It makes my head spin."
—*Ruben, married 8 years, 2 kids*

Swollen with pride at the gurgling, giggling, ball-tossing evidence of their manly prowess, guys become increasingly involved in the life of their growing family. It helps that the older kids, are, well, getting older, and therefore significantly more interesting (not to mention easier to care for) to a man than a newborn is. They get great satisfaction from the relationships they form with the kids, and they often find they are relating better to their more-chilled-out wife as well. Of course, they also can't help but notice that their slice of the pie keeps getting smaller, and that their free time has virtually disappeared. With the increased pressure to provide, and a life that often seems out of their control, they can feel worn down by the double treadmills (work and home) of their existence.

The Pack Mule

Getting the Dad Thing Down

> "The good news is that with the second, you're more skilled. You
> get better, faster, smarter. You know what corners you can cut."
> —*Greg, married 10 years, 3 kids*

Argh! Always cutting corners! But hey, maybe they're on to something
after all ...

> "I have so much fun with Catherine, our four-year-old; she just
> cracks me up. She's a real little person now. The baby is cute,
> but it's not much fun to hang out with him. It feels like work.
> Catherine doesn't feel like work anymore."
> —*Howard, married 7 years, 2 kids*

Like their wives, men also gain perspective on the process and can adjust
their expectations accordingly. They know, for example, that the Twilight
Zone doesn't last forever—that they *will* sleep again and their wife will
eventually return to a fairly recognizable version of her former self.

> "I remember with Luke that I bought these alphabet letter
> cards and taped them on the ceiling above his changing table,
> thinking he'd learn to read his name by the time he was two.
> I'm a little more realistic about things with the baby and just
> try to have fun playing with him."
> —*Scott, married 8 years, 2 kids*

Aha!

> "Most of your time at home seems to be 'kid focused' when you
> have two or more kids. Whether you're getting lunch or dinner
> ready, changing diapers, playing, getting them ready for naps,
> or bathing; it seems there is always a kid activity going on. I
> finally realized, 'Shit, this is hard.'"
> —*Curt, married 5 years, 2 kids*

> "Paradise is watching one kid!"
> —*Andy, married 5 years, 3 kids*

Once they get more involved in the heavy lifting (especially on the weekends), most men, as we noted, finally "get it." *They do, therefore they understand.* Of course, a few enlightened men got it the first time around, but for most, the proverbial light bulb does not go off until the second arrives. This understanding translates into empathy, appreciation, and willingness to help. When their wife is nursing the baby, and the toddler is about to take a flying leap off the kitchen counter, they can see how their participation is important. They realize their wife can't "fight two alligators" (change two diapers) at once.

> "With three kids, I saw that I needed to pay more attention to each of them, to invest that time. My wife is a great mom, but she can't read to Jenny, stack blocks with John and Katie, and load the dishwasher at the same time."
> —*Jeremy, married 7 years, 3 kids*

What Happened to My Life?

> "Guys are haunted by the ghosts of their past life. They remember the guy who used to go out after work and have a couple of drinks. They remember (or they imagine) the days of wanton women and wild sex. They remember when they had the freedom to sit around all day on Saturday watching sports. As they have more kids, though, they finally realize they have to kill those ghosts."
> —*Alan, married 9 years, 3 kids*

Our friend Pat said, "Having the first kid was a cakewalk, but that second one was a car crash." He was not alone. It's almost as if it takes men an extra child (or two) to catch up with their wives. Her world was upended the first time; his was merely shaken. For him, the additional kids bring on the earthquake. Why is this?

With one child, men can maintain their extracurricular pursuits—albeit at a reduced frequency—but they can find the time to do it. Our friend Gary told us, "When we had our first kid I realized I had to transition my weekend motorcycle racing from an obsession to a hobby. And I did. But now, with the second, I had to pretty much give it up. If I can get out there once a month, I'm doing well." It's that whole *freedom* thing again. The incremental loss of freedom or downtime adds up and it wears a guy down—more than we realized, actually. Some feel like their lives are nothing but a series of "have-to's." "I have to suit up and perform at work. I have to suit up and perform at home."

Julia's first instinct was to call this section "Poor, Poor, Pitiful Me," but Cathy and Stacie were much more sympathetic to men's "plight" and talked her down from her sarcasm. After all, we know where they're coming from. We need some freedom too. Some men, however, can lose sight of the relative sacrifice and get a tad dramatic:

> "For a guy domestic life can be emasculating. When there's no hope of escape and little to no chance of hooking up with your wife at the end of the day, you might as well castrate a guy. Diapers, baths, naps, time-outs ... it goes completely against our biological drive, and if we don't get a break from it all we end up climbing the walls."
> —*Sam, married 9 years, 2 kids*

(Julia says, "Boo hoo, cry me a river." But in the name of building mutual understanding here, she's trying her best.)

Beasts of Burden

The comedian Bill Maher weighs in on the subject of domesticated men: "I'm like the last of my guy friends who has never gotten married. And their wives, they don't want them playing with me. I'm like the escaped slave. I bring news of freedom." He acknowledges the argument that married men live longer than single men and quips, "Ah, yes, and an indoor cat also lives longer. It's a fur ball with a broken spirit that can only look out on a world it will never enjoy. But it does, technically, live longer."

If things are *so bad* for married men, why is it that when they do escape, they come right back for more? The recidivism rate is astounding. Most widowers/male divorcees remarry within three years of a divorce or death.[3] What's more, married people have sex twice as often as single people.[4] We know that's still not nearly enough sex for most men, but if you're married, chances are you're getting more than your single buddies, no matter what they might tell you.

So there, Bill. Put that in your pipe and smoke it.

How They Feel About Their Wives

Not So Nutso

Most guys we talked to agreed on this one: their wives chilled out big time after the second kid.

> "When you just have one kid, that child is always in the cross-hairs, the parents have laser-like focus on that one target. But with two, you have double bogeys, two moving targets. My wife can't hyper-control everything anymore and it is such a relief. We feel more balanced now that she is not so obsessed—more like a family."
> —*Ryan, married 8 years, 2 kids*

Most women stop acting like control freaks. Some even learn to let their husbands play a larger, maybe even a leading role. A more relaxed Mom is good news for everyone. It makes the men breathe a sigh of relief. Now if they put the baby's dress on backward, Mom won't quibble. She's just happy that the baby is dressed.

... But Then Again ...

According to most men, although their wives were more relaxed when it came to caring for the kids, they sometimes became more uptight as far as running the household and running the family were concerned.

> "My wife built the nest. My wife runs the nest. I just sleep there."
> —*Paul, married 9 years, 2 kids*

A man can understand that organization is critical in a multi-kid household, but he doesn't like it when his wife, the newly *Self-Appointed Family*

CEO, starts treating him like an employee. She makes the decisions and controls family life, he is merely taking orders. If she wants him to hang the curtains in Joey's room, he hangs the curtains in Joey's room. If she wants the family to spend Saturday at Grandma's house, they spend Saturday at Grandma's house.

Where's My Piece?

"I feel like I don't have a wife anymore. I get ten minutes a night if I'm lucky. Sometimes she doesn't even say good night to me. I'm watching TV and the next thing I know, the lights are off in the kitchen and she's gone to bed."
    —*Jared, married 7 years, 2 kids*

Another kid often means that the husband slips further down the family totem pole. Hanging out in last place waiting around for the scraps isn't fun for any guy. But with more kids in the picture, he can at least start to understand why his wife is less able to make time for him. As long as he is not forgotten entirely, he can adjust his expectations and survive quite well on a reduced portion of the wife-pie.

"I don't know if it's acceptance or resignation, or both, but in terms of sex, I've just accepted that you have to do it when you can—when one kid is watching a movie and the other is napping—you have to take what you can get. You're just going to have to bang it out, so to speak."
    —*Ian, married 7 years, 2 kids*

Some of them even have the long-term vision to see that the condition is temporary. They can at least intellectualize, if not be thrilled about the fact that someday, in a galaxy far, far away, the kids will be older and they will regain some of their former glory.

SOLUTIONS FOR BOTH

"Once you have that second, your old life is over, so *over*."
    —*Brian, married 6 years, 2 kids (Authors' Note: He said it, we didn't.)*

Brian's right. Our old lives *are* over. But that's kind of the point, isn't it? Becoming a parent is a whole new way of living. In many ways, our lives are just beginning. Most couples we spoke to underscored this sentiment by telling us that adding to their families, and increasing their overall workload, actually gave them clearer perspective about what's really important. They said it made them more aware of what they were gaining and less focused on what they were losing.

Of course raising kids is a tough business. How many times have you exchanged a sympathetic glance with another frustrated parent wrestling with a screaming two-year-old in the grocery cart? We're all just hanging on by a thread. (And those who appear to have it really and truly under control are on drugs. We know they are.) But hanging back and looking longingly over the fence (or out the window, for all you indoor cats) doesn't get us anywhere.

Once we have kids, they aren't going to go away. We've entered a new reality. The question becomes, as someone put it earlier in this chapter, *how are you going to make it work for you and your family?*

Two Ways: Surrendering and Thinking like a Team.

(Authors' Note: We're all about promoting Team Spirit in this chapter, so this solutions section is addressed to both members of the team. Where there is specific advice for men or women, you'll find it within the bigger idea.)

Surrender Already

If *you* haven't surrendered already, it's time. The people that are happiest with their lives have made that step, committed themselves to their families, and given in to the madness. Not sure how? We have a Four-Step Surrender Plan. It's not foolproof—of course there will be flare-ups. That *person-you-used-to-be* won't disappear entirely. As we were writing this chapter, for example, Gordon took down all the baby gates in the house because, "It just looks nicer without them."

Once as a teenager, Julia almost drowned in the Guadalupe River. The lifeguard who pulled her out of the water later told her, "You were caught between two opposing currents, one going downstream, one going upstream. If this ever happens to you again, sink to the bottom and let the downstream current carry you away from the rapids before you try to come up for air." Ah—the perfect metaphor for parenting: sink, so you don't drown.

Step One: Lose the 'Tude

"The greatest part of our happiness depends on our dispositions,
   not our circumstances."
   —*Martha Washington*

Time to suck it up. In our minds, surrendering is a conscious decision. It's a *choice* we make about the attitude we're going to have. Running a full house and staying meaningfully employed can wear anybody down. It's easy to develop a bad attitude. Problem is, a bad attitude doesn't solve anything; it only makes you unhappier. If you dwell on your "how tough I have it" feelings, you won't see all the wonderful things that you do have in your life.

> "When you have a house full of kids, it's either going to be really crazy and really fun or it's going to be hell. Whether it's fun or it's hell is up to you. You can try to laugh or you can bitch and moan your way through the early years."
> —*William, married 8 years, 2 kids*

Example A: Take Stacie, for example. After a few weeks of loading kids into the car headed for the preschool, Stacie remembers thinking that there might as well be prison bars surrounding her SUV.

> "I felt like I was in a jail cell. One day I realized what I was saying ... 'a jail cell?' and snapped out of it. I reframed my attitude. I knew that my kids needed an education, and as long as homeschooling was not an option (unfathomable!), they had to get to and from school. I started to see the school run as something valuable and important that I did for my kids rather than just another chore."

Example B: Our friend Jim used to dread taking his kids to Home Depot.

> "I was so annoyed that it would take at least two hours to get in and out. Then I got it. I wasn't running an errand, I

was hanging out with my kids, and if I had to answer their
questions about lawn mowers that was OK."

He made an attitude adjustment and, voilà, he started having fun.

Example C: Ross will tell you that anyone wanting three kids should have
their head examined. (Stacie talked him into the third.) So whenever
he feels frustrated about his chaotic life, he checks his attitude and
thinks about the big picture:

> "When I'm eighty years old, am I going to regret having the
> third? Am I going to wish that I played more golf or played
> more with my kids? Am I going to wish that I worked more,
> or spent time with my family? I think the answer is pretty
> obvious."

Nothing worthwhile is easy. But is there any endeavor more worthwhile
than being the best parent and partner we know how to be? The very
things that we might be complaining about—how much we are sacrific-
ing and how hard we are working—are, in reality, the building blocks of
a great life. Parenthood and family take everything we have to give and
then some. But we all know, we reap what we sow. What we invest in our
kids and our spouses comes back to us in ways we can't even imagine.

Step Two: Change Management

> "Now with two kids, we just have to give ourselves up a little
> bit to the chaos. I feel like I've figured that out but, Bruce hasn't
> yet, or isn't willing to. I'm ready to use my sense of humor,
> throw up my hands, and say, 'Oh well!' to a lot of things, while
> he's still feeling really frustrated. I think he's coming around,
> but only time will tell. I've noticed that his realization of the
> need for change is about six months behind mine."
> —*Katherine, married 8 years, 2 kids*

For most of us, change doesn't come easy. Think about the millions of dollars
in advertising spent each year just to get us to switch our brand of toothpaste.
We dusted off some of Julia and Stacie's old business-school textbooks to

check out how companies deal with change. In a nutshell: when a company has to make a change, it needs a *plan* to maximize the understanding and buy-in of its employees, and minimize the risk that people will fight the change and/or quit. The business types call it Change Management.

There are two elements of change management to consider as your family grows:

- Becoming a parent for the second/third time might not be as traumatic as the first time around, but it is a huge change nonetheless. It's not just about adjusting to having a new family member—our schedule, attitude, and expectations have to change, too. That's a tall order for most of us.

- Your spouse may take longer, or find it more difficult to change than you do, and you may have to wait around awhile for him or her to catch up.

We wondered if there might be some change management strategies that could be applied when you add more kids to the mix. So we did a little digging and found a few gems:

- **Make small, but incremental changes.** OK, that's great in theory, but babies are an all-or-nothing deal. One day you don't have one and the next day you do. But you can adjust your schedules gradually. Start with giving each other half an hour off on Saturday and slowly work your way up to half a day.

- **Maintain consistency in as many areas as possible.** How many people do you know who move to a new house or start a remodeling project when they are expecting? At least half, right? Julia and Gordon's big move happened when she was eight months pregnant—new house, new job, new town, new school for the older child, new obstetrician, new pediatrician, new everything. It was a long year. They highly recommend maintaining as much of the status quo as possible when you have another baby.

- **Let yourself grieve.** Change, no matter how wonderful and wanted, also means loss. When you have that second, third, etc. kid you lose a bit more of your old life. The experts say it's OK to feel upset and even a little bit nostalgic. So don't beat yourself up. And don't beat your spouse up if they're dragging their feet (for a while, anyway).

- **Recognize your capacity to adapt.** We are remarkably adaptable creatures. It is one of our most impressive traits. No matter how much a new baby upends our lives, we will adapt to the changes and wonder how we ever had a life without him or her.

- **Go with the flow.** At least for a little while and see where you end up. When you resist change, it's a lot more painful. Remember? It's the "sink, don't drown" philosophy.

Step Three: Surrendering for Women, or Time to R-E-L-A-X

Parenting advice from Frankie Goes to Hollywood? Why not? Relax. Don't do it.

> "I finally learned to just look at everything and laugh. If the kids are not dressed perfectly for school, who cares? Sometimes I forget to take them to their activities, or I forget the permission slip for the field trip. That doesn't mean the world is going to stop spinning on its axis."
> —*Ruth, married 11 years, 2 kids*

> "After high-maintenance-baby number three came along, we go to bed with a lot fewer baths, eat a lot more cereal for dinner, and tend to leave the grocery store before all the shopping is done."
> —*Maggie, married 7 years, 3 kids*

Taking Our Own Advice:
Relaxation Lessons Learned the Hard Way

If only we had known when we had our first babies . . . How much easier our lives would have been. But no, we had to learn the hard way. Here are some things we got right the second (and third) time around:

Baby Care
- Didn't sterilize bottles in boiling water
- Ignored the baby advice books and followed our guts
- Didn't wrap the baby in a Michael Jackson–style mask/ blanket
- Stayed in bed whenever we could/didn't feel guilty about taking a nap

Shortcuts (!)
- E-mailed the baby announcement (well, that was just Cathy)
- Left the house in a mess
- Asked for and accepted help
- Stopped writing meticulous accounts in the baby books— now throw notes in a pile (Well, that is just Julia. Stacie didn't buy baby books the second or third times, and Cathy has never bought one.)

Keeping Things in Perspective
- Learned to laugh at ourselves
- Didn't worry about getting our figures back
- Savored the moments instead of rushing to the next one
- Stopped caring about everyone else's opinions
- Quickly learned about "mother's day out" programs for the older child

After Number Three (well, this is just Stacie)
- The newborn stage didn't faze me—it was still hell, but it just didn't faze me

- Understood the meaning of zone defense—they weren't kidding
- Accepted that my old life is over and learned to love my new one (on most days, anyway)

Step Four: Surrendering for Men, Kill the Ghost

So guys, have you given up your ghosts? Or are you still fighting your own little private Battle of the Alamo? If you choose to die fighting, you won't be a hero to anybody.

> "I think playing golf for half a day on a Saturday is just not on after you have kids. That's just selfish. Those guys are missing out. It's just about being a man. Suck it up. This is it. What else are you going to do, spend the rest of your life in bars picking up women? Playing sports? That's not a life. This is what it's all about."
> —*Pat, married 10 years, 2 kids*

Ah, words of wisdom—from one of your own, no less.

The three of us know now what a big step it is for you to come to terms with the fact that you will not spend an entire Saturday lying on the couch in your boxer shorts watching replays of the 1992 Masters for quite some time. One day, when you're fifty, you'll be able to do that again, because by then the kids won't want to hang out with you anyway. In the meantime, try to figure out a way to participate in the lives you helped create. Take responsibility for your contribution to the overpopulation of the planet. We bet your wife will be willing to work with you if you work with her. And your kids will remember you as the Dad that showed up.

Team Think (Only Four More Steps, We Promise!)

When there's more than one kid in the house we have to pool our resources and act like a team. If we don't, our marriage could be the first casualty in the relentless kid assault. It's sink or swim. It's life or death. We either get up and take our place in the game, or sit on the sidelines and wait for those divorce papers. So go team!

Step One: The Team Needs a Game Plan—You Gotta Have a System

A number of couples we know compare raising kids and maintaining a home with running a business. They have budgets and quarterly goals and strategy meetings. Yeah, we thought it sounded a bit anal, too, but apparently they're on to something. The couples with a system of kid hand-offs and job trade-offs seem to fight less and be a little less exhausted than the rest of us. They *Divide and Conquer* (our old Scorekeeping prevention strategy) and trade off responsibilities. Here are some thoughts from the more process-oriented among us:

Divide and Conquer: "We manage the logistics and the routines like we are running a business: 'You take Ally to the birthday party at 3:00 P.M. and I'll run Peter to his soccer game at 4:00 P.M. Then we'll meet up for pizza at 5:30 P.M.'"

Systemic Thinking: "We follow our unwritten rules to make sure we're constantly taking turns. Like at bath time: 'I'll run the water while you undress the baby. Then you bathe him, and I'll get the towel and his diaper and pajamas ready. Then I'll dress him, and we'll both read him *Goodnight Moon.*'"

Planning Ahead: "Michael and I sit down once a month to talk about our work schedules (I travel, he doesn't) and figure out who needs to do the pickups: what we want to do around the house, and what errands need running. We also make sure to work in some fun time, too, for each of us and with the kids."

Trading Off: "In the morning I take care of the kids so that Molly can get ready for work; it takes her longer than it does me. Then I drop the kids off at day care, and Molly does the evening pickup."

Picking Up the Slack: "When one of us is trying to meet a book deadline, the other one gets home early to pick up the slack."

Warning

Remember how we noted that with more kids, Dad steps up and Mom chills out? Well, not doing these things can really chip away at the team's morale.

Men: The Fastest Route to the Couch: Lack of Empathy and Assistance

Guys, try not to be an insensitive piece of luggage. Check out Exhibits A and B:

Exhibit A: "I remember having two kids hanging on my legs and trying to make dinner and looking out at my husband watching the news. When I made a comment, he barked that he needed to watch the news to relax."

Exhibit B: "We had a baby nurse to help with the twins for a week. I turned to Dave after she left and said, 'I don't know how I'm going to do it.' I'm expecting him to be supportive, but all he said was, 'Suck it up.' I said, 'Suck it up? Who do you think I am—one of your football players? You are not my coach, you are my husband.' That is as much sympathy for my situation at home as I got. Let's just say that attitude did not encourage sex. That put a damper on things. And he had no idea why."

A + B = Your ass is sleeping on the couch tonight.

Women: The Fastest Route to the Therapist's Couch: Uptight Antics

Girls, we all can act a little crazy. Our exhibits don't look much better:

Exhibit A: "You let him do something and then you jump in and tell him he's not doing it exactly how you want it done. I realized I'd gone too far when I started telling him he was stacking the diapers in the thing the wrong way."

Exhibit B: "The other night I was going to bed and my wife was still on the Net searching for a Baked Alaska recipe to make for my mother's birthday. I said to her that I'd buy Mom a cake; after all it's not her problem, it's my mother, and that she should just come to bed. She told me that she had to make a cake and that I just didn't understand. Then she comes to bed an hour later, furious with me because she has to make a cake for my mother!"

A + B = Your ass is calling Dr. Shapiro on Monday.

Step 2: Team-Building Activities

There are two aspects to a successful team—getting the job done (what we've just discussed) and working well together. You can do a fabulous job of running the family business, but you can get consumed with it and wind up neglecting your relationship.

So, to help you build a little more team spirit (Go Grown-ups!), we researched popular corporate team-building activities (you know the drill—build trust, respect, and cooperation by creating a shopping mall out of paper clips and leaping from great heights while shouting the company slogan) and retooled them for babyproofing purposes.

And just remember, if it's good enough for corporate America, it's good enough for the two of you.

The Scavenger Hunt

The *BPYM* version of *The Amazing Race*! Your mission: be the first to get all the items on your shopping list and get home to claim your rightful position on the couch. One of you goes to Target, one of you to Babies R Us, with an equal number of kids in tow. If you have an odd number of kids, the contestant with the extra kid gets a ten-minute head start. This game can also be played within the same store if you just have one place to go on Saturday (fat chance).

The Date Night Challenge

Try, just try, to talk your way through this one! Go out on one of your regular date nights (hint, hint) and see if you can get through the *entire* meal without talking about the kids, the house, or your finances. Betcha can't do it! We know from experience how challenging this is, so here are a few possible topics of conversation (so you can prepare your statements ahead of time):

- Politics (on second thought, nah)
- Global warming: myth or just a problem for your kids to deal with?
- Favorite sexual positions
- The existence of God
- List of things you want to do before you die (cycling the Alps, running a marathon, getting a pedicure)
- List of things you wish your spouse would do for (and/or to) you before you die
- Which celebrity you'd most like to sleep with, and, if you ever meet them, do you have permission to do so?

Judges will be watching, and they will award (or deduct) *Marriage Capital* points on your scorekeeping ledger based on successful (or unsuccessful) performance of the following elements:

- Physical contact: including eye contact, hand-holding, and hugging action, but not necessarily ending up with sex (minus ten points for that one)
- Emotional displays: laughter, tears, laughter-through-tears, etc.
- Listening skills: i.e., no electronic gadgets allowed

The Annual Corporate Retreat

Our favorite! Get your heads out of the daily grind and go somewhere beautiful to contemplate the state of your union or just to have some fun together. Can also be done in your basement if scenic vacations are not an option at the moment. Outline of discussion questions available for an additional fee. We know of one couple who go to a weekend marriage conference every other year. It's less about the couple workshops and more about just getting away together. But either way we think it's a neat idea. (The husband jury is still out on this one, however.)

*And most important, lest we forget ... **Sex** is a team-building activity!*

Step Three: Get Out of Jail Free Cards

We need to be liberal with the *Get Out of Jail Free Cards* to keep the Married-with-Kids-Machine humming.

> "I think we're generous with each other with 'time off' since we
> agreed that we don't both need to be home every night to share
> in the joys of heating up chicken nuggets."
> —*Brandy, married 8 years, 2 kids*

Everyone needs and deserves a break. Dealing with work and kids and household stuff without a break is honestly more than any one person can bear. We each need a chance to recharge and refuel. This is true on a short-term, weekly basis, and also on a long-term, getting-away-for-a- weekend basis. If you can manage, letting each other out of the trenches for an entire weekend pays huge dividends into the family business. Having some time to step back refreshes our perspective: we renew our appreciation for how much we have. By the time we get back we can't wait to see the kids and (conceivably) get our hands on our spouse.

We'll talk in the next chapter about why it's necessary to take time to do what recharges you, but for the moment, just try to be generous when it comes to giving each other some time off.

Cheers!

Step Four: Couple's Cocktail Hour

"All we do is take care of the kids. That's all we do. We don't have any other outlets. We just manage the chaos all day, then collapse on the couch at night with a glass of wine and say, 'We did it.'"

—*Greg, married 10 years, 3 kids*

SEVEN

Balancing Priorities

Where Do We Go From Here?

"What's the hardest thing about being a parent? Getting in and
out of the car is hellacious! And the crap. Every time I sit down
something squeaks. The thing is, you can't imagine life any
other way once you have a kid, and I wouldn't want it any other
way, but things used to be so much easier: one plus one equaled
two. It's all a negotiation now. And I wasn't so fat."
      —*Jeff, married 4 years (to Elizabeth), 1 kid*

"I do love being a Mom, but, boy, I feel drained a lot of the time.
I don't like it that Jeff and I don't get to have fun together very
often. I really miss that. We didn't even manage to celebrate our
last anniversary. I think that makes us argue more. But are we
unhappy? I don't think so. We're not living just for ourselves
the way we were."
      —*Elizabeth, married 4 years (to Jeff), 1 kid*

We are all fundamentally happy with our choices, right? Our children
are our greatest joy, and we'll make whatever sacrifices are necessary in
exchange for the privilege of being a parent. But the trade-offs that we so
willingly make for the kids come at a price; whatever life balance we once
had takes a hit. Don't we all have days when we want to run screaming
out the front door and hitch a ride to anywhere that Barney cannot go?
You might even find yourself, like the three of us, fantasizing about getting sick—nothing too serious—just sick enough to have our husbands
(or George Clooney) wait on us hand and foot for a few days. And of

course let's not forget our husbands who've all tried to marathon, fish, and cycle their way to freedom.

We're Smart People. Why Does This Seem So Hard Sometimes?

What's going on? Why do people report that their marriages falter during this time, when, really, having kids should make us closer than ever? Why is keeping body and soul and spirit together so difficult for us? Are we just a bunch of whiny, self-indulgent complainers who don't know how good we have it? Is a collective kick in the ass really what we need? Or is parenthood just plain difficult? A little of both, actually. . . .

1. **It is difficult, and some of it is no one's fault.** There is so little time and so much to do. We are forced to cut activities out of our lives that recharge and refuel us as individuals and as a couple.
2. **We do things that aggravate the situation (this is the kick-in-the-ass part):** Sometimes we make our married-with-kids life harder than it has to be. In our effort to do and have it all, we can end up focusing on the wrong things and overlooking what's truly important.

Something's Gotta Give

It's not as if everything was in perfect alignment before we had kids and we were both scoring off the happiness charts. We're not saying that life was better before, just that it was simpler. Once kids enter the picture, though, "couple time" and "me time" get squeezed, and the consequences take a toll on how we feel.

When we neglect our marriage, it wilts. Like a houseplant, all it needs is some regular watering (i.e., real intimacy—and we don't just mean sex), but so often we find other things to do that seem more important. Marriage is one of the few things we can ignore without immediate and dire consequences. If we ignore our job, we'll get fired. If we ignore our kids, they'll starve. But if we ignore our relationship, our spouse can live off the scraps for a pretty long time.

After kids, because we are so busy, the marriage can slip into auto-pilot. We coast along, paying very little attention to where we're going. There are no more "deep and meaningfuls." Instead it's "time to make the donuts" … every single day. Here's an example, a "Come on Baby Light My Fire" e-mail that Julia recently sent to Gordon (careful, this is hot stuff …):

1. Not sure what to do on the 401K. Call when you have time to discuss.

2. Do you have any of this year's tax stuff at the office? Where do you want to keep the file?

3. I keep getting cards for the new insurance plan in the mail. Who should I talk to at the office to figure out which ones we are supposed to be using?

4. Don't forget to call your Mom about Saturday before you leave town tomorrow.

5. When do you want to try to have a dinner party?

6. What should I do about getting the rug fixed?

7. Blah. Blah. Blah. My list is just as long, and before you start groaning, just take a close look, most of these things on "your" list are actually things on my list.

Hard to believe she once left poems for him in his briefcase, isn't it?

Marriage on Autopilot

In the same way, when we neglect ourselves, we wilt. Parenthood means reducing many of our critical life-maintenance activities. We aren't talking about how giving up carousing in bars or a weekly pedicure is kind of a bummer; we're talking about losing some of the basic components of a happy, well-lived life that recharge us and make us whole: time with friends and family, exercise, sleep, sex, work, or volunteer activities.

> "My life is very well balanced if you exclude myself."
> —*Anna, married 6 years, 2 kids*

> "I'm thirty pounds overweight. I've gained fifteen pounds with each of my daughters. The thing is, I leave the house at 7:00 A.M. and I don't get out of work until 7:00 P.M.—if I go to the gym, my kids will be in bed by the time I get home. So it's exercise or see my kids."
> —*Anthony, 210 pounds, married 8 years, 2 kids*

> "You know those before and after pictures you see of presidents, before they take office and then four years later after the first term? They look like they have aged at least ten years. I feel like motherhood does the same thing. My oldest is four and I feel and look like I'm a decade older than I was when she was born."
> —*Alicia, married 8 years, 2 kids*

Sometimes it's self-neglect that can cause a marriage to wilt. Scaling back on sanity-saving/happiness-inducing activities can make us feel overwhelmed, vaguely dissatisfied with life in general, and possibly even depressed. Any of the above can make us damn difficult to live with.

Stuff We Do That Aggravates the Situation

There's more to this happiness issue, though, than not having enough time for each other and for ourselves. Being human, we can all do things that make our happiness more elusive than it needs to be:

- **Ignorance (We mean that in a nice way.)** We don't realize that we need to prioritize. Most of the time we don't even know *what* to prioritize.

"I'm not quite sure what's happened. I feel like I'm trying to force really big square pegs (all the stuff I want to do) into really small round holes (how much time I have to do those things)."
—*Barry, married 9 years, 2 kids*

• **It's Never Enough!** Even though we effectively "have it all" when we have our marriage, job, and offspring ducks in a row, we are perpetually longing for "more."

"We drive ourselves so hard, but we feel like we are never on top of everything. We focus too much on what isn't right instead of all that is right. Why can't I say, 'Oh, everything's so great?' I keep saying, 'Let it go, let it go,' but I can't really let it go."
—*Margot, married 7 years, 2 kids*

• **Pining for Perfection.** Just trying to keep the fridge stocked, the checkbook balanced, and the kids healthy is a pretty substantial undertaking. But instead of feeling good about ourselves when we manage to do just that, we pine for the washboard abs, the granite countertops, and/or a new car.

"I hate checking out at the grocery store because there is inevitably a celebrity on a magazine cover in a bikini six weeks after the birth of her third baby, and there's advice on how to boost your baby's IQ and your soufflé-making skills all in the same article. It makes me feel bad every time I look at those. Our life is just so chaotic."
—*Laurie, married 9 years, 3 kids*

The Extreme Parenting Phenomenon

Then there's our eminently reasonable and admirable desire to give our children the best possible opportunities in life. Unfortunately, the pressure of it all can make us feel like we're just not doing enough, no matter how much we do. How many of us think that we would fail as parents if we didn't get our kids into the best preschool, schedule X number of playdates, and expose them in their early formative years to a martial art, a musical instrument, and a foreign language?

"Sometimes I worry that the kids see more of the back of my head than my face. They spend so much time in the back of the car being driven to all their activities."
Dawn, married 10 years, 3 kids

Are You an Uber-Mama?

Plenty of men get caught up in extreme parenting, but it's the Moms who really make it an art form. Our desire to be the best Mom we can be can get out of hand; the Mommy Chip goes haywire, like HAL 9000, the computer in *2001: A Space Odyssey*.

While there's nothing wrong with hand-making birthday party invitations and kitting out your home and yard for every holiday (and if you have genuine creative tendencies and really enjoy that stuff, rock on), *the problem with uber-mama-ing activities is that they are high in cost and low in return*. We spend weeks organizing a big Elmo extravaganza for our child's first birthday, which he proceeds to sleep through. Meanwhile we're annoyed with our husband because he didn't help out more and didn't give us any kudos for throwing the party. He didn't share our

The Uber-Mama Olympics

enthusiasm because he just didn't see the point. *Who*, we asked ourselves, *is benefiting from this kind of activity?* And why do we do it? It's the pressure—pressure we put on ourselves and pressure we absorb from society.

> "It's so easy for Michael to tell me I'm crazy to be looking at drama camp for Gavin, but he doesn't know how nuts it is out there. Moms are getting math tutors for their preschoolers!"
> —*Dana, married 6 years, 2 kids*

Attack of the Uber-Mamas

It's hard to fight our inner manic-mom tendencies when it seems that the world is conspiring to turn us all into ubermamas. The three of us have been there:

Cathy: "I casually mentioned to another mother that I should really start putting Kate into a gymnastic class or something. This woman looked at me aghast and listed all the classes her two-year-old was doing: dance, music, art. I think she thought I was clueless. I told myself that this woman was overscheduling her child, but really, she made me feel guilty. So what did I do? I stayed up until the wee hours researching every conceivable activity for a three-year-old. Did you know that they can take yoga?"

Julia: "The other day I was demoralized by a four-year-old. She was over playing with my son and she said, 'Your house is really messy,' and, honestly, I was upset. I thought, 'She's going to tell her mother … maybe I can buy her silence with chocolate chip cookies.'"

Stacie: "It's time I confess. I threw a big *Nemo* party for two of my kids who both have September birthdays. I invited fifty people, it was catered, there were two piñatas for both age groups, and our pool looked like an aquarium with all the plastic Nemos swimming around in it."

Men can also get caught up in the competitive parenting game. A few of them can be worse than women. As Darren told us:

> "You know how guys measure things ... They look at their friends, coworkers, neighbors and size up where they stand. It's not just about acquiring things, either, like a big house or a nice car, it's also about ranking. Who's the best? Guys want their kids to excel at school and at a sport."

How Much of This Is a Generational Thing?

The fact that we approach parenthood with such high expectations is not surprising. We are the first generation in human history where "having it all" was not only possible, but what we expected. And until we became parents, it was quite often the reality we made for ourselves. Reconciling the perfectionist/have-it-all philosophy with the parent who has to make trade-offs is very difficult for us. Here's what one writer had to say about it:

> "Unfortunately, it's not until you've had children that you discover how selfish you actually are. That's one of the paradoxical aspects of becoming a parent: at the very same time you realize precisely how selfish you are, you are forced to become less selfish. "[1]

From Benign Neglect to Anger and Resentment: Marriage in a Vicious Cycle (Hey, Wasn't This Chapter Supposed to Be about Happiness?)

Marriage on Autopilot/Self-Neglect situations or harboring a bad attitude can degenerate into a *Vicious Cycle. We don't realize how easy it is for these issues to spiral out of control at this stage of life.* One partner's unhappiness contributes to the other's and we both start to take our frustrations out on each other. There is no technical starting point. Once we're in a Vicious Cycle it doesn't really matter who started it, because it takes two to keep it going. Here's what it can look like:

"My husband and I spent the first year of Charlie's life in a state
of perpetual aggravation. We were both really, really angry.
Bitter. It was about all the stuff you've been talking about here:
him wanting sex and me not wanting it, me counting up all
the things he 'just didn't get' and wouldn't help out with, him
feeling rejected, me feeling ignored. After a while, you almost
start to look for it—to look for the things the other person
does that prove, once again, how it's all his or her fault. I was
jealous of his job, and really pissed that he expected me to do
everything around the house. He was pissed that I complained
so much and never seemed to be happy. Neither one of us
wanted to leave the marriage, but we thought we were in big
trouble. We've worked a lot of this out now, but it took a long
time."

—*Gwen, married 11 years, 3 kids*

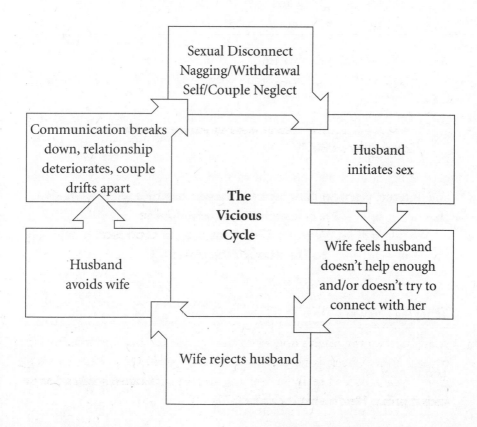

No one wants to end up in a Vicious Cycle, so what are the signs that you might be drifting out of autopilot into low-burn resentment or even bold-faced anger?

You Play the Blame Game
It's all his or her fault. When we start blaming our spouse for our unhappiness: "If only he'd do the dishes, I'd be happy," or, "If only she'd put out a little more often, I'd be happy," we're headed for trouble. It's not that big a leap to "If only I were married to someone else, I'd be happy."

You Become a Basement Dweller/Potential Porn Addict/Book Club Refugee
When we stop focusing on each other, important physical and emotional needs go unmet. When their other half seems too busy, too tired, or too annoyed to care, both men and women look for ways to fill the void.

A lot of men become *Basement Dwellers*. They retreat into their self-made caves and spend all their free time down there playing with their electronic toys (among other things …) to avoid the "cold fish" upstairs. If a guy's basement looks like Circuit City, he's probably not getting much sex or anything else from his wife.

Sexually deprived men will go to extraordinary lengths to fill the physical void as well. They'll even agree to have more children if they think it's going to get them laid a few times. So a *Potential Porn Addict* getting his dollar bills and credit card number ready for the strip clubs and Internet porn should come as no surprise to anyone. A husband channeling all his sexual energy into a computer screen spells trouble.

Women will, of course, also look for ways to fill the emotional gap. Sometimes we immerse ourselves in the kids. Or we become *Book Club Refugees*. We'll seek out the understanding and empathy we need from other social outlets like a book club where husbands and their various annoying behaviors are the main topic of conversation, not great (or even mediocre) works of literature.

You Ponder an Affair
Having an affair is a huge jump to make. But *thinking* about it is not inconceivable when there's an emotional void in marriage. Sweet Gina in

Accounts Payable, or the tennis coach, or the work colleague in the San Francisco office suddenly appears in our mind's eye. Maybe *they* might fulfill all the things we are missing in our relationship?

You Become "That Couple in the Restaurant"

You know, the ones with nothing to talk about. There's a country song for every situation in life. When you start humming, "Is It Cold in Here, or Is It Just You?" you know you're in trouble.

The D-Train

Of course there are plenty of truly bad marriages out there. But maybe yours isn't one of them. Some marriages are just imperfect: they're suffering from neglect, or low-burn resentment, or any of the other problems we've talked about in this book. It might seem like a marriage is faltering, when in reality it's imminently salvageable.

The Myth of Gina in Accounts Payable

Plenty of people are tempted into that *"grass is always greener"* way of thinking. They figure that life would be better if they leave Nest A to either strike out on their own, or find another mate and set up Nest B. Guys, Gina in Accounts Payable just might be the perfect woman: the nymphomaniac who also really understands you. And hey, girls, what about Dave, your kids' handsome pediatrician? Newly divorced. Nice suits. He just might be the sensitive guy who won't pressure you to have sex and can whip up a delicious Lobster Newburgh at the drop of a hat.

Let's Take a Ride on the D-Train, Shall We?

If there are times when hopping on that D-Train sounds like an option you want to consider, maybe stop a minute to think about where it's headed. *It's a train that runs straight to Vegas.* Let's say a woman leaves her husband and starts playing house with the doctor. What are the odds that he'll actually prefer doing the dishes to doing her? Let's say the guy divorces his wife and marries Gina. More than likely, she'll want to procreate as well, so a couple of kids later, *he'll find himself right back where he started*. Imagine that. Now he has two "nests" to tend, another un-horny hausfrau, and a ton of baggage. The cold, hard truth is that Bird B might be just as fallible and imperfect as Bird A.

> "I watched some of my work colleagues make the same mistakes
> over and over. They would marry a woman, have a couple of
> kids, cheat on her, leave the first wife to marry the girlfriend,
> have a couple of kids, cheat on her, and so on and so on. Some
> of them married and divorced two and three times and had five
> and six kids. These guys never matured. They never understood
> what marriage and commitment were all about. They kept
> trying to get back to the romantic, fanciful stage. But they just
> wound up in the exact same place. Most of them ended up
> alone and financially ruined."
> —*Tom, married 42 years, 2 kids, 5 grandkids*

The three of us are not here to moralize. We obviously don't know any-one's particular set of marital circumstances. We're just saying that tak-ing a crack at making Nest A a better place to be might be another option to consider.

SOLUTIONS

> "Every person in every marriage should wake up every day and
> say to themselves, 'This is a choice. I choose to be married. I
> choose to be happy.' You can't take it for granted. You must be
> proactive. This is my relationship and this is my life and I will
> get out of it what I put into it."
> —*Richard, married 11 years, 3 kids*

> "Most people are about as happy as they choose to be."
> —*Abraham Lincoln*

So how about you, has your happiness taken a hit since you became a parent? Or are you generally in a pretty good place, even on those days when you want to strangle Barney and all his furry friends?

Thinking Inside the Box

We accept that the constraints that come with having kids are part of the deal. Unless we're holding on to the "sell the children to the gypsies" idea as a reserve option, we're pretty well stuck inside the box. But we do have a choice about how we react to how our lives have changed.

1. We can wallow in blame or self-pity and limp through our remaining fifty years under the weight of the giant chip on our shoulders.
2. We can throw in the towel and leave our marriage.
3. We can be proactive. We can choose to be happy and figure out what we need to do to get there.

We don't know about the rest of you, but we thought we'd give Door Number 3 a try here.

The Duty to Be Happy (Happiness Is Serious Business)

Happiness may be more than a choice, actually. Duty is a pretty strong word for it, but that's exactly what it is. When we have kids, personal happiness is a responsibility, not a luxury. We all need to cultivate our own happiness in order to be happy in our marriages, *and* to be good parents. We call it *The Trickle Down Theory of Familial Happiness*: Happy

The Route to Happiness

Self—Happy Marriage—Happy Family (i.e., happy kids). Here's why: if we are unhappy, it can suck the life out of our marriage and take innocence and joy from our kids' childhoods. We can wind up taking the whole ship down with us.

We'll even take this duty idea a step further. We also each have a duty to facilitate our spouse's happiness. Not only do they deserve our best efforts to help them to be happy, but if either spouse's unhappy state leads to divorce, we might handicap our kids' happiness, too. So, hey, no pressure or anything.

> "I realized a few years into our marriage that I'm Ross's best shot at happiness. What I 'let' him do, whether or not I support his dreams and help to make them happen, determines whether or not he's going to be happy in life. We all have so much power over our spouse's lives. It's not just about 'me.' It's about 'us.'"
> —Stacie, married 9 years, 3 kids

The *BPYM* Guide to Happiness

So how do we do it? The first step is to identify what we need in order to be happy, and then make those activities a priority. As Stephen Covey would say, "*The main thing is to make the main thing the main thing.*"[2]

Just as important, we really do need to "have it all." Balance is essential. We might be making it to the gym every other day but if we haven't hung out with friends in months we'll probably feel pretty off-kilter. There are a few key areas that one might consider fundamental to leading a life well-lived: Health, Marriage, Parenthood, Relationships, and Self-Actualization (work, hobbies, volunteer efforts, etc.). All these "cups" need to stay relatively full.

"Well, how on earth are we going to do that?" you ask. Good question. We've wondered the same thing ourselves, especially on those nights when we can barely manage to wash our faces before collapsing into bed. There's no easy way around this one. The only way we can figure this out is to be strategic and disciplined about how we use our time. We have to (1) use it wisely and well—on the things that really matter—and (2) find ways to make more time for the essentials by cutting out the things that *don't* really matter.

The Balancing Act

How to Live Happily Ever After in Four Easy Steps (Ha!)

Step One: Make a happiness short list. (Avoid a case of self-neglect). What do you need to have in your life in order to be happy? What are the things that really matter to you?

Step Two: Your spouse gets to make one, too. Because if he or she isn't happy, you won't be either.

Step Three: Water the houseplant (Avoid a case of couple-neglect). Compare your lists and figure out a plan of action.

Step Four: What should give? In other words, stop doing things that aggravate the situation. Think of it as a diet (boo). Some things will have to go (but they are bad attitudes and low-value activities, so you won't mind).

Step One: The Happiness Short List

What Do You Need?

Know thyself. It's not just what we like to do, or want to do—we could all come up with lists a mile long on that one. It's knowing what *really and truly recharges us*. Regular self-maintenance is vital to our happiness.

What do we *need* to make us feel like we're living a life, not treading water? For some it's a good book; for others it's a good walk; for most men, it's a good you-know-what. What do *you* need, on a daily, weekly, monthly, or annual basis, to sustain your happiness?

- "Staying connected with good friends and family in Ireland," said Cathy.

- "Self-actualization, doing something for myself—like working on this book with interesting people that I like," said Stacie.

- "Brain Food: books, movies, going to see someone speak, etc.," said Julia.

- Doing "girl stuff" or "guy stuff" on a regular basis: book club, poker night, (or, if you live in Texas, "going to the shooting range and drinking beer," as our friend Dan suggested).

- "Red wine and goat cheese," said our more cultivated friend Paul.

- "Time alone," said our introverted friend Allison.

- Exercise. "If I don't exercise, I go nuts. That's pretty much the only thing I do for myself, but I put it above a lot of other things and go thirty minutes, three days a week," said Emily.

And, let's not forget the universal key to personal happiness: *sleep.*

> "I know that when I start feeling annoyed, it usually just means I need to take a walk alone, call a friend, or hang out with Mike a little more. Simple and not earth-shattering stuff. I get amazed that the smallest amounts of self-care seem to do the trick in our household."
> —*Cathy, married 7 years, 2 kids*

Step Two: Your Spouse Gets to Make One, Too

What we need as individuals is just one part of the equation. We also need to understand what makes our spouse happy, a) because they deserve it, and b) because if they aren't happy, we won't be either. This is not just our opinion. Happiness experts have weighed in with the same idea. A recent study of over 10,000 married people showed that, "A married man is significantly more satisfied with his life when his wife becomes more satisfied with hers, and vice versa."[3] The same study also showed that happiness is contagious. It can overflow from one spouse to the other, even when one spouse has dire health or financial problems. "Married people have become more satisfied with their lives over the years merely because their spouses have become happier with theirs."

Step Three: Water the Houseplant

> "When you are partners, you can survive anything. You have to make that your goal. You put each other first and everything else falls in line."
> —*Karen, married 30 years, 3 kids*

We love each other. We have kids together. We hitched our stars to each others' wagons a long time ago. *Our kids mean the world to us, but the marriage has to be a priority, too.* A little water keeps the houseplant thriving.

Man the Controls: Avoid, or Get Out of, Autopilot

Regular marriage maintenance is all that's needed.

Make Time for Each Other's Needs

Help each other have it all, don't compete with each other to have it all. Take out your happiness short lists and compare notes. How different are they? Do they make you wonder how you've managed to stay married so long? In the process of figuring out how to give each other some of what we need (he gets to do his dirt-bike thing on Saturday morning; she can go shoe shopping on Sunday afternoon), we build tremendous goodwill that will fuel the marriage. As simple as it sounds, these feelings can kick-start a marriage out of Autopilot and keep the Vicious Cycles away.

> "Melinda really needs time with her friends. I used to get annoyed by that, but then I figured it out. If she misses a couple

of book clubs in a row, she is harder to deal with. It is better for
me to make sure that she can go."
—*Bobby, married 7 years, 1 kid*

"I finally realized Jay needs his alone time since he never has
any during the week. The stuff he loves to do: running, golf,
gardening are all solitary pursuits. I've learned to give him
that instead of demanding he be 'fully present' all weekend.
And I think he's learned that I need more couple time than he
naturally would, so he's making an effort to be more engaged in
our relationship more often."
—*Vanessa, married 7 years, 2 kids*

Make Time for Each Other

A little water goes a long way. It really is as simple as a regular date night,
a hug and a kiss at the end of a long day, or a thoughtful note at the bottom of the e-mail about the 401Ks. If we're not talking about running the
empire, we're talking about the kids. Being slightly baby-crazy is normal,
but it's hard to sustain a marriage when our whole adult relationship is
defined by being parents, and we let our happiness and/or tension be
tied up in the kids. It's tricky, though. We love them so much, we can get
carried away.

Practice Virtuous Acts

Otherwise known as extending the olive branch (or the whole damn
tree), *Virtuous Acts* are the selfless actions we take for the benefit of our
marriages, even when we are feeling far from virtuous.

These acts often run counter to our emotional instincts, so even
though they're baby steps, they seem to require Herculean effort. Try telling a tired mom she needs to muster the energy for a quick Five-Minute
Fix at the end of the day. You might as well suggest she hop a flight on
over to Nepal and give Mt. Everest a quick scaling before she hits the hay.
Try telling a man who's been rebuffed for weeks that he just needs to take
his haggard wife out for one more dinner at the local Chinese restaurant.
Watch him roll his eyes and say, "but I tried that already and it got me a
whole lotta nothin'."

We've learned, however, that when we each make some effort, we *can* break the cycle. When we acknowledge that our spouse is working hard for us, it makes it easier to work for them. We get what we give. We reap what we sow. In the grand scheme of things, *these efforts really aren't that hard, yet their impact is tremendous.* If you're feeling less than altruistic, another way to think about them is just changing your tactics to get what you want.

Virtuous Acts for Men

- **Ask her out on a date.** Try this: "I want to spend time with you because you are beautiful and smart and I'm still attracted to you. Let's go out and have dinner Saturday."

- **Plan family fun.** Initiate and orchestrate a family activity, rather than (or at least prior to) your own escape attempt.

- **Remember the finer things.** It's all that crap you can't stand, but used to do because it got you laid (same principles still apply): writing a note, initiating a "deep and meaningful." *It's always the thought* that leads straight to a woman's heart (and other vital body parts).

- **If you are a basement dweller, step into the light.** Explore the possibility that life upstairs with your family at bedtime might be better than the one you have created for yourself underground. Withdrawing won't help your cause.

- **Do the domestic crap.** Do what needs doing and give yourself a gold star just for being such a champ.

Virtuous Acts for Women

- **Implement the Five-Minute Fix.** *Warning*: if you are deep into a No Sex Vicious Cycle, it might take you five minutes a day for an entire week to extricate yourself. But, as our friend Ellie said, "If you just need your asparagus patch weeded, it won't take long." (She really does have an asparagus patch in her backyard! This is not some weird sexual innuendo, we swear!)

- **Implement the Training Weekend.** Maybe he just doesn't get it. He doesn't realize how hard it is or how much there is to do. This eliminates nagging. They do, therefore they understand.

- **Leave the house a mess for forty-eight hours.** If the nagging or debating about the division of labor has reached fever pitch, cut and run. Eat out, or eat on paper plates, for a two-day cool down period.

- **Retrieve your basement dweller (if you dare).** Venture down there and spend a couple of hours playing video games/watching sports or sharing in *whatever* activity it is that he does down there.

- **Praise something about him.** Find something to thank him for. Anything. Washing a fork. Combing his hair. Remembering to zip his fly.

- **Tell him what you want.** Guys told us loud and clear: "I hate having to guess what she wants." If he knows what you want him to do, he'll generally do it. Make your expectations and desires clear.

Virtuous Acts for Both of You

- **Talking.** Ask, "How are you, Babe?" or otherwise break the silence.

- **Listening.** Turn off all electronic gizmos (this includes televisions, iPods, computers, Crackberries, and cell phones, for those of you who think those things are actually bodily appendages) for an entire evening.

- **Change the setting.** Get out of the house if it has become a battlefield. Meet your spouse downtown after work. Try a new restaurant for dinner or a new park for a walk.

- **Give surprise Get Out of Jail Free Cards.** Unexpected personal time can boost anybody's sagging spirits. Or you could give yourself a break, too, by organizing the child care and then doing something together.

- **Practice role reversal.** If you always do the same chores and are sick of them, trade places for a week. He cooks dinner and she mows the lawn—or, if your marriages are like ours, vice versa.

And finally, the most virtuous of all acts, and the most necessary if you are in a cycle of extreme self-neglect or anger:

• **Accept responsibility.** Maybe it's not all your spouse's fault. If you're unhappy about something, maybe it's self-neglect or harboring an attitude that aggravates the situation.

> "How many of us stop to ask ourselves, 'Maybe I'm the problem? Maybe I need to fix myself not the environment.' When two people have that approach, a marriage will work."
> —*Elise, married 38 years, 4 kids, 3 grandkids (divorce attorney)*

Taking a proactive, "hmm, what can I do?" (as opposed to an accusatory, "why doesn't he/she just …?") approach is one of the best things we can do for our marriages.

Wow, we can see your halo glowing from here.

Step Four: What Should Give?

> "I accept that right now the children need and deserve a huge amount of time, but it's only for a short period, and it's been such a wonderful experience that I wouldn't begrudge it for anything. I am very focused on being a good husband and a good Dad and spending time with my family. I just wish I could find a way to make some time for myself without feeling selfish."
> —*Joseph, married 7 years, 2 kids*

Now we understand that we cannot squeeze round pegs into square holes. We know we have to prioritize. There are two things we can let go of that will make more time for the things we need: harboring unhealthy attitudes and striving too hard for perfection.

Attitude Is Everything

The three of us are not life coaches here, but as far as those 'tudes go, we can all at least be aware of them and consider whether or not they are contributing to our general unhappiness. As Todd put it, "You basically have to reorient yourself after you become a parent. Your happiness comes from different things than it used to." (What a lovely sentiment ... It sounds much nicer than "this is the 'kick in the ass' part.")

"Perfectionism Is the Voice of the Oppressor."[4]

Perfection is a myth, and it is certainly not worth having at the expense of forgetting we already have everything we need to be happy. We don't live in a magazine. We live in our aging, leaky house with our aging, nagging/withdrawing spouse, and our noisy children who will one day leave home and forget to call us.

> "So many women worked so hard to get women out of the kitchen, to get away from this notion that a woman's worth is tied to how her house looks. And now it seems like we are pushing ourselves right back to the place that they ran away from."
> —*Justine, married 6 years, 2 kids*

> "I'm trying to master the art of blowing things off. I have to tell myself that it's OK that the spare bedroom is not going to be decorated for four years, that it's OK to have a dinner party with pizza and beer. I'm learning to prioritize. I'm learning to let go."
> —*Sarah, married 7 years, 2 kids*

Mothers for a Saner Life

> "There is no way to be a perfect mother, and a million ways to be a good one."
> —*Jill Churchill, writer*

In an effort to bring some sanity to our own lives we talked to a child psychologist about the extreme parenting phenomenon. This was his response:

> "Parents want to give their kids an edge by putting them in all these activities. What they don't seem to realize is that the best edge they can give them is gained by sitting down with them

at the dinner table, just being with them, just hanging out as
a family. Kids who are truly secure in themselves have the real
edge. Ultimately that's what's going to make them a success."

We all want what's best for our kids. But perhaps, before we sign up for
more work, we should make sure that the return on an activity is worth
the blood, sweat, and tears of our investment. The three of us now apply the following common sense test (whether it is planning a birthday
party, adding another activity, or agreeing to participate in the school
bake sale):

A. Is this really going to benefit my child, me, or my marriage? (*If the answer is no, we say no. If the answer is yes, we move on to question B.*)

B. If I do this will I complain about it later? (*If the answer is yes, we don't
   do it. If the answer is no, we go to question C.*)

C. Is there a less painful way to make it happen? (*For example, buy, don't
   bake cookies for the school; trade off driving responsibilities with another
   Mom, etc.*)

Or, as Pam put it, "You have to be strong enough to set priorities in life—
just say no."

Family time is where it's at. We can give our kids every bit of a design-
er lifestyle, but most of them are more interested in just being with us.
Think back to your own childhood. What did you care more about? Getting Steve Austin, The Six Million Dollar Man, for Christmas, or reading *'Twas the Night Before Christmas* with your parents? OK, you wanted
Steve Austin. But what do you remember now, as an adult? It's the vague
"we made cookies and went to Aunt Betty's and had a big dinner" memories
you treasure. Those are the experiences that gave you the security and
warm inner glow you needed to grow up into the fine human being you
are today. Spanish lessons are great, but the time you spend together doing a thousand inconsequential things is what culminates in a meaningful childhood for your kids.

The *BPYM* Call to Inaction

Can't we all just lighten up? One of the reasons we invest so much time pursuing perfection is societal pressure. We're expected (or think we're expected) to live a certain way. But each of us is a member of society; so we have the power to change those expectations.

A Sticker and a Fruit Snack

Birthday parties are wonderful and important. There's nothing better than celebrating the day our darling children arrived in our lives, and the fact that we've all survived another year. But things have gotten out of hand. (Stacie is still recovering from that *Nemo* bash she put on a few years ago.) If the kid can't remember it, or is likely to sleep through it, they might not be old enough for a party. Get a cake, take a few cute pictures, and consider your job done. And for any age child, when you do have a party, as our friend Theresa said, "The contents of a goodie bag should be a sticker and a fruit snack. Those moms who put lip gloss in them are Satan. My six-year-old got it all over our couch."

Join the Revolution

A Playdate Is Not an Open House

One of us actually went to a playdate with our two-year-old where the hostess mother had filled the house with fresh flowers and made a point of saying she'd done so just for the playdate. We didn't want to buy her house, we just wanted to hang out in it for a couple of hours! Why do we feel compelled to go into *Open House Overdrive* whenever we have friends over? Let's stop cleaning up before playdates and presenting show-palace perfection for our dinner parties. Why not let our friends see that our lives (and houses) are just as chaotic and messy as theirs? Our friend Leslie wishes things could be more casual, "Like when we were in college and people would think it was cool that you had a couch—not whether your pillows were custom-made to coordinate with the love seat." Yeah, those were the days, and we miss them.

Reflections: A Little Perspective from the Other Side

"Going through it, there's nothing funny about it. After you survive it, it's very funny."
—*Jerry, married 27 years, 3 kids, 1 grandkid*

The View from the Weeds

It's hard to have perspective about this stage of our lives. We are down in the weeds. We can't see too far beyond the next milestone: "Things will be so much easier when he's potty trained/in preschool/making his own lunch/driving a car." Like all of you, the three of us are slap bang in the middle of it. So we looked for that perspective elsewhere—from couples who'd been down this road many years ago. Even though marriage and parenting have changed dramatically in a generation or two, the fundamental experience of adjusting to parenthood remains basically the same. They found it as shocking as we did. They felt their way along in the dark just like we're doing now.

The veterans wanted us to understand three things: this is just a stage; it might just be the most difficult one our marriages will go through, but ultimately, sharing the parenting experience will be the biggest reward of our lives. It's good stuff.

The View from the Rearview

"Couples need to remember that this is just a season. It will pass. You will have time and energy for each other again."
—*Nancy, married 30 years, 3 kids, 2 grandkids*

"I remember when my kids were little thinking I might die I was so tired. I do remember that very vividly. But now, when I look back at that time I just remember the good things—how a baby feels in your arms, or the funny things a toddler says. At the time, you don't know how you'll get through it, but after it's over, trust me, you'll miss it like you wouldn't believe."
—*Sylvia, married 18 years, 3 kids*

The Good News: This Is Just a Stage

According to those with hindsight, right now we are living just one chapter in the great book that is our marriage. Hard to believe it now, but we'll have decades of sleeping in on Saturday morning, reading our newspapers, sipping coffee, and having uninterrupted conversation with our spouse.

Can you imagine a day that doesn't begin with someone screaming and hurling a sippy cup across the kitchen in a wave of toddler fury? A day that passes without a single time-out? Julia recently realized things were changing when her five-year-old didn't get any immunizations at his last doctor's appointment. No more shots? It was the beginning of the end of an era.

The kids, we've been told, will get older and quite simply, won't need the same level of care and attention. One pastor told us, "I've counseled hundreds of couples at this stage in their marriages. By the time the youngest child is in first grade, most of these problems seem to disappear."

Married With Kids Journey

Before Kids: Starry-Eyed Lovers:
4 Years

Baby/Toddler Stage: Ass-Kicking Part I
8 Years (Ages 0–5)

Empty Nest:
24 Years

School-Age Stage:
8 Years (Ages 6–13)

Teenage Stage: Ass-Kicking Part II
6 Years (Ages 14–18)

(Assumptions: You marry at age 25 and you both live to age 75. You're married for a total of 50 years. You have 3 kids, all born 2 years apart. So the span from birth of the oldest to birth of the youngest is 4 years. Kids are at home for 22 years. It's just the two of you for 24 years.[5])

Even Better News: This Stage Is Uniquely Difficult, So Hang in There
Most couples we spoke to said transitioning from carefree couple to partners in parenthood, is one of, if not the biggest, tests our marriages will likely face. Don't just take our word for it: some research indicates that women are more likely to suffer depression when they have young children *than at any other time in their lives*, including menopause and the empty nest years.[6]

> "Having young children is the ultimate time of stress in
> a marriage. It is the most demanding time of life, really,
> especially for mothers. The teen years are hard, too, but the
> baby stage is harder because of their total dependency on you. It
> requires so much time to keep them fed, and so much physical
> effort to keep them safe. And now, in modern life, with all
> the things your generation wants to do and have, it is almost
> impossible."
> —*Phillip, married 22 years, 2 kids*

Maybe, if we can at least intellectualize that *this is not it* for the next fifty years, the diapers and the tantrums (the kids' and your spouse's) won't seem so traumatic. Maybe we can all breathe a sigh of relief and stop freaking out about how our spouse just doesn't get it, and move forward with confidence that things will get easier with time.

Ridin' the Storm Out?

All the long haulers we spoke with stressed that their marriages had gone through cycles—literally, waves of good times and bad. "If you know you married a fundamentally good person, hang on during the tough times; there are better ones around the corner," was their message. We can at least envision this, even if it's hard to see the bend in the road at this stage. It's another message that's supported by some scientific evidence. A study published in 2002 reported that two-thirds of unhappy marriages right themselves within five years. In fact, *seventy-eight percent of people who reported being in "very unhappy" marriages said that the marriages were "happy" when they were asked about it five years later.*[7]

The Happily Ever After ...

"Life is not a journey to the grave with intentions of arriving
safely in a pretty, well-preserved body, but rather to skid in
broadside, thoroughly used up, totally worn out and loudly
proclaiming ... *Wow!* What a ride!"
—*Anonymous*

One day, in the very distant future, we will look back over our lives. Our gray-haired gurus reminded us that it will be our children and our spouse that will define what our lives were all about. Whether or not we feel proud of the way we have lived will hinge mainly on our marriage and our parenting. Here's another way to look at it: the work and time we invest in our kids and marriage today will determine what our lives will be like tomorrow.

> "Being a parent is the role of your life. It is both the toughest and the most rewarding thing you will ever do. Even with all the worry and the self-doubt, in the end, your world grows as your kids grow, and there's no question that it's worth it."
> —*Al, married 34 years, 3 kids, 2 grandkids*

> "When you have kids, you and your wife will go to hell and back. Your kids will take you there. Looking back, though, it was the 'worst' times, not the 'better' times that made Jackie and me as close as we are today."
> —*Fred, married 38 years, 4 kids, 10 grandkids*

> "I think I'm a much better person since I became a Mom. I'm more patient. I'm more compassionate. I know the meaning of selfless love. Those are three of the most important lessons in life, don't you think?"
> —*Karen, married 30 years, 3 kids*

> "I'm closing in on the final chapters of my life now, and looking back, what has really mattered are my wife and my kids. I've made money, we've been very comfortable, but really it doesn't matter a damn compared to my family. It's your family that validates your entire existence."
> —*Tom, married 42 years, 2 kids, 5 grandkids*

So, Did We Learn Anything?

The three of us started this book with plenty of questions and very few answers. Now, though, we have all the answers and our marriages are perfect in every respect ...

Hardly.

Let's just say that things have improved enormously, but our marriages are still—and always will be—works in progress. We're happier today than we were two years ago, that's for sure. And leaving aside their occasional high-drama high jinks, "Whaddaya mean I have to watch the kids again so you can write? What about *book*-proofing this marriage?" our husbands are happier, too (yes, we asked them). Writing this book helped us (and, thanks to osmosis, our husbands) become better navigators of the perilous early-parenthood seas.

So after two years, three more kids (one for each of us), hundreds of conversations, and the occasional meltdown, what have we learned?

Sometimes It's Better to Accept the Great Mom/Dad Divide

This was a tough one for us. But when you hear the same complaints, as we did, over and over again, "He just doesn't understand how tough it is for me." "Why does she get so upset if I buy the wrong diapers?" you start to see that we want and need different things, and that that's OK. Compulsive Mom behavior is normal. Shortcut-seeking Dad behavior is normal. Hound-dog husband behavior is normal. Shut-down-the factory wife behavior is normal. Faced with these sorts of unavoidable differences, sometimes the best course of action is to hold our noses and tolerate a few of our spouse's incomprehensible behaviors (her obsessions with bug spray and sunscreen) and demands (his desire for sex on a regular basis).

Action Matters. A lot.

Just accepting that we're different is not really enough, though. We've all got to give a little. Giving our spouse some of the things that he or she really needs, at this stage of our lives, goes such a long way.

- For women, those things are: a husband who thinks and acts like a team member, not an escapee; validation; romance and attention to the finer things; and off-leash time.

- For men those things are: sex, validation, sex, lower standards, sex, being part of the new family unit on their own terms, sex, and off-leash time.

It's Not All His/Her Fault

As we wrote this book, we realized that some of the reasons we felt annoyed and/or disappointed had nothing to do with our husbands and everything to do with the books we weren't reading, the exercise we weren't getting, and the friends we weren't seeing. This took a lot of pressure off the marriage. It's up to us to figure out what our "thing" is and make a little time to do it. Obviously, the same goes for the ball and chain sitting next to us on the sofa.

We Are Not Alone

Ask anyone how having kids impacted their marriage and watch them roll their eyes at the ceiling with half a grin and half a grimace. We're all in the same boat, which is really reassuring. This stuff is normal. Most of the problems we're having are not personal, but instead universal. What the three of us have taken away from this is the belief that with a little perspective, a handful of strategic actions, and as much good humor as it is possible to maintain on four hours of sleep a night, we can survive these trying years with our marriages and our happiness intact.

This Time Is Unique

It's uniquely tough, but also uniquely fabulous. Just accepting that the growing pains are inevitable makes them more bearable. When the three of us feel overworked or even just slightly deprived (as we often do), we remind ourselves not to wish away these precious chubby-thighed, drooly-smiling years. Can you think of any person with older kids who *doesn't* say, "Oh, enjoy this time. It goes by so fast." Clearly, their memories are also damaged by several years of major sleep deprivation, but maybe they have a point.

This difficult time will end. As soon as it does, we'll miss it and we'll want it back.

ACKNOWLEDGMENTS

This book would not be what it is without the wit, wisdom, laughter, and tears of so many people—whether dear, lifelong friends, or poor, unwitting souls who had the great misfortune to sit next to us on an airplane—who shared their stories. Our heartfelt thanks to all of you, who, though you will forever remain anonymous, let us peek into your hearts, minds, kitchens, and bedrooms.

Thanks to our agent, Richard Abate, at ICM, for your thoughtful guidance, unwavering support, and strictest adherence to the male perspective. Whatever drove you to take a chance on three first-timers, we'll never understand, but we will always be grateful for your recklessness. Thanks also to Kate Lee, our bonus agent, and the rest of the talented staff at ICM. And where, oh where, would we be without Allyn Magrino, time-honored friend and one of the most well-connected women in New York?

Everyone at HarperCollins has made this experience truly a joy. We are particularly grateful for the enthusiasm and support of our editor, Mary Ellen O'Neill, whose warmth and talent and humor have propelled us forward, challenged our thinking, and kept us laughing from start to finish. Joe Tessitore amazed us with his relentless energy and commitment to make this book a success. Paul Olsewski, Shelby Meizlik, Jean Marie Kelly, Felicia Sullivan, and Laura Dozier are simply the best in the business.

To Larry Martin, thank you for your fabulous illustrations and for the extraordinary patience and humor with which you always responded to our bizarre, last-minute requests, such as, "Can you make the male rabbit look hornier?"

We'd like to thank our dear parents—Richard and Judy Harris, Brendan and Mary O'Neill, and Lou and Julie Pirkey—for a lifetime's worth of love, encouragement, and "fit to burst" enthusiasm. We are also deeply indebted to our fabulous parents-in-law: Susan Cockrell and Will Lapage, Mohinder and Krishna Kadyan, Jerry and Evelyn Stone, and Tom and Weezie Duff, who in no way resemble any of the Outlaws in Chapter 5, and who have gone above and beyond the call of in-law duty throughout this process. Our warmest thanks as well to the wonderful women who've helped maintain peace in our kingdoms, and therefore in our minds: Dorina Hinosja, Sharlene Parker, Barbara Timko, and Brandy McDonald.

We'd also like to thank our children: Jaclyn, James, Ross, Kate, Maeve, Theo, and Henry; in a way, we wrote this book for you. We want to be the best Moms (and Dads) we can be, and we hope this book will help us do that. We appreciate your (occasional) patience and (limited) understanding. It's more than we deserve. Thank you for helping us make this dream of ours come true. One day, we promise to do the same for you.

And most of all, we want to thank our husbands, Ross, Mike, and Gordon, our biggest fans (*Are you done yet?*), harshest critics (*Here's a diagram of all the things you got wrong in Chapter 3.*) and greatest sources of inspiration (*I didn't say that!*). For all the times you found yourselves enslaved in a weekend of child care; trawling the supermarket aisles for diapers, milk, and kitty litter; and even bedecked in Pretty Princess jewelry in a last, desperate attempt to keep the little ones entertained, at the end of the day, you made it all possible. This book springs from the very best places in our hearts, and from the happiness we find in being married to you.

GLOSSARY OF TERMS

Bait and Switch—A tactic employed to "get the girl or guy" in which a certain behavior is displayed and then discontinued once the objective (e.g. marriage) has been achieved. Both men and women feel like their other halves pull a Bait and Switch once they have kids. Men complain that their wives pull one in the bedroom *(Why doesn't she ever want to have sex?)*; whereas women feel that their husbands pull a **Reverse Bait and Switch** in the romance department *(Now all I get is a tap on the shoulder . . .)* and/or a **Domestic Bait and Switch** on the home front. *(He used to make dinner all the time . . .)*

Basement Dweller—What some men become to avoid the cold fish upstairs. Men go underground to develop a hobby or play with their electronic toys (among other things) when they feel like their wives are too tired/busy/annoyed to care about them. Some Dwellers are **Potential Porn Addicts**. Most Basement Dwellers are retrievable, however. Wives who venture down below to share in their husbands' subterranean activities can usually persuade their men to step into the light.

Book Club Refugees—Often married to uncommunicative **Basement Dwellers**, these women flee to monthly book clubs to fill the emotional voids in their marriages. Husbands who sharpen their romance and communication skills will find their wives eager to migrate back to the sanctuary of home.

The Bottom Head on the Family Totem Pole—How many men feel after kids arrive: unnoticed, unappreciated, and weighed down by the task of supporting everyone else in the family.

The BPYM Call to Inaction—A plea to mothers everywhere to embrace lower standards and end the *Uber-Mama* insanity. The movement's manifesto includes calls to a) abolish *Open House Overdrive* (e.g. setting out fresh flowers before play dates) and b) limit the contents of all birthday party goodie bags to a *Sticker and a Fruit Snack*.

The BPYM Family Management Plan—Policies and procedures developed by Mom and Dad for handling extended family members. Strategies include clarifying *The Pecking Order* (see below), *Running Interference* (each spouse deals with his/her own offending relatives) and establishing unique family traditions.

Clash of the Grannies—A high stakes *"who will have the greatest influence on the grandkids"* tournament played by each set of grandparents. Competitive categories include: *The Title Championship* (who gets to be called "Grandma"), *the Battle for Floor and Wall Space, the Battle for Face Time, Exclusive Access, Equal Access, and Gratuitous Grandparental Gift Giving.* Winners get to claim *Alpha Grandparent* status.

Cut the Cord—What Mama's Boys and Daddy's Girls should do after they become parents. Failure to cut the cord can lead to *Turf Infringement*, a distraught spouse or, in cases of extreme attachment, divorce papers.

Deer in the Headlights—The stunned "I just got whacked over the head" sensation experienced by most new parents.

Did-Enough Dads—These are the Dads who do just enough to get by. Domestic *Shortcuts* (skipping baths and teeth brushing) are Standard Operating Procedure, and they make liberal use of *Convenience Cards* (TV, McDonald's, 1-800-Grandma).

D-Train—That's D for Divorce. While hitching a ride is appropriate in various circumstances, the D-Train often brings its passengers right back to the place they left. Same shit, different spouse. Changing partners won't change millions of years of the biological hardwiring that drives much of our post-kid behavior.

Divide and Conquer—Unless you have a fleet of staff and unlimited cash, this apportioning of household and parenting responsibilities between spouses is the only way to reduce Scorekeeping.

The Everything List—Drawing up this list of *all* the required parenting and household to-dos is the first step in the Divide and Conquer solution to Scorekeeping.

Extreme Parenting—The tendency to overparent, overschedule, and overeverything our children. All parents who want to give their kids the best possible opportunities can fall into extreme parenting behaviors; although *UberMamas*, and the occasional UberPapa make it an art form. It can cause us to neglect ourselves and our marriages.

Family Tug-of-War—The conflicting familial pulls experienced by new Moms and Dads. Opposing sets of grandparents pull at opposite ends of the rope, and heave extra hard during holidays and birthdays. Sometimes a spouse joins his or her family in the tugging.

Five-Minute Fix—An underutilized, relatively easy, and most importantly, (for women, at least) non-time-consuming sex act. Its weekly implementation can transform a marriage.

Free Pass—What some men think their wives enjoy when they stay at home with the kids.

Get Out of Jail Free Cards—A "no strings attached" break given by one spouse to the other. The recipient isn't expected to use *Marriage Capital* (see below) to "buy" his/her freedom (e.g., promising to do all the laundry and/or baths for a week). There is no quid pro quo with these cards. The paroled spouse usually returns with renewed energy, appreciation and a willingness to help.

The Getting vs. Giving Equation—This formula for marital happiness requires that both spouses focus on what they can do for the other, rather than on what their spouse is *not* doing for them.

Global Conspiracy of Silence—The iron curtain of secrecy that hides the reality of the *Parenthood Ass-Kicking Party*. No one, not even our own parents, will tell it like it is. Some cryptic messages do make it through the silence, though, like advice to stockpile couple time for the famine ahead: *"Make sure you go to the movies/out to dinner/sleep in because you'll never, ever get to do it again."*

The Granny Grab—A Grandma's involuntary, uncontrollable impulse to snatch a baby right out of whoever's arms it happens to be in. This is a force to be reckoned with. Attempts to intercede a Grandma, mid-grab, can result in serious bodily harm.

The Great Sex Negotiation—Heavy-duty peace talks held between husband and wife to address supply/demand problems and work toward *Sexual Equilibrium*. Diplomacy skills rivaling those of Kofi Anan are required to achieve a mutually agreeable outcome.

Hardwiring—The genetically programmed instincts that kick in when we become parents. Although both men and women are compelled to maximize their genes' chance of survival; they have different, and often, incompatible hardwiring. She ensures her genes' survival by focusing on her baby. He, on the other hand, seeks to proliferate his genes through sex.

Helpful Man vs. Passive Man—The superhero that lurks in the heart of every husband, a man who will pitch in without being asked; and his alter-ego, the guy who parks his ass on the couch and whose sole contribution is to point out that the baby is crying and/or has grabbed the remote. Passive Man drives women nuts. Helpful Man, however, always gets the girl.

Hound Dog/Ice Queen Vortex—The highly-scientific BPYM term for people's post-baby hardwired response to sex. He (the Hound Dog) wants sex, baby or no baby, because men proliferate their genes through sex. She (the Ice Queen) focuses on the baby to the exclusion of all else because women are compelled by nature to nurture their young.

The Hourglass Effect—This is how many men respond when their wives say no to sex. They tip the sands and make it clear that she needs to "make it up" within a 24-hour time period and indicate (usually with stooped shoulders and a sulky look) that failure to do so will result in supremely grouchy husband behavior. Most women, however, are supremely annoyed by the Command Performance and become even less interested in putting out.

The Ick Factor—The slimy, gross reality of mothering small kids. One side effect of dealing with all the Ick (i.e. bodily fluids and messy baby food) is less interest in sex. What woman wants to deal with another mess after a slog through the *Trenches of Muck*?

It's Never Enough!—The collective howl of protest from hardworking Dads across the land, who say that no matter what they do, at home and at work, it is never enough, and certainly never *good* enough, to satisfy their wives.

JV/Varsity Squads—The teams Moms and Dads "join" after having a baby. When it comes to caring for the baby, Moms demonstrate remarkable talent, fit for the Varsity Squad; while Dads show only "B-Teamer" JV capability. The JV players are quite happy to let the superior players do battle on the field while they wait out the game on the bench. Other Varsity team members include grandmas, sisters, and aunts.

The Lioness Effect—The fiercely powerful instincts of motherhood. In particular, this is the standard instinctive Mom response to Turf Infringement. Even the mildest of women will bare her fangs, sharpen her claws and make an almighty roar if she feels her supreme authority as Mom is threatened.

Marriage on Autopilot—This is the most common marital state for couples parenting small kids; we're not quite asleep at the controls, but no one is actively flying the plane. The *"deep and meaningfuls"* are gradually replaced by *"time to make the donuts"* repetition and routine.

Marriage Capital—Scorekeeping points that are traded back and forth between husbands and wives. Usually wives determine how much capital, if any, to award for a specific activity. (For example, emptying the dishwasher counts, but changing the oil in the car doesn't.) The capital can be positive (he got up with the kids on Tuesday) or negative (he forgot to pick up milk). Positive capital has a use-by date. Negative capital can be used against the holder, indefinitely.

Marriage: A Houseplant—Like a houseplant, all a marriage needs to thrive is some regular watering (i.e., sex, SGIs, the occasional *deep and meaningful*) and maybe a bit of fertilizer (an annual couple-only weekend getaway). Neglected ones die easily.

Martyr Badge—A self-awarded insignia of suffering *(I've been up since 6:00 A.M. Yeah, well I got up with the baby last night.)* worn by both men and women in the post-baby battle over the division of labor. A *Perma-Scowl* often accompanies the Martyr Badge to complete the look.

Maternal Gatekeeping—The tendency of many Moms (a.k.a. the *Self-Appointed Family CEOs*) to micromanage their husbands' fatherhood. Dad is often relegated to the sidelines with the meaningless title (like Vice President) of Assistant Mom.

Midnight Chicken—Also known as Who Will Blink First? In this battle of the wills, each parent's objective is to make the other think that they are sound asleep and cannot hear the screaming down the hall. Victory is achieved when one parent (a.k.a. the sucker) gets up and goes to the baby. Experienced contenders play a mean game of *Advanced Midnight Chicken*, nudging their spouses and whispering, *"You're up, I got her last time,"* when, in fact, there was no last time.

The Mom Pie—How a Mom starts to feel after she has a second kid. Everyone (including Dad) wants a piece of her and there just doesn't seem to be enough to go around. With each new kid the portions get even smaller.

Mommy Brain—The sizable portion of a mother's brain that is consumed with both the day-to-day and long-term minutiae of parenting: carpool logistics, doctors' appointments, a toddler's social development and potty-training progress. There is little mental real estate left over for her husband or herself.

Mommy Chip—A hardwired circuit that is activated when women become mothers. Once triggered, this chip hums 24/7 and cannot be turned off. The chip drives, what men refer to as, crazy Mom behavior. It contains a *Worst Case Scenario Program* that feeds a mother's fears *(Let me just make sure the baby is breathing)* and is plugged into a *Guilt Circuit* that makes her constantly question whether or not she is doing enough for her kids.

Mommy Mode—A condition that describes any woman with a Mommy Chip and Mommy Brain. Mommy Mode is at the opposite end of the female-state-of-being spectrum from Lover Mode.

Mommy Shock—The astonishment women experience when the Mommy Chip is activated and primal maternal love kicks in. The shock is especially acute for women who, pre-motherhood, had a *"what's the big deal?"* attitude toward babies.

Parallel Phenomena: Mom Chills Out and Dad Steps Up—Complimentary Mom and Dad behaviors usually triggered by the arrival of kid number two. When Mom relaxes her standards, Dad is more motivated to get involved, and vice versa. One behavior reinforces the other.

The Pecking Order—The post-baby family hierarchy. Ideally, one's spouse and kids should be in the top position, with family of origin members in second place. If the order is reversed, the resulting Turf Infringement commonly produces tears, tantrums, and often downright misery.

Perfect V-Formation—How groups of men arrange themselves when they sense an opportunity to escape the home front. Their organization is seamless. They can mobilize at a moment's notice, equipping themselves with golf clubs/fishing rods/skis/hiking boots before their wives have a chance to say, *"Hey, where are you going?"*

Provider Panic—The hardwired compulsion many new fathers feel to adequately provide for their growing family. Men, caught in the grips of The Panic, can be found gazing over the crib muttering, *"I better go make more money."* It stimulates a laserlike focus on work, and occurs regardless of current household income or their wife's contribution to such. Morbid thoughts like *"What if something should happen to me?"* are often outgrowths of Provider Panic.

The R Word—That's R for romance, a word that most husbands retire from their active vocabulary after they bag their deer. Reinstating this word and putting it into play can have remarkable effects on a man's life, namely that his wife will want to have sex with him.

Ramping Up—The process of adjusting to life with more than one kid. In addition to adapting to more work and chaos, parents must master man-to-man and/or zone defense and learn to deal with social ostracism (usually occurs with the arrival of the third child).

Repeat Offenders—These are Dads who, in spite of their wives' selfless efforts to educate and reform them, continue to do and/or say the wrong thing. Most wives deal with Repeat Offenders by listing their husbands' *Prior Convictions* and referring to the *Log of Evidence*. Many men feel there is no statute of limitations.

The Romantic Stage—How women remember life with one kid after they have a second. Adding another child can make Moms nostalgic for the earlier *"and baby makes three"* days as they recall having the time and energy to savor all the special moments. Few of us, however, appreciate the uniqueness of this stage until it is over.

Schlep-Fest—What our vacations become after we have kids. Dad becomes the ***Family Pack Mule***, and we all have moments when we wonder if the holiday is really worth the packing and unpacking, disrupted sleep schedules and lost blankies.

Scorekeeping—An exceedingly complex, often relentless, tit for tat war waged by husbands and wives over the division of parenting responsibilities and domestic chores.

SGIs (Small Gestures of Intimacy)—These are the simple acts of affection (hugging, kissing, handholding etc.) that start to disappear as sex diminishes. Women withhold them because they worry that kissing etc. will send the wrong *"I'm up for some action later"* signal to their husbands. Men in turn become frustrated when the SGIs don't land them in the sack and so give up on them altogether.

Something's Gotta Give/The Great Escapees—Mind-sets that usually coincide with the addition of more kids. Moms feel that giving up an activity (from a weekly spinning class to a career) is the only way to move forward. On the other hand, many Dads respond to the additional demands of more children by looking for more elaborate and time-consuming ways to fly the coop (i.e., golf, fishing trips, campaign work).

Surrendering to the Madness—What happens when Moms and Dads accept that their old lives are really and truly over. The surrender to the chaos and rewards of parenthood often marks the beginning of happier days.

Team Think—A prerequisite for a happy marriage and happy family. The only way a marriage can survive the Grown-ups versus Rugrats battle is for Mom and Dad to work together as a team.

Ten O'Clock Shoulder Tap—Considered by many men to be a form of foreplay. A paw on a wife's shoulder is how some men indicate their desire for sex. The Tap is never accompanied by a term of endearment, or any other verbal form of communication, and is rarely well-received by the often sleeping/almost always exhausted wife.

Training Weekend—A 48-hour Navy SEALS-type experience for Dads. Mom takes off and Dad is left, unassisted, to man the kid and house ropes for the weekend. If done correctly (i.e., Dad has *absolutely no backup*) a reinvigorated Mom is likely to return to an enormously appreciative and surprisingly helpful husband, and newly confident Dad.

Trickle Down Theory of Familial Happiness—The belief that marital and familial happiness begin with personal happiness. A Happy Self leads to a Happy Marriage, which leads to a Happy Family (i.e., happy kids.)

Turf Infringement—When an extended family member or in-law steps over the line and invades a fledgling family nest.

Vessel Syndrome—The practice of some grandparents and grandparents-in-waiting wherein they treat their own children as little more than vehicles for genetic proliferation (i.e., grandkids).

Vicious Cycle—Where a marriage can end up when the small neglects and seemingly minor offenses go unchecked. A Vicious Cycle usually includes some, if not all, of the following: no sex; nagging; lack of appreciation; self-neglect, and patently unfair division of labor.

Virtuous Act—A small but entirely selfless action that can stop a Vicious Cycle and/or keep a marriage out of Autopilot.

Weekend Warriors—What Moms and Dads feel like on Saturday and Sunday. Scorekeeping escalates on the weekend as couples battle it out for some precious alone time. We wrestle with the logistics of taking care of the kids and dealing with all the household crap that accumulates during the working week. Weary from combat, we limp into work on a Monday morning and kiss the desk.

Whiplash—The sensation experienced by many stay-at-home moms that they have been yanked out of the 21st century, and hurtled back in time to the 1950s where they have to cope with gender inequality and never-ending, unappreciated housework.

That Whole 50:50 Thing—The expectation of many women that the equality they expected, and often had, in their pre-baby marriages would continue forever; and the abject disappointment and anger they experience when the lion's share of the post-baby domestic crap falls squarely on their plates.

ENDNOTES

Chapter 1: How Did We Get *Here?*

1. Jay Belsky and John Kelly, *The Transition to Parenthood: How a First Child Changes a Marriage* (Delacorte Press, 1994).
2. Alyson F. Shapiro and John M. Gottman, "Effects on Marriage of a Psycho-Communicative-Educational Intervention With Couples Undergoing the Transition to Parenthood, Evaluation at 1-Year Post Intervention," *Journal of Family Communication* (2005):1–24
3. R.J. Evenson and R.W. Simon, "Clarifying the Relationship Between Parenthood and Depression," *Journal of Health and Social Behavior,* 46, (December 2005): 341–58.

Chapter 2: Baby ... Boom!

1. F.M. DeLeon, "Rocking the Cradle—and a Marriage—After D-Day: Programs for Parenthood," *The Seattle Times,* October 24, 1999. (p. 31) John Gottman, Alyson Shapiro, and Sybil Carrère, "The Baby and the Marriage: Identifying Factors that Buffer Against Decline in Marital Satisfaction After the First baby Arrives," *Journal of Family Psychology,* 14 (1), (March 2000): 59–70.
2. John Gray, *Men Are from Mars, Women Are from Venus: A Practical Guide for Improving Communication and Getting What You Want in Your Relationships* (HarperCollins, 1992).

Chapter 3: What's the Score?

1. This MSNBC survey results are cited by Courtney Ronan in an article titled "Divvying Up Those Dreaded Household Chores," *The Realty Times,* June 16, 1999.
2. John M. Gottman, and Nan Silver. "Coping with Typical Solvable Prob-

lems," in *The Seven Principles for Making Marriages Work* (Three Rivers Press, 2000), Chap. 9.

3. Katya Adder, "Housework Looms for Spanish Men." BBC News. June 17, 2005. http://news.bbc.co.uk/2/hi/europe/4100140.stm.

4. "John Leguizamo: One-Man Firebrand," *Psychology Today* (March-April 2005): 49.

Chapter 4: The Sex Life of New Parents

1. Robert Wright, *The Moral Animal* (First Vintage Books, 1995) p. 41.

2. Sean Elder, "The Emperor's New Woes," *Psychology Today* (March-April 2005): 44.

3. Kathleen Deveny (with Holly Peterson, Pat Wingert, Karen Springen, Julie Scelfo, Melissa Brewster, Tara Weingarten and Joan Raymond), "We're Not in the Mood," *Newsweek*, June 2003.

4. Kathleen Deveny (with Holly Peterson, Pat Wingert, Karen Springen, Julie Scelfo, Melissa Brewster, Tara Weingarten and Joan Raymond), "We're Not in the Mood," *Newsweek*, June 2003.

Chapter 6: Ramping Up and Giving In

1. "What is the Ideal Family Size?" survey (results as of July 9, 2006) http://www.babycenter.com.

2. Center for the Ethnography of Everyday Life.

3. Arthur Norton and Louisa Miller, "Marriage, Divorce, and Remarriage in the 1990s," *U.S. Bureau of the Census, Current Population Reports, 1992.* Barbara Foley Wilson and Sally Cunningham Clarke, "Remarriages: A Demographic Profile," *Journal of Family Issues 13* (1992): 123-141.

4. "Sex in America: A Definitive Survey," *The New York Times*, August 4, 1998 (University of Chicago Press, 1995).

Chapter 7: Balancing Priorities

1. Mark Cleary, "The Awful Truth about Parenthood." *The Age*, February 7, 2005, http://www.theage.com.au/news/Opinion/The-awful-truth-about-parenthood/2005/02/06/1107625057169.html.

2. Stephen R. Covey, A. Roger Merrill and Rebecca R. Merrill. *First Things First: To Live, to Love, to Learn, to Leave a Legacy* (Free Press, 1996).

3. Miranda Hitti, "Recipe for Happiness in Marriage," *Web MD Medical News*, March 22, 2005. http://www.webmd.com/content/article/102/106708.htm. Cited research conducted by Nick Powdthavee at University of Warwick, Coventry, England.

4. Anne Lamont, writer and mother.

5. U.S. Census 2005. Median age for first marriage for women: 25.8 years,

for men: 27.1 years. National Center for Health Statistics, *National Vital Statistics Reports* 52(3) (September 18, 2003). Average male/female life expectancy in U.S. is 77 years (as of 2002).

6. E. McGrath, G.P. Keita, B.R. Stickland, and N.F. Russo, Women and Depression: Risk Factors and Treatment Issues (American Psychological Association, 1990).

7. Study by University of Chicago sociologist Linda Waite reported in, Tiffany Kary, "Don't Divorce, Be Happy: Miserable Unions That Morph Into Wedded Bliss," *Psychology Today* (November-December 2002).